Employment, Poverty and Rights in India

In comparison to other social groups, India's rural poor – and particularly Adivasis and Dalits – have seen little benefit from the country's economic growth over the last three decades. Though economists and statisticians are able to model the form and extent of this inequality, their work is rarely concerned with identifying possible causes.

Employment, Poverty and Rights in India analyses unemployment in India and explains why the issues of employment and unemployment should be the appropriate prism to understand the status of well-being in India. The author provides a historical analysis of policy interventions on behalf of the colonial and postcolonial state with regard to the alleviation of unemployment and poverty in India and in West Bengal in particular. Arguing that, as long as poverty – either as a concept or as an empirical condition – remains as a technical issue to be managed by governmental technologies, the 'poor' will be held responsible for their own fate and the extent of poverty will continue to increase. The book contends that rural unemployment in India is not just an economic issue but a political process that has consistently been shaped by various socio-economic, political and cultural factors since the colonial period. The analysis which depends mainly on ethnography extends to the implementation of the 'New Rights Agenda', such as the MGNREGA (Mahatma Gandhi National Rural Employment Guarantee Act), at the rural margin.

Challenging the dominant approach to poverty, this book will be of interest to scholars working in the fields of South Asian studies, Indian Political Economy, contemporary political theories, poverty studies, neoliberalism, sociology and social anthropology, as well as development studies.

Dayabati Roy is a sociologist by training and currently attached with the Centre for Studies in Social Sciences, Calcutta, India. She has published articles in various journals including Modern Asian Studies, and she is the author of *Rural Politics in India: Political Stratification and Governance in West Bengal* (2013).

Routledge Contemporary South Asia Series

Media as Politics in South Asia
Edited by Sahana Udupa and Stephen D. McDowell

Death and Dying in India
Ageing and End-of-Life Care for the Elderly
Suhita Chopra Chatterjee and Jaydeep Sengupta

Documentary Film in India
An Anthropological History
Giulia Battaglia

The Rule of Law in Developing Countries
The Case of Bangladesh
Chowdhury Ishrak Ahmed Siddiky

New Perspectives on India and Turkey
Connections and Debates
Edited by Smita Tewari Jassal and Halil Turan

The Judicialization of Politics in Pakistan
A Comparative Study of Judicial Restraint and Its Development
in India, the US and Pakistan
Waris Husain

The Appeal of the Philippines
Spain, Cultural Representation and Politics
José Miguel Díaz Rodríguez

Employment, Poverty and Rights in India
Dayabati Roy

For more information about this series, please visit: www.routledge.com/Routledge-Contemporary-South-Asia-Series/book-series/RCSA

Employment, Poverty and Rights in India

Dayabati Roy

Routledge
Taylor & Francis Group

LONDON AND NEW YORK

First published 2018 by Routledge

2 Park Square, Milton Park, Abingdon, Oxfordshire OX14 4RN

52 Vanderbilt Avenue, New York, NY 10017

Routledge is an imprint of the Taylor & Francis Group, an informa business

First issued in paperback 2020

British Library Cataloguing-in-Publication Data
A catalogue record for this book is available from the British Library

Library of Congress Cataloging-in-Publication Data
Names: Roy, Dayabati, author.
Title: Employment, poverty and rights in India / Dayabati Roy.
Description: Abingdon, Oxon ; NewYork, NY : Routledge, 2019. |
    Series: Routledge contemporary South Asia series ; 125 | Includes
    bibliographical references and index.
Identifiers: LCCN 2018006663 | ISBN 9781138479586 (hardback) |
    ISBN 9781351065429 (ebook)
Subjects: LCSH: Rural unemployment—India. | Manpower policy,
    Rural—India. | Poverty—India. | Rural development—India.
Classification: LCC HD5710.85.I4 R39 2019 | DDC
    331.12/0420954—dc23
LC record available at https://lccn.loc.gov/2018006663

ISBN: 978-1-138-47958-6 (hbk)
ISBN: 978-0-367-59030-7 (pbk)

Typeset in Times New Roman
by Apex CoVantage, LLC

Contents

Preface and acknowledgements

When I was about to finish fieldwork in the year 2008 in rural part of an Indian state, West Bengal, for my doctoral thesis, I was struck by a major question. Why employment is hard to find even in agriculturally prosperous villages of India? This question had been carried over to my future research. I saw Pakhi Murmu, one of my informants, was in terrible shape throughout. Pakhi Murmu was a landless peasant, but one among those 2.8 million fortunate peasants in West Bengal who had managed to obtain 3200 sq cubic of vested, or patta, land meant for cultivation thanks to the redistributive land reforms during the Left Front Regime (1977–2011). He and his wife used this land to cultivate a very small portion of land leasing in from different landholding families, and to work as day-labourer if available on others' land in and around the village over the years. How can they manage then the whole year to eke out a living? This might be an interesting question, but this question had not motivated me so that I would undertake the current research. The question which motivated me most is: why is rural employment scarce in India? What is the impact of the so-called achievements of green revolution technology (GRT) and the programme of land reforms on the rural poor?

After doing a decade-long empirical research into this major question, this book explains why the peasants in India have continually been confronted with predicaments posed by economic uncertainties, unemployment or underemployment, and why even the non-farm work as well as the remittances cannot rescue the jobless villagers. Through navigating the history of policy interventions on behalf of the colonial and postcolonial state in regard to alleviation of unemployment and poverty in India and in West Bengal in particular, it explores how unemployment has been created and shaped complexly at the rural margin. In theoretical terms, this book argues that rural unemployment in India is not just an economic issue but a political process that has consistently been shaped by various socio-economic, political and cultural factors since the British period. It also looks at the way the issues of unemployment have been reconstructed as consequences of the implementation 'New Rights Agenda' like the MGNREGA at the rural margin.

This book has taken a longer time to write than I planned initially. So it has no doubt that the list of intellectual debts I have accumulated along the way is long. First of all, I express my gratitude to those villagers who speak through the pages of this book in their own voices. They are not just my informants in fieldwork, but the ones who have shaped my understanding about rural employment through their wit and wisdom. I acknowledge the support of the Danish Agency for Science, Technology and Innovation, Denmark. The post doctoral grant I received from this agency enabled me to accomplish this research, to engage in collaborative effort and to interact with many people in this field. I would like to mention the helpful attitude of Prof. Ravinder Kaur as well as other faculty members of the Department of Cross-cultural and Regional Studies, University of Copenhagen. Supplementary financial support was obtained from the Eastern Regional Centre (ERC), Indian Council of Social Science Research, which made it possible to write this book. I am immensely grateful, particularly, to Prof. Manabi Majumdar, the Honorary Director, ERC, for her kind gesture in providing this book-writing grant for completing this book.

The University of Copenhagen as well as the Centre for Studies in Social Sciences, Calcutta, was very supportive in facilitating my research and manuscript preparation respectively. I had intensive interactions with the officials of West Bengal government and a couple of non-governmental organizations (NGOs). Their willingness to share their views with me was immensely helpful. Earlier drafts of some chapters have been presented at various conferences and seminars in the universities and institutes of India, Denmark, Sweden and Finland. I thank the organizers of these events as well as the participants who stimulated me with their insightful comments. I thank the Routledge editors for their patience and support, and the anonymous reviewers for their useful comments and suggestions. It will be impossible to mention all the people who have helped me in conducting fieldwork, in sharing their views with me, in guiding me to others, providing me with data. They gave me their time, often regardless of their busy schedules and pressing commitments. Without their help, the research would have been impossible.

Dayabati Roy
Kolkata, India

Abbreviations

AIDMK	All India Anna Dravida Munnetra Kazhagam
ALC	Assistant Labour Commissioner
BDO	Block Development Office
CPI	Communist Party of India
CPI (M)	Communist Party of India (Marxist)
DM	District Magistrate
DTW	Deep Tube Well
DVC	Damodar Valley Corporation
GC	General Caste
GoWB	Government of West Bengal
GP	*Gram Panchayat*
GRT	Green Revolution Technology
HYV	High Yield(ing) Variety
HYVP	High Yielding Varieties Programme
IAAP	Intensive Agriculture Area Programme
IADP	Intensive Agriculture Development Programme
ICS	Indian Civil Service
IRDP	Integrated Rural Development Programme
IAY	Indira Awas Yojana
JRY	*Jawhar Rojgar Yojana*
LF	Left Front
MGNREGA	Mahatma Gandhi National Rural Employment Guarantee Act
MLA	Member of Legislative Assembly
MP	Member of Parliament
NGO	Non Government Organization
NREGA	National Rural Employment Guarantee Act
NREP	National Rural Employment Programme
NRI	Non Resident Indian
NSSO	National Sample Survey Office
OBC	Other Backward Castes
PIL	Public Interest Litigation
PRI	*Panchayati Raj Institutions*
RLEGP	Rural Landless Employment Guarantee Programme

RSP	Revolutionary Socialist Party
SC	Scheduled Caste
SDO	Sub-Divisional Officer
SECC	Socio-Economic and Caste Census
SEZ	Special Economic Zones
SGRY	*Sampoorna Grameen Rozgar Yojana*
SGSY	*SwarnaJayanti Gram Swarozgar Yojana*
SHG	Self-Help Group
ST	Scheduled Tribe
STW	Shallow Tube Wells
SUCI	Socialist Unity Centre of India
TMC	Trinamul Congress
TPP	Twenty Point Programme
UF	United Front
UPA	United Progressive Alliance
WBHDR	West Bengal Human Development Report
WDR	World Development Report

1 Introduction

Land, capital and well-being in India

At the onset of this book, I make two senses very clear. These two senses, I believe, are enormously significant to understand the logic not only of my emphasis on politics as an angle to analyse the issues of employment, but also of my focus on employment rather than poverty as an analytical category. First, I take it as axiomatic that unemployment is nothing but a political process. Second, I propose to focus on employment, instead of poverty, as an analytical category to gauge the degree of well-being of a particular society. These two senses, I argue, would together engender both a theoretical possibility of a change in viewpoint to conceive the issues of well-being and social justice in a better way, and a practical possibility of essaying a politics in the field of power with an aim of 'transformative social development'. In other words, what I analyse here is the way unemployment has politically been created and recreated in the present regime as part of the complex relationship between capital, class and the state in India. Furthermore, I explain why the issues of employment and unemployment are the appropriate prism to understand the status of well-being of a particular group of population. Conversely, the question of poverty which is being recognized as the main focus of several scholars who are concerned with the well-being of population, or even with the social justice, I would argue, is just one of the techniques of the government to manage the population in want of well-being for the sheer purpose of governance. Poverty is itself an apolitical technical concept originated for the purpose of governance by the state 'bureaucracy' particularly of the developing countries. Departing from the Harriss's argument (2014, 9) that 'the narrow focus on measurement in the analysis of poverty' has a tendency to reduce the problem of poverty to a technical question, I contend that not only does the focus of measurement, but also the discourse of poverty as a whole, in any form and on any level, have the potential to reduce the issues of well-being to a managerial question on the part of the government.

The entry point of my argument to the poverty issues is a recent provocative article titled 'State of Injustices: The Indian State and Poverty', by John Harriss, the veteran scholar on Indian political economy, who draws the inference that (2014, 17) 'even the new rights agenda is more about the management of poverty, in the interest of capital, than it is about the realisation of social justice'. While the statement is partially correct when it says that the 'New Rights Agenda'[1] is about the management of poverty, the statement carries a sense of expectation that the 'New Rights Agenda' has the potential 'that is inherent in the way in which the legislation has cast some socio-economic entitlements as legally enforceable rights' for the realization of social justice. I argue by problematizing the concepts like social justice, its means of realization, its relation with both the issues of poverty and poverty alleviation programmes that there is hardly any inherent potential in the way the 'socio-economic entitlements' have become 'legally enforceable rights' in regard to social justice since these policies including the New Rights Agenda are meant for the management of poverty. The policies, legislations or agendas which are aimed at managing issues of poverty have undoubtedly little prospect to deal with the realization of social justice. The issues of social justice are essentially related with the issues of entitlement or, more specifically, with the well-being of the population. In other words, the sphere of social justice is more about the processes of well-being through which the population of a given society enable themselves to have their socio-economic entitlements. The state unsuccessfully tries to mediate between the two processes, or rather the two classes, in order to fulfil the capitalist agenda. If the process of capitalist accumulation is one among two such processes, another must be the process of intervention in citizens' well-being. Why the state often fails to keep a balance between these two processes is actually due to the inherent fallout of capitalist processes, which I discuss in the following chapters, but what is important in our context is that the state somehow successfully manages the dynamic manifestation of the deficiency of well-being among its population.

The manifestation of the deficiency of well-being, this is to say, of the effect of accumulation of capital can generally be called as poverty. The term 'poverty' is so influential in the administrative terminology of governance that the state politics in contemporary period has mainly been revolved around this term. The state does its politics in, or manages, the domain of poverty in such a way that all the concerned actors presuppose poverty as an end in itself. This is to mean, we all endeavour to target the concept of poverty as both cause and effect. The real cause of poverty, it seems, has increasingly faded into oblivion. The more the governed people would become oblivious to the real root of poverty, the more the state and its institution would try to manage the issues of poverty only for the purpose of governance. As long as poverty, either as a concept or as an empirical condition, remains a technical issue to be managed by governmental technologies, the 'poor' would just be thought to be responsible for their own wretchedness and misery. And, therefore, not only would the extent of poverty continue to increase, but also market capitalism would remain as a default condition in all societies. In the book *Poor Economics*, Banerjee and Duflo (2011) describe the nature of poverty across the globe and explain the ways of fighting global poverty. They have attempted, not surprisingly, to explore the dynamic reasons why the poor are poor, and to prescribe some steps about what is to be done to remedy the poverty or, in a way, to improve the lives of the poor. What the book reveals throughout its pages, interestingly, is that poverty is the reason of poverty. The poor themselves are, as it were, liable for their sorry state. Thus the poor themselves should step forward to improve their lives, and, if they desire, they can undertake the lessons chalked out by the authors. Evidently, the authors are against the view of political economy which presupposes 'politics has the primacy over the economics'. So there is, as such, no politics or class politics or the politics of capital, in their world of poverty, which does play consistently in creating and recreating the issues of poverty. The authors, or the so-called poverty specialists, are rather quite optimist that they identify the poverty traps, armed with patient understanding 'why the poor live the way they do', and know which tools they need to give the poor 'to help them get out of them' (Banerjee and Duflo 2011, 272).

I argue that we all, within the academy as well as in popular discourse, have been familiar with this kind of narrative since long from the beginning of the practice of liberal thought. The normative theories of liberal politics are actually nothing but a capitalist narrative in which the state mediates the issues among its citizens in terms of well-being. But the issues of well-being in the toolbox of the statist discourse almost always remain as a technical, or bureaucratic, purpose of governance throughout all the countries. In the postcolonial countries as well, it has no doubt that, the politics of well-being, rather the politics of governance, mainly revolves around the management of poverty, not around the social justice. Even the Marxist tradition, though having contrary views to liberal political thoughts, rarely offers an effective alternative to liberal political theories. Because, as Chatterjee (2011, 4) correctly analyses the failure of Marxist thoughts, the tendency in a great deal of Marxist thinking is to subordinate 'the political to the economic', and thus to regard 'political principles as the instrumental means for securing economic ends'. The poverty narrative of Banerjee and Duflo simply reflects the mainstream liberal thoughts with which many among the academic milieu perhaps agree. Not only does economics as a discipline conceive this kind of narrative, but the academics in other disciplines also conceive the issues of well-being in terms of the idea of poverty, and thus believe that the latter's eradication requires only an apolitical intervention. The class or capitalist agenda, or the politics in any form, never get a primacy in this narrative of capitalist development. Regardless of the perspective or broader context which set the dynamics of social justice, the dominant liberals try only to understand the nature of poverty, and various means of its eradication. As a result of these deliberations, Harriss (2014, 5) argues that, all 'attention began to be directed at measurement of the incidence of poverty' and its alleviation, at least to some extent, 'which has subsequently become a major academic industry'. But, the question arises whether the attempts or attentions which are to be directed towards the issues of poverty may at all deliver the social justices to the population. Harriss, who correctly recognizes that all the policies including the 'New Rights Agenda' are actually more about the management of poverty, holds some expectation that the policies have potential, since his arguments remain in the same discursive practices. It is the urgent call of the present to the scholars who are seriously constructing their arguments in terms of social justice for a departure from this dominant liberal discursive terrain.

Why I urge for a departure from the liberal discourse is actually due to the very reason that the genuine arguments in favour of social justice are incompatible with the discourses in liberal thoughts. Interestingly, like the Marxists, as mentioned by Chatterjee (2011), who, although critiquing the liberal discourse, are nevertheless failing to offer an effective alternative, the scholars who, though having a tendency to critique often the liberal way of thinking, actually are limiting their arguments to the same discursive mode. I would strongly recommend for a framework which departs from the liberal discursive level toward a new discursive level, and would try to understand the issues of social justice in a newer way. The new framework intends to construct its arguments on the basis of new discourses, and makes sense of the current regime of hegemonic strategies. The question arises: how does Harriss's social justice look like? In fact, Harriss possibly still dreams of the realization of social justice which Nehru had set out in 1947 as a promise.[2] He believes that the policies including the recent New Rights Agenda in India still fall (2014, 17) 'far short of the Nehru's promise of social justice'. Harriss has referred to Nehru's statement that was made during the question and answer session on his draft resolution in the Constituent Assembly where he (Nehru 1947) had affirmed very clearly that '(T)he first task of this Assembly is to free India through a new constitution to feed the starving people and cloth the naked masses and to give every Indian fullest opportunity to develop himself according to his capacity'. However, interestingly, two months ahead of this session, Nehru (1946) didn't hide his concern while moving the resolution that

> this Constituent Assembly is not what many of us wished it to be. It has come into being under particular conditions and the British Government has a hand in its birth. They have attached to it certain conditions. We shall endeavour to work within its limits.... But ... governments do not come into being by State Papers. Governments are, in fact the expression of the will of the people.[3]

Here probably lies a part of the dynamic reasons behind why the government in our context still lacks its essence.

Although Nehru's vision of social justices as declared by him in 1946–1947, and considered by Harriss very recently as kind of exemplary model are essentially based on the principles of liberal politics, his grave concern over the circumstances under which this Constituent Assembly was going to be originated in accordance with the conditions attached by the British Government is significant here to further our discussion. Instead of referring to latest Nehru in the period of 1946–1947, if Harriss could have turned his attention to Nehru's thoughts and arguments a little earlier in the 1930s, particularly in the period of 1933–1936, he could have found another Nehru whose senses of social justice was quite different from the former one. Jawaharlal Nehru grew more and more radical in the period of 1933–1936, and had become a 'Marxist revolutionary anti-imperialist' and written in 1933 (Chandra 1975, 1307), 'the true civic ideal is the socialist ideal, the communist ideal'. The renowned historian Bipan Chandra had written a beautiful and insightful piece about how the radical Nehru would produce consternation among the Indian capitalists and the right-wing in the Congress. Nehru writes, as quoted by Chandra (ibid.), 'I see no way of ending the poverty, the vast unemployment, the degradation, and the subjection of the Indian people' and 'the ending of vested interest in land and industry' and also the ending of private property 'except through socialism'.[4] But, surprisingly, he was gradually, after his Presidential address at the Lucknow session in 1936, abandoning his radical stance only to be engrossed once for all in the liberal fold. Why did this happen? Discussing vividly about how the capitalist class were being frightened upon Nehru's radical political stance, and stepped down wholeheartedly to cut-into-size Nehru, Bipan Chandra clarifies reasonably that (1321) 'many factors, forces, and events went into the making of post-Lucknow Nehru'. While the inherent weakness in Nehru's Marxism and socialist commitment is, no doubt, one of the main causes behind the transformation of Nehru, the multi-pronged attempts of the capitalist class, who became frightened owing to his radical stance, to tackle Nehru at any cost did accelerate this process. This narrative of Nehru's transformation from one pole to another would be of our interest when we discuss the role of the Communists in the sphere of employment in the context of West Bengal.

The main problem regarding the issues of social justice and its achievement seemingly lies the way we are to conceptualize it. Many a time, the scholars who endeavour to use the terms viz. social justice, well-being and poverty alleviation usually use them interchangeably. Although these terms are apparently identical, interpretation of the processes is going to be complicated by the interchangeable use of the terms. It is undeniable that all these terms can be defined in a number of ways on the basis of the standpoints of different schools in social sciences. Social justice is, everyone perhaps agrees, justice in terms of the distribution of wealth, opportunities and privileges within a society.[5] If this is the definition of social justice in just a rational expression, it is clear that the attempts of poverty alleviation and the deliveries of social justices have their own different purpose. The policies which are aimed at poverty alleviation can hardly deliver anything related to social justice. However, the social policies which are aimed at social justice can have the potential to alleviate, or even eradicate, poverty. Almost all the social policies in India, as mentioned by Harriss, have more or less failed to deliver social justice simply due to the fact that these are only aimed at poverty alleviation. Nehru's senses of social justices that Harriss has considered as models of social justice, and also equated with that of Sen's concept of social justice are actually pseudo–social justice being, as it seems (Harriss 2014, 2), 'a common-sensical statement of what would be regarded as fair and reasonable by very many people'. What Nehru had aspired, or rather concerned about, in concrete terms, since a major part of his statement is commonsensical and vague, to achieve at the time of first Constituent Assembly, is nothing but the alleviation of poverty thus having very limited scope and potential in terms of the issues of social justices. Sen's theory of capability approach is, instead, evidently well-thought, reasonable and focused when it defines freedom as to achieve well-being in terms of people's capabilities. This approach is broader, fine and deeper in comparison with the established approaches which focus on economic criteria such as poverty measure and economic growth per capita. In his approach (Sen 1999), 'poverty is understood as deprivation in the capability to live a good life'.[6] While being solicitously defined and morally significant, Sen's approach lacks the strength to explain convincingly about the roots of unequal distribution of wealth, opportunities and privileges in a particular society. We do not get an answer from his theories why some sections of a particular society are deprived from capabilities they require 'to live a good life', and why the people, despite having required capabilities, fail 'to live a good life'. Even Dreze, a staunch protagonist of Sen's idea, finds 'chance' as the only answer when he asks himself (2017, 2), '(H)ow come they (poor) are in their situation, and I in mine?'

In fact, Sen, like late Nehru, tries to explore the meaning, means and solution of social justice within the confine of liberal thoughts. Therefore, he inevitably reckons a standpoint wherein the capitalist development and its predicament are seen as a predetermined context which cannot be altered anyway. Instead of considering this larger perspective, Sen, like late Nehru, thus tries to understand the issues of social justice and poverty considering only the available frameworks that suited with liberal ideologies. I argue that the issues of social justice cannot be understood, let alone be resolved, without bestowing due importance to the root causes of injustices. Put differently, it can be understood, as Parry (2014, 3) asserts, 'only in the context of a broader analysis of the distribution of power'. It must be required to know about, if one intends to address the issues of social justice, on the one hand, how the capitalist relations create the deficiency of social justices, and on the other, the way the social structure influences and reshapes the nature and treatment of justices. In other words, as the issues of social justice would be inexplicable without considering the dynamic reasons of capitalist predicament, so would be its realization. The capability approach, as imagined by Sen, by contrast, reasons the lack of social justice in deprivation in the capabilities, and so does its realization in expansion of capabilities. Likewise, Nehru who had become a hardcore Marxist radical at some point in his colourful life, and whose conception of social justice, while often being exemplified, unsurprisingly laid down a pathway toward progress which soon, as commonly recognized, ended in vain. It was ended in vain as because the pathway recommended by him and his followers who could not but follow his pathways, didn't take into consideration the role of capital in the issues of employment or, more broadly speaking, in the lives and livelihoods of the masses. As a consequence, the successes of his avowal of delivering justice in the Constituent Assembly in 1947 have become ever more and more elusive. Had it been taken into consideration, as did he earlier, he would have explained in a better way the actual reasons behind the lack of social justice in India, and taken actions accordingly.

It is thus evidently important to find out the obstacles behind the failure of 'the redistributive measures and institutional reforms adopted by the Indian state' in reducing poverty as 'the Nehruvian planners had hoped and expected' (Parry 2014, 18) for an effective reprieve therefrom. However, another question which is equally important, if not more, is about how potential these redistributive measures and institutional reforms are in delivering social justice. I argue that we ought to give more emphasis on the analysis of redistributive measures and institutional reforms adopted by the Indian state for finding out the extent of their actual potentiality to deliver social justices than on the obstacles behind the less-effectiveness of the said interventions to reduce poverty. It sounds like a paradox when the scholars like Parry, on the one hand, note that the situation of the poor 'is explicable only in terms of the wider system of class and power relations in which it is embedded' (6), on the other, believe that the above measures of the government are having some potentials to reduce the poverty. Although Parry himself does not deny the fact, when he says that 'over the course of a decade, many (poor) might escape, while many others fall into it (poverty)', and 'democracy cannot be relied upon to provide the solution' (30); however, his statements become ambiguous since he fails, it seems, to recognize these intervention policies as ineffective in itself in question of social justice. If he had recognized that, he would have concluded, as did Frankel (2005) at least to a greater extent, that the democracy for which these kind of social policies are going to be possible does actually create such a condition in which current inequalities instead are aggravated. Despite being in agreement partly, I would disagree with Frankel in some points, and would rather extend some of her arguable points further than what she touches but misses to carry forward. Frankel (2005), it seems, has no dispute over the nature and potentiality of the Nehruvian socialist programme, and so she believes that poverty could be alleviated if these policies were to be implemented properly. Her main point is that as a result of the prevailing democracy, 'the privileged dominant castes and classes were able to subvert the goals of social policy' (Parry 2014, 21), and thus 'the promises of the policy makers could not be redeemed' (Frankel 2005, 491). I argue that even if the privileged dominant castes and classes had not been able to subvert the goals of social policy, poverty would have not been alleviated, let alone the realization of social justice.

This book explains through a narrative of (rural) West Bengal the reasons why the redistributive measures and institutional reforms could do very little within the existing structure of political and economic power in India. The question that arises then is in what way we would characterize the existing structure of political and economic power in India. Why and how far does the existing structure of political and economic power cause inequality which in turn inevitably creates and recreates poverty in India? Why the issues of social justice are 'explicable only in terms of the wider system of class and power relations in which it is embedded' (Parry, 2014, 3)? In order to explore the answers of these questions we have to deal with the root at which the existing structure of political and economic power began to originate in colonial India.

Colonialism, land and landlessness

The history of undivided Bengal, the state of West Bengal in India and Bangladesh presently, has featured relentless poverty for more than two and a half centuries since 1757 in such a way that Bengal has long been synonymous with hunger. However, before 1757, the features of Bengal were just opposite, and as Clive (1772) narrates, 'the country of Bengal, by way of distinction' was 'the paradise of the earth'.[7] Bengal, a miniature of India, was really a very prosperous settlement before the British and other colonialists came in for trade and business in the seventeenth century. Bernier, a physician and traveller in the Mughal period, found Bengal as 'the finest and most fruitful country in the world' as early as in late 1665, and there was a proverb (Bernier 1891, 439) 'in common use among the Portuguese, English and Dutch, that the kingdom of Bengale has a hundred gates open for entrance, but not one for departure'.[8] The villagers, I quote Mukerjee (2010, xv–xvi),[9] it seems significant, 'owned the lands they tended, and not even bankruptcy could evict them.... Agricultural taxes – a fifth of the harvest – could be paid in kind', and 'the state recognizing farmers, spinners, weavers and merchants as the source of its wealth, tried to protect them'. However, Bengal soon would fall down into subjugation, ruin and bankruptcy as consequences of the company and its masters' conspiracies, plunders, corruption and above all, abusive domination. The vivid accounts of the historians like Dirks (2006) and many others reveal about how the royal treasury became empty; local merchants began downing shutters, and the villagers in general became ever more destitute and land-poor.

What is particularly significant in our context is that the existing norms of land ownership of the villagers were changed once for all. Now all lands belonged to the state which meant that the villagers or the farmers who could not pay the rent would lose possession of their land. And, unsurprisingly, their inability to pay agricultural tax was more than obvious fact as consequences of frequent crop failure, rain shortage and the exorbitant revenues charged by the Company. Such an exorbitant exploitation, however, would not go for ever, and it exacerbated the problem toward a general bankruptcy which, in turn, caused a famine in 1770 due to, as well, the failure of rains.[10] Hunter describes (1868),

> (T)he husbandmen sold their cattle; they sold their implements of agriculture; they devoured their seed-grain; they sold their sons and daughters, till at length no buyer of children could be found; they ate the leaves of trees and the grass of the field; and in June 1770 the Resident at [Murshidabad] affirmed that the living were feeding on the dead.[11]

Actually, the policies of the British East India Company were liable to a great extent to aggravate the famine. The Company, instead of distributing relief[12] and granting exemption from tax revenue, forced the villagers to pay the rent 'owed by dead neighbours' (ibid.) despite the fact that there were very few hands available then for tilling the lands, and subsequently Bengal's fertile lands virtually became a total waste like jungles. Thus the amount of taxes that the Company expected could not be met any longer. The Empire was afterwards evidently required to regulate and reform the land revenue system. Cornwallis added to the villagers' distress by returning to the *zamindars* their hereditary role of collecting taxes, and 'fixed the annual revenue owed to the state' (ibid.). This new system, which is called as Permanent Settlement, had two obvious purposes. One, it would inspire the *zamindars* to tend their fiefdom. Two, the East India Company tried to annex other regions of India upon using the steady income from Bengal. As a result of the changing nature of tax, from one which varied with the harvest to the other, which was fixed rent, the villagers, the landowners, rapidly became labourers after losing their lands to the moneylenders, and began to work for low wages in 'what had been their own fields' (ibid.).

The historical trajectory of the early period of colonialism in India explicates about how unemployment and poverty had been constructed due not to the individuals' lack in their capabilities but to 'the wider system of class and power relations' (Parry 2014, 3). And, the western colonialists, who could ably develop their countries by maintaining an apparent balance between the processes of capitalist accumulation, and the intervention in well-being of the population, failed considerably to maintain the balance between these two processes in their colonies like India and, I argue, subsequently devastated these societies during, at least, the initial period of colonial rule due mainly to their focus only on the accumulation of capital. However, the colonial rule since then could successfully construct a new discursive terrain wherein India, particularly Bengal, began to be identified as a country or state of poverty and wretchedness, and the subjects of which, as the British rulers believed, were waiting to be liberated by the colonial modernists. Many influential scholars and intellectuals as well would describe the situation of Bengal in such a way that, it seems, Bengal, or India, as it were, originated out of poverty and unemployment, and would keep carrying on this feature until and unless the colonialists aid them to salvage from their destitution.

But the British colonialists would soon realize that it is not only just significant but also an essential prerequisite for governing a subject-population, particularly who have been colonized, to maintain a fair balance between the extent of accumulation of capital, and the level of intervention in people's well-being. While a brief initial period of colonial rule (1757–1793) in India witnessed the anarchy, rampant plunder and brutal exorbitant taxation, and also ensuing famines and a series of rebellions of the hungry and destitute people, the latter period (post 1793) of the colonial regime did attest supposedly more controlled, strategic and well-thought governance. While, in the earlier period, the British colonialists neglected to maintain a balance between the capitalist accumulation, and the survival of the subject people, they had tried to take care of maintaining a balance between the two processes in the subsequent period. In colonial Bengal, Chatterjee (1984, 6–7) correctly notes that, 'after much debate and several experiments, it (the colonial government) went into an arrangement' 'with a class of Indians who were designated as proprietors', to accomplish 'the primary and abiding interest' that is the extraction of a part of the surplus in the form of land revenue. Floud, the Chairman of Bengal land revenue commission appointed in 1939, after meticulously analysing the system of land revenue in the colonial era, commented (1940, 19) that 'the primary object of the East India Company ... was to safeguard the punctual receipt of the land revenue'. For this purpose, he added, 'the expansion of cultivation was indispensible, and ... Lord Cornwallis hoped that it (Permanent Settlement) would result in the creation of a class of landlords who would supply capital for the improvement of land and the extension of cultivation'. The Floud Commission (19, 36) has also noted, 'in the opinion of the government', the expansion of cultivation 'could only be achieved by giving to all people interested in the land down to the actual cultivators a sense of security'. Although the Permanent Settlement remained operational throughout the nineteenth and the first half of the twentieth centuries 'as a basic institutional form through which revenue was collected' (ibid.), the colonial government had always been concerned about the 'protection' of small peasant economy. The report of the Bengal land revenue commission, popularly called as Floud Commission, describes thoroughly why a policy like Permanent Settlement was not economically sound, and why the rights and securities of the actual cultivators were more than essential. Simply put, one of the main reasons was purely economic in nature. An unimpaired system of economy, the British rulers seemed to have realized, might 'ensure a steady source of revenue'. They had also tried to protect the rights, be it customary or the legal, to both proprietorship and occupancy, of the small peasants keeping in mind that any such alternation could cause law and order problem in the respective areas. Notwithstanding the fact that the colonial government tried to check the (ibid., 7–8) 'thoroughgoing capitalist reorganization of agricultural production' mainly in order to continue their expanded process of colonial appropriation, neither could they succeed in curbing the risk of law and order problems among the peasantry, nor could they prevent the decay of the small peasant economy. The small peasant economy, in fact, was going to be pushed down gradually causing enormous crisis in employment situation particularly in the latter period of colonial rule.

After the periodic famines occurred in the initial period of colonial rule which had devastating effects on their lives and livelihoods, the peasants of Bengal began to experience the ramification of unemployment since the middle of the nineteenth century, when the demands of land was relentlessly increased by deindustrialization,[13] and the enhancement of rent was frequently made. However, it was not the fact that 'the burden of the rent on the raiyat was just about the utmost that he could bear' and, as Chatterjee (1984, 16–17) describes, it was enhanced when 'the erstwhile constraint on the enhanceability was no longer effective'. The earlier constraint meant by them was the likelihood that 'the *raiyat* would leave his land and run' resulting in a crisis of availability of *raiyats*. Had it been the case that the colonial rulers always consider the grounds on which (ibid.) 'enhancement of rent would be permitted', the Bengal's economy would not have been so distraught in the colonial period. Floud Commission Report (1940, 37) notes that 'a steady reduction is taking place in the number of actual cultivators possessing occupancy rights, and there is a large increase in the number of landless labourers'. The labourers 'now constitute 29 percent of the total agricultural population'. Conversely, the same report informs that the army of rent-receivers was increasing even by 62 per cent in the same period. Due to the reasons like subinfeudation, absence of rent remission and unscientific rent rate, many *raiyats* were becoming *bargadar* at that time after losing their occupancy rights in land. In fact, the colonial policy, right from the Permanent Settlement, of taxation and revenue accumulation was framed in such way that neither did the small tenants prosper, nor did the small proprietors or tenure holders flourish to be rich. The small *zamindars* or tenure-holders were so distressed, particularly after early

1930s when the collection of rents reduced drastically in Bengal as a result of widespread agrarian distress, due to their insufficient earnings from the land that, I quote from Chatterjee (ibid., 22), 'it is known that the number of unemployed amongst the *bhadraloks* is large and that the circumstances of many families are pitiful and their sufferings vary great, in some cases falling little short of death by slow starvation'.

Several petty *zamindars* or tenure-holders in Bengal, particularly in its western and northern districts, were thus propelled to transfer or sublet their land or tenures often to the traders and moneylenders who, in some cases, were the rich *raiyats*. Conversely, a section of the landlords, small or big, instead of distributing all land to the *raiyats*, did retain some *khas* land in their possession for direct cultivation by the labourers. As a result, some of the rich *raiyats* had become rent receiving tenure-holders, whereas some of the tenure-holders could retain in their possession new land which was either brought under cultivation or kept as uncultivable land. While more than 70 percent of the land in the districts of eastern Bengal was in the direct possession of cash-paying settled *raiyats* (ibid., 27), 'the situation in western and central Bengal was in sharp contrast with the distribution of occupancy rights'. This was the beginning of the process of differentiation among the peasantry in western part of Bengal. At the start of the twentieth century, this process of differentiation among the peasantry took an interesting turn when the substantial tenure-holders could well utilize the new development that occurred in the agricultural sector. An analysis by Chatterjee (1984) on the basis of data available from the Census of India (1921) reveals that 'whereas 83.75 percent of the agricultural workforces in British Bengal were tenants', this proportion was below 80 per cent in the south western districts. The proportion of labourers and tillers, those don't have any legal rights to land in these districts, on the contrary, was much higher.[14]

We would also see that there were a significant number of rentiers who did not belong to the class of proprietors and tenure-holders. Conversely, a large number of *bhagchasi* (sharecroppers) peasants, who instead of being considered as independent tenant cultivators,[15] were usually recognized as labourers, constituted huge proportions of agricultural population in these districts. Chatterjee informs us that a large proportion of those having land in their possession were not cultivators themselves in these districts. Their land was actually cultivated by the sharecroppers or, in other words, the labourers.[16] As a result of this phenomenon of differentiation among the peasantry, the districts of south-western and northern part of Bengal did rarely witness such kind of mass agitation of the peasants against the *zamindars* and tenure-holders as did in the eastern part of Bengal. Not only was the peasantry differentiated herein, but was also no agricultural class that being clearly defined. For instance, take the category of sharecropper peasants for analysis. The sharecroppers were not only included in the category of labourer, they were also differentiated into many sub-categories like *adhiars*, *bargadars* and *sanja*. Although the classification of agricultural population was usually the discretion of the colonial government, in practice there were various kinds of occupation in land, and of sharing of crop/produce rent. Besides, many of the sharecroppers, or the *bargadars*, were themselves small owner-cultivators. As a result of these practices, only a lesser proportion of agricultural population could be classified as *bargadar*.

This trajectory of land ownership, land occupation and land alienation in Bengal was in point of fact conditioned by colonial capital, and was subsequently driven to recreate various class relations in agrarian field. The older categories got fragmented, and new categories emerged in the evolving agrarian structure particularly in its western and northern part. Despite the consistent endeavour of colonial power to 'protect' both the proprietor class and the small peasantry, neither did the *zamindars* remain stable, nor did the small peasants. While the landed *zamindar* class continued to decline, a new rich peasant/*raiyat*-moneylender-trader class emerged at the rural grass root. The small peasantry also got disbanded into a composite class of poor peasant, sharecropper and labourer who were steadily going to be controlled by the emerging rich peasant/*raiyat*-moneylender-trader class. The conditions of colonialism under which this transformation in socioeconomic formation had occurred itself eventually began to be questioned by the vulnerable classes resulting in a class conflict causing agrarian unrest in Bengal. The British state who long seeking to maintain an equilibrium between two major agricultural classes, the *zamindars*-tenure-holders and the small peasantry, was neither able to arrest the threat of high unemployment experienced by the class of poor peasants, sharecroppers and labourers, nor able to succeed in controlling the peasant unrest in Bengal. The colonial state had compellingly been trying to intervene with its governmental legislations and policies in the growing agricultural crisis, and the subsequent peasant unrests for their broader purpose of regularizing the expansion of colonial appropriation. Until the declaration of the Floud Commission Report in 1940, the legislations like Bengal Rent Act (1859), Bengal Tenancy Act (1885) and the Bengal Tenancy Amendment Act (1928) are notable among various acts passed by the colonial government meant for mediation between two major conflicting classes. However, these acts and legislations failed to achieve due success not because only of the intrinsic dynamic reasons cropped up in rural Bengal, but also due to some other crucial factors operating in the broader context.

The agrarian structure in which these legislations/acts were administered, and subsequently ended up with a mess was, in fact, pre-muddled with a number of undefined and conflicting issues regarding the question of right. One of the two pairs of conflicting rights that did factor in our context was between the right to proprietorship and the right to occupancy, while another was between the customary right and legal right. Neither of the pairs, or neither side of each pair regarding the question of right, was at that time agreeably and categorically defined among different stakeholders, and therefore, the discourse on right in terms of land question did always generate confusion, debate and conflict at the rural margin. However, the fact is that, for instance, in case of Bengal Tenancy Amendment Act (1928), as Chatterjee's influential study on land question in the colonial period shows, despite the original bill of this legislation providing some safeguards in the interest of the tenants and the under-*raiyats*, its amendments were inclined only to the interest of the *zamindars*. The historical narrative, ever since the introduction of this bill (1928), explains the ways in which some pro-tenant clauses scripted on the proposed bill were amended in favour of the *zamindars* in the Council, and several protests and political formations were consequently organized around various recommendations, amendments and interests of different agricultural class groups. But everything took a new turn when a land revenue commission was formed under the chairmanship of Francis Floud in 1939 as an urgent response to, on the one hand, escalating unemployment, poverty and landlessness in terms of right to occupation and proprietorship, and on the other, inconstancy of revenue earning in Bengal. Above all, peasant unrest was also the reason that the said commission was set up. After critically examining the land revenue system with reference to the Permanent Settlement, the effect of this system on economic and social structure of Bengal, and the economic conditions of the actual cultivators, the commission notes that the province was in a state of tremendous jeopardy both from the perspective of revenue collection, and from that of agricultural prosperity. The main concern of the commission had been the steady increase in number of *bargadar* sharecroppers and landless labourers almost all of whom had lost their land due to subinfeudation, rack-renting and indebtedness. As part of the recommendations, the report asserts, 'it is practicable and advisable for government to acquire all the superior interests in agricultural land so as to bring the actual cultivators into direct relation with the government.' In other words, the report considered the proposal (sec 10) 'to abolish the *zamindari* system in its entirety'. Also, by expressing their concern over 'a large and increasing proportion of the actual cultivators' (*bargadars* and sharecroppers) who had (39; Para, 87) 'no part of the elements of ownership, no protection against excessive rents, and no security of tenure', the commission (69; Para, 146) recommends that 'all *bargadars* should be declared as to be tenants' and 'the share of the crop legally recoverable from them should be one-third, instead of half'.[17] The Floud Commission report and recommendations clearly reveal that the economy of rural Bengal had become devastated in terms of land and employment issues in course of and due to British colonial rule for around last two centuries. This report also shows that it was really a difficult task to maintain a balance, which the colonialists intended for, on the one hand, between two agendas, the capital accumulation and the general masses' well-being, on the other, between two classes, the proprietors and the tenants. But let's see now the fate of Floud Commission's report, and what it could deliver in the field of employment and well-being in rural Bengal.

Land, land reform and employment

The postcolonial rural Bengal thus set out on its journey carrying a strong existence of landlessness, indebtedness and unemployment in the rural landscape as well as with a strong sense of expectations for agrarian prosperity grown out of India's independence as well as of recommendations and suggestions by the Floud Commission for the remedy of the ongoing rural predicament. Nehru correctly recognizes the challenges before the political architects of new India when he expresses his concern about the fulfillment of the expectations of the peasantry at the inception of Constituent Assembly in 1947. Actually, he identifies the future challenges long before India's independence, and warns (Nehru 1938, 235),

> they (the peasantry) are expectant and if the Congress call does not reach their ears, some other will, and they will respond to it. But the call that will find echo in their hearts must deal with their own sufferings and the way to get rid of them.[18]

This is to mean, the leaders were aware all along of the political consequences of the failure to fulfill the rural expectations. They could not but pay heed to the recommendations by the Floud Commission for managing the issues like land-lessness, *bargadar* rights and unemployment, apart from taking some community development projects in rural areas. The Nehru-led government of independent India thus first took an urgent attempt to enact the land reform laws in line of instructions that scripted for colonial interest by Floud Commission. On the basis of this enactment, all states including West Bengal did subsequently reform their own land policies.

In case of West Bengal, the history of land reforms can roughly be divided into three phases. During the first phase (1953–1966), while the West Bengal Estate Acquisition Act (1953) aimed to eliminate the interests of intermediaries i.e. *zamindars* and tenure-holders on all lands except that they 'self-cultivate' (using hired labours, of course), the Land Reform Act (1955) intended to restrict the landholders' ability to transfer land (to avoid ceiling), and to provide protection to the *bargadars*. But, little of these two acts were implemented since much of the above-ceiling land was retained until 1966 by the rural gentry through evasive transfers to relatives, friends and fictitious persons. On the contrary, the latter act supposedly led to widespread eviction of cultivators from land by the landlords who wanted to evade the provisions of the act, thereby increasing the percentage of agricultural labourers in the state (Dutta 1988). The second phase (1967–1976) saw the installation of two United Front (UF) governments in West Bengal, and a surge in peasant movement principally to reclaim the *benami* lands so far held by the landlords through their connection with the administration and the political leaders in power (Bandyopadhyay 2007). But little could be done in this period to grant greater security to the *bargadars* due to the lack of a proper legislation. In the third phase (since 1977), however, success was achieved to an extent in safeguarding the rights of the *bargadars*, and distribution of ceiling-surplus land when the erstwhile Left Front government launched 'Operation Barga' under which the names of *bargadars* were recorded.

The question arises as to what sort of changes have occurred in employment condition after the relative success in implementation of land reform policies in rural West Bengal. Have the policies of land reform which was once thought to be the panacea for all rural ills resolved the employment question in the state? The data suggest that after a forceful effort of land reforms like estate acquisition and legal protection of *bargadars* for more than a half century, nearly half of the rural households still appear to be landless in the state, and the rate of landlessness is fast increasing (HDR 2004). SocioEconomic and Caste Census (SECC) (2011) data demonstrate that 49 per cent of rural households in the country show signs of poverty, and 51 per cent of households have manual casual labour as their source of income.[19] The same source also reveals that one out of three families living in villages is landless and depends on manual labour for livelihood.[20] The economic data from various registers actually present a dichotomous view of West Bengal – on the one hand, there has been a phenomenal growth in agriculture,[21] and on the other, there seems to be a steady decline in regular employment in rural areas.[22] Though the amount of land distributed in the state was more than any other state in India, there has been a simultaneous increase in proportion of landless people among the rural population who work in agriculture (Roy 2013). According to the census reports, the per cent of owner-cultivators has decreased from 53.9 per cent to 43.4 per cent while the per cent of agricultural labourers has increased from 46.1 per cent to 56.6 per cent in just one decade (GoWB 2004).

Actually, it is not surprising that the occurrence of landlessness and unemployment increases in recent times in rural West Bengal. Despite the successful tenancy reforms and initial production boom in agriculture in West Bengal, many small cultivators are losing their land, be it their own land or the *barga* land, and facing job scarcity in their vicinities at the rural margin. The rural elites or the erstwhile prosperous farmers are also not in a reasonable position to continue agriculture since it has turned often into an unprofitable sector. This phenomenon of crisis in agriculture has further accelerated the job scarcity in rural West Bengal. All these factors thus prompted a huge migration of these jobless marginal villagers from rural to rural, rural to urban and even rural West Bengal to abroad in search of jobs. This research finds that the rural men leaving their families at home are even venturing out for unfamiliar and risky jobs to distant places in the foreign countries. My field survey notes that there are simultaneous instances of reverse migration when some of the rural migrants are back home either after earning a lump sum amount of money or recognizing the migrant jobs more uncertain and vulnerable. The point is that the phenomenon of landlessness and unemployment which was defined by Floud and his associates as early as in 1940 in Bengal as consequence of Permanent Settlement, and lack of any right of the *bargadars* to land has still been evident in recent period though in a different fashion even after a major change in land relations. The question that remains to be answered: how could we interpret this phenomenon of unemployment afresh?

In fact, it is true that agriculture and its growth has expanded and improved due to the implementation of land reform policies formulated in conceptual line of Floud Commission. But it is also true that the expansion of market as well as capital has enormously grown as a result of land reforms during the same period. Floud thus seems to be considered as right in his position, if we judge the potential of his recommendations from the perspective of capital. However, in our context, interestingly, not only does agriculture become unprofitable, but the small peasantry also turn out to be the most vulnerable section for the very purpose of capital. Actually, capital as well as market gets increasingly thriving ever since at the cost of agriculture, and the lives and livelihoods of small peasantry. By exploiting the input provision and the harvest procurement in the agricultural sector, the market has become strengthened, and capital thereafter gets accumulated at a higher level at the rural grass roots. The application of GRT, which is deemed as a dream project by a section of academics, has prompted not only to increase the application of inputs in cultivation but also to reduce the fertility of the soil, and subsequent slump in production which one can assume once s/he sets foot in the village. In course of all these major steps on the part of the government in regard to land reforms and expansion of agriculture, capital only gains its strength through utilizing the thriving sphere of peasant economy. Hence, the agenda 'to feed the starving people and cloth the naked masses and to give every Indian fullest opportunity to develop himself according to his capacity', as set by Nehru, to be taken into action, have still mostly remained as an agenda. And it has remained as an agenda even after six decades or so as Indian democracy has had to work, in Nehru's words, 'within its limits'. The limit, i.e. British Government's hand, as argued, which had imposed certain conditions, is actually the capital both in the past and the present. Those sections of small and marginal peasantry are still experiencing the predicament of being unemployed and landless, and so waiting to be relieved by poverty alleviation programmes of the government. However, the formulation of poverty alleviation programmes for the rural poor is not new and has begun to implement just after independence in 1952. Its scope and intensity have, however, amplified day by day, but there is certainly some doubt about the validity and applicability of every precedent policy and legislation. What are the roles of these policies in lives and livelihoods of the rural people, anyway? What has necessitated the government to enact the 'New rights agenda' like MGNREGA (Mahatma Gandhi National Rural Employment Guarantee Act) after these long years of sustained efforts since independence to resolve the crisis of unemployment and poverty? Drawing on the ethnographic findings from field work in 18 villages of 18 districts in the state, the book examines, first, the nature and dynamic reasons of unemployment, and second, whether these 'New Rights agenda' contain any new potential which enables the rural citizens to recognize their right to employment.

Outline of the book

The present chapter sets the hypothetical and empirical context for explaining why the issues of employment and unemployment should be the appropriate prism to understand the status of well-being of a population. It also explains the way the poverty vis-à-vis unemployment is going to be created and recreated in different regimes as simple consequences of complex relationship between capital, class and the state in rural West Bengal, India.

Chapter 2, 'Right to Work! Politics of Poverty Alleviation Policies in India', delves into the genealogy of governmental reasoning behind employment generation in rural India. Upon understanding carefully the rationale of various policies and acts regarding employment generation that have been enacted since 1947, it tries to explore why unemployment has been a perennial phenomenon at the rural margin. Does the enactment and implementation of the MGNREGA create any enabling condition for the people in rural areas to get employment as entitlement? The chapter explains the dynamic trajectory of emergence of this act, and the ways different stakeholders engage with it in terms of employment and rights. It explains, by analysing the laws, by-laws and various rules and regulations scripted in the act, why the same fails to fulfil its claims of guaranteeing work to the rural citizens in India.

Chapter 3, 'Political Parties, Employment Generation Policies and Governance', deals with the roles played by the political parties in shaping and determining the creation and fate of social policies, in India particularly in context of West Bengal. It explains, in other words, the way the political parties are mediating between two sets of confronting classes as well as capital and the broad masses, and thereby shaping the nature of capitalist expansion at the rural margin. The roles of political parties seem to be enormous in a country like India since the citizens here often assess the legitimacy of a government, and the parties in power or the parties in opposition, on the basis of the latter's performance/promise in delivery of well-being. This chapter discusses how the roles of different political parties do change in different time and place based on their position in relation to power.

Chapter 4, 'Caste, Class and Rural Employment', engages the issues of caste and class, the most significant components in realm of public policies, which have been operational in rural areas of West Bengal. It explores, on the one hand, the trajectory of transformations in land relations, and the role of the upper caste landholding group in shaping the phenomenon of landlessness, and on the other, the implication of the policy interventions on all rural classes in employment terms. It explains the social dynamics of ascendancy of the rich peasantry to power by means of land ownership and authority over labour, and its subsequent politics in shaping the condition of rural unemployment in West Bengal. The chapter concludes that owing to the determinant role of capital whatsoever in agriculture, the state of rural economy of India, particularly of West Bengal, has deteriorated leading to transform the class configuration further by means of marketization of farming and other occupations.

Chapter 5, 'Civil Society, NGOs and Rural Employment', focuses on the roles of 'civil society', 'non-party formations' and the NGOs in making and shaping various policies and acts like the MGNREGA that were meant for alleviating rural poverty. It critically analyses why the people of civil society who enjoying the privileges of exploiting the spaces of accumulation economy would try to mediate with the government for the benefit of rural subordinate groups. It begins with a conjecture that the NGOs have basically been the part and parcel of the civil society, and their relationship with the state is, instead of being tensional and conflicting, in most cases 'one of strategic alliances and interdependence'. This chapter elucidates by analysing the functioning of three NGOs working on the domain of rural poverty and unemployment that the initiatives on the part of all kinds of 'civil societies' are more or less same as far as their aims and objectives are concerned. All these 'civil societies' are actually venturing into the lowest strata of people in order to accommodate them in the grand narrative of state formation and capitalist development. Instead of being the opposition to the state, the people of these 'societies' do act as appendages of the state so as to aid in its duties to govern the distressed people who are the creation of the underlying processes of this unequal structure of the postcolonial societies.

Chapter 6, 'Gender, Women and Rural Employment', deals with women's work in rural West Bengal in order to understand, on the one hand, the prevailing gendered structure of power in the domain of work and employment, and on the other, the impact of the changing governmental policy on gender and women in rural West Bengal. The chapter interrogates whether and how the dichotomous conception of private and public shapes the women's access to employment, work and local representation, and thereby creating a condition that affects their right to various entitlements. The chapter concludes that the *ghar* and *bahir* dichotomy still determines the women's performance in employment, and in rate of wages. The women can hardly use the MGNREGA for equal opportunities in employment, and thereby pursuing a larger political process in gender terms. Even the greater participation of women in the MGNREGA doesn't necessarily ensure greater representation on the employment front. Rather, women' labour which is otherwise invisible, is being used to make the land and agriculture more productive.

Chapter 7, 'Conclusion: Employment, Capital and the State in Rural India', concludes that unemployment is nothing but a political process. Understanding poverty as a manifestation of unemployment that is rooted in dynamic relations of classes and castes, the chapter analyses the limit of the dominant theorizations to understand the causes of poverty as well as its eradication. It investigates through the lens of employment the way in which poverty is being recreated in the context of neoliberal restructuration. The chapter reveals by analysing the implementation of Employment Guarantee Act that while the present policy regime tries to strengthen its hegemony by introducing a new kind of governance, the eradication of poverty remains mostly as an unfinished agenda since the fundamental causes of poverty have mostly been ignored.

Notes

1 'New Rights Agenda' is now a popular phrase (since its coinage by Ruparelia (2013)) among the scholars who are concerned about the welfare policies in India.
2 Nehru stated these words on 22 February 1947 in course of discussion of the Resolution moved by Nehru on 13 December 1946, when the Constitution Assembly of India met in the Constitutional Hall, New Delhi.
3 Nehru gave a short introduction regarding the context considering which he was going to move the resolution on 13 December 1946.
4 Chandra has beautifully written this article on the basis of historical evidences including Nehru's own writings, letters, news statement, interviews as well as many communications and pamphlets issued on behalf of the industry owners, merchants and traders particularly in Mumbai (then Bombay).
5 See *New Oxford American Dictionary*.

6 See Internet Encyclopaedia of Philosophy. Downloadable from www.iep.utm.edu/ sen-cap
7 See the lecture of Robert Clive (1772) who founded the British Empire by conquering Bengal.
8 See Bernier (1891, 437–438) and Majumdar (1973, 177–178, 184). Bernier has described in detail in his travelogue how prosperous Bengal is in the period of Mughal. He writes, '(F)oreign merchants worked the wholesale markets, offering to buy produce in exchange for silver. They could not trade goods with native business, because Bengal was in need of virtually nothing.'
9 Mukerjee uses historical findings of Majumdar (1973); Sinha (1981); and Sen (1988) to establish the fact that the villagers would enjoy some sorts of securities on land before the East India Company's domination came into being.
10 Historical sources reveal that the Calcutta Council, or the East India Company, put the task of collecting taxes up for auction, and handed over the right to collect tax to whoever promised the greatest return for the territory (Majumdar 1973; Mukerjee 2010).
11 I quote from Hunter (1868), the Kindle version.
12 The East India Company did spend a small amount on famine relief, mainly by buying rice from the districts only to distribute the same in the cities like Calcutta and Murshidabad.
13 Numerous researches on the economy of both pre-colonial and colonial India reveal that the Indian economy, particularly of Bengal's, was much better in the pre-colonial period. It was even better than the contemporary British economy. There were lots of petty commodity producers who used to produce many handicraft products in the manufacture industries in Bengal and to export those to the entire world including Europe. But the British colonial rule did ruin entirely the indigenous industries in India as a part of the process which is known as deindustrialization. For details, see Bagchi (2010).
14 The proportion is above 20 per cent in western part of Bengal, whereas it is only 12.23 per cent in case of Bengal. See Chaterjee for details.
15 But, exceptionally, in some parts of northern Bengal, like Jalpaiguri district, there were a large number of tenant cultivators who cultivated the land of *zamindars* independently but having no permanent rights of occupation. They were called as *adhiar* in this region.
16 Interestingly, a much smaller proportion of the agricultural population was classified as mainly sharecroppers or *bargadars* since many of them were small owner-cultivators.
17 Flood Commission actually recommends that the John Kerr's Bill should be restored, 'by which it was proposed to treat as tenants *bargadars* who supply the plough, cattle, and agricultural implements'. After anticipating that some difficulties may arise in the way to define the *bargadars* who supply the aforementioned components, the commission recommends that all *bargadars* should be considered as tenants.
18 See also Nayar (1960) who took quotation from Jawaharlal Nehru (1938).
19 See also the *Times of India*, 4 July 2015. Though the focus of SECC (2011) was equally on caste-like other socio-economic classes, the findings on castes have not been published due to the fear of social upheaval.
20 See again *Times of India*, 3 July 2015. According to that census, the total number of families in India is 24.39 crore, of which 17.91 crore live in villages.
21 There was an unprecedented growth in the production of food grains including paddy, the main staple food in the state, during the 1980s, i.e. the first decade of the Left Front rule in West Bengal. See for details Rawl and Swaminathan (1998) and Roy (2013).
22 According to the Planning Commission, the proportion of population below poverty line in 1999–2000 was 31.85 per cent in the whole state, which is higher than the national average of 26 per cent. Significantly, 84 per cent of the absolutely poor population lived in the villages, compared to 74 per cent in India as a whole. See Roy (2013).

References

Bagchi, Amiya, ed. 2010. *Colonialism and Indian Economy*. New Delhi: Oxford University Press.

Bandyopadhyay, Debabrata. 2007. *Land, Labour and Governance*. Kolkata: Worldview.

Banerjee, Abhijit V. and Esther Duflo. 2011. *Poor Economics: A Radical Rethinking of the Way to Fight Global Poverty*. New York: Public Affairs.

Bernier, Francois. 1891. *Travels in the Mogul India (AD 1656–1668)*. London: Archibald. Downloadable at Archive.org

Chandra, Bipan. 1975. 'Jawaharlal Nehru and the Capitalist Class, 1936.'*Economic and Political Weekly* 10 (33–35): 1307–1324.

Chatterjee, Partha. 1984. *Bengal: 1920–1947: Land Question*. Calcutta: K P Bagchi.

Chatterjee, Partha. 2011. *Lineages of Political Society: Studies in Post-Colonial Democracy*. New Delhi: Permanent Black.

Dirks, Nicholas B. 2006. *The Scandal of Empire: India and the Creation of Imperial Britain*. Cambridge: The Belknap Press of Harvard University Press.

Dreze, Jean. 2017. *Sense and Solidarity: Jholawala Economics for Everyone*. New Delhi: Permanent Black.

Dutta, P. K. 1988. *Land Reforms Administration in West Bengal*. New Delhi: Daya Publishing House.

Frankel, Francine R. 2005. *India's Political Economy 1947–2004: The Gradual Revolution*. New Delhi: Oxford University Press.

Hunter, William Wilson. 1868. *The Annals of Rural Bengal*. London: Smith. Downloadable at Archive.org

Majumdar, R. C. 1973. *History of Medieval Bengal*. Calcutta: Bharadwaj.

Mukerjee, Madhusree. 2010. *Churchill's Secret War: The British Empire and the Ravaging of India during World War II*. New Delhi: Tranquebar.

Nayar, Baldev Raj. 1960. 'Community Development Programme: Its Political Impact.' *Economic and Political Weekly*, September 17: 1401–1410.

Nehru, Jawaharlal. 1938. *Eighteen Months in India*. Allahabad: Kitabistan.

Parry, Jonathan. 2014. 'Introduction.' In *Persistence of Poverty in India*, edited by Nandini Gooptu and Jonathan Parry, 1–31. New Delhi: Social Science Press.

Rawl, Vikash and Madhura Swaminathan. 1998. 'Changing Trajectories: Agricultural Growth in West Bengal, 1950–1996.' *Economic and Political Weekly*, October 3: 2595–2602.

Roy, Dayabati. 2013. *Rural Politics in India: Political Stratification and Governance in West Bengal*. New Delhi: Cambridge University Press.

Ruparelia, Sanjay. 2013. 'India's New Rights Agenda: Genesis, Promises, Risks.' *Pacific Affairs* 86(3): 569–590.

Sen, Amartya. 1999. *Development as Freedom*. New Delhi: Oxford University Press.

Sen, Ranjit. 1988. *Economics of Revenue Maximization in Bengal 1757–1793*. Calcutta: Nalanda.

Sinha, Narendra K. 1981. *The Economic History of Bengal*, 3 Vols. Calcutta: Firma KLM Pvt. Ltd.

Newspapers, magazines, reports and other media

Clive, Robert. 1772. Speech in Commons on India. Downloadable at http://sourcebooks.fordham.edu/mod/1772clive-india.asp

Government of West Bengal. 2004. *Statistical Hand Book*. Kolkata, West Bengal: BAES.

Harriss, John. 2014. 'State of Injustice: The Indian State and Poverty.' CAS Distinguished Lecture Series, JNU, New Delhi. May 2014 CAS/DL/14-1.

HDR (Human Development Report), West Bengal. 2004. Development and Planning Department, Government of West Bengal. Downloadable at hdr.undp.org/en/content/west-bengal-human-development-report-2004

Nehru, Jawaharlal. 1946. Constituent Assembly of India, Vol. 1, 13th December. Downloadable at parliamentofindia.nic.in/ls/debates/vol1p5.htm

Nehru, Jawaharlal. 1947. Constituent Assembly of India, Vol. 2, 22nd January. Downloadable at parliamentofindia.nic.in/ls/debates/vol2p3.htm

Report of the Land Revenue Commission, Bengal (Floud Commission Report). 1940. Downloadable at Archive.org

SECC (Socio Economic and Caste Census). 2011. Downloadable at secc.gov.in/

2   Right to work!
Politics of poverty alleviation policies in India

During the last 10 years or so, since after the introduction of the 'New Rights Agenda' that has legislated some kind of guarantee to various socio-economic entitlements like employment in India, there has seemingly been a growing scholarly consensus (Ruparelia 2013; Harriss 2014; Jenkins 2014) that these legislations at least in their deliberation are progressive and innovative in question of governance, and, have (Ruparelia 2013) 'the powerful long-term ramifications', though 'its direct impact has been limited'. Among those who have critically engaged with the dynamics and trajectory of enactment of these 'New Rights Agenda', Ruparelia (2013, 569), though pointing out some of its risks, forcefully emphasizes that new laws 'devise innovative governance mechanism that enable citizens to see the state and provide fresh incentives for political coalition', while Jenkins (2014) believes that these, particularly the MGNREGA, 'represent an important step towards a meaningful social safety net'. Another analysis, however, seems more ambitious when it comments on the MGNREGA in Tamil Nadu that it has produced (Carswell and De Neve 2014, 564) 'significant transformative outcomes for rural labourers, such as pushing up rural wage levels, enhancing low-caste workers' bargaining power in the labour market and reducing their dependency on high-caste employers'. This is to say, the New Rights Agenda is often being considered as progressive and innovative even in some critical analyses let alone the other analyses which generally gauge the importance of policies only on the basis of its cost-effectiveness. Before going to enquire insightfully into the prospects and challenges of these enactments, particularly the MGNREGA in our context, it seems to be urgently necessary to explain their emergence since the dynamics of enactment process does most often determine and shape the nature of its impact. The first section of this chapter portrays the political trajectory of formation of various employment generation policies on the part of the government throughout the postcolonial period since 1947, and explains the general rationale behind these policies and enactments. The second section analyses the conception of right or otherwise that is scripted in the MGNREGA's structure of conjecture, and explores potential or otherwise of this 'New Right' enactment for guaranteeing employment to the rural people. The chapter concludes that while there has been a series of initiatives on the part of the government in policy formulation in the name of employment generation, the said policies fail to provide employment for the rural people simply due to the sheer fact that these policies have limited potential in regard to employment generation.

Employment generation: the reasoning

It has been discussed in the last chapter about how Nehru had expressed his concern in the first Constituent Assembly on the year 1947 regarding the sorry state of general masses of India, and about how he made the leaders conscious of the immediate tasks before the assembly. Nehru would also never forget to remind us the limit, i.e. certain conditions put by British government, within which the assembly had to function. Nehru was aware of the extent of fallout of the failure to fulfil the aspirations, grown in course of the nationalist movement, of the peasantry who were then politically conscious for the very reason of consistent political training imparted by the Congress Party. He says, this wind (political consciousness) (1938, 235–236) 'is blowing to the villages and to the mud huts where dwell our poverty-stricken peasantry, and it is likely to became a hurricane if relief does not come to them soon'. It is thus a truism that the postcolonial India would embark its new journey with, on the one hand, the expectant general masses, particularly the peasantry in rural front, who do not 'continue to be starving', and, on the other, the supposedly concerned government who are liable to build a new India, even if only for their own interest of the maintenance of the Congress Party in power. The new leaders of new India, i.e. the Congress party, could hardly afford to remain to be indifferent about the plight of the peasantry at the beginning of the postcolonial era. It is true, as Nayar (1960, 1401) says,

> the continuance of a stagnant, backward economy, with the masses living at subsistence level, and the presence in that society of radical elements ready to exploit the resulting discontent, could thus be fatal to the continuance in power of the Congress party.

However, it seems not to be reasonable to assume that the Congress-led government took initiatives to ameliorate poverty only due to its political goals of retaining power by evading law and order problem.

The recommendations of the Floud Commission (1940) in context of rural Bengal still remain operative as an instance, or rather a revelation, that the government, or the ruling class, would take pro-poor or pro-peasantry measures as well in interest of over-all market or capitalist expansion. The essential prerequisites for the development of capitalism are, in fact, the pre-existence of vibrant market, and the expansion of production, in this case, the cultivation. This is to say, tapping new areas full of natural resources into the emerging market is crucial to further capitalist accumulation. While the British colonial government had always been supposedly keen, except a brief period only at the initial phase of colonialism, to protect the small peasant economy, the members of Floud Commission had gone one step further, and recommended a number of radical measures and policy revision for the apparent interest of overall peasantry including the small peasants. The Commission had not only categorically criticized the existence of uneconomic landholding, and the lack of agricultural development in Bengal resulting from subinfeudation, rack-renting and lack of occupancy rights, but suggested also immediate tenancy reforms and termination of Permanent Settlement. The policy of tenancy reforms formulated by the said commission was so radical in essence that even the Communists in India could hardly imagine those as their future programme.

The point is, I argue, that the policy reforms which are often recognized as progressive and revolutionary, and proposed to be undertaken with an aim of poverty alleviation by the political parties both in power and in opposition, are also concurrently the proposals both of the protagonists of capitalism and of the pro-market thinkers. For the sake of the market expansion and development of capital, they would put forward these kinds of policy reforms and propose the same for implementation to the government. We have noted earlier that the implementation of tenancy reforms recommended by the Floud Commission could actually impact a little on the lives of small and marginal peasants of Bengal in terms of unemployment and poverty. After long years of land reforms, nearly the same proportion of peasantry still comprises the category of poor and unemployed in rural West Bengal. The all-India level data on land reforms too are indicative that despite the successful implementation of land reforms, a little has been improved in regard to employment. Apart from the more than 20 million tenants of former intermediaries who have become owners of their land as consequences of land reforms in independent India, 3 million or so tenants and sharecroppers in *raiyatari* areas have acquired ownership over nearly 3 million hectares of land (Dandekar 1986). However, as far as the issues of unemployment and poverty are concerned, the question arises, as Dandekar recognizes (1986, A-90), 'whether removal or alleviation of so dismal a poverty could be left to the general course of economic development or whether a direct attack would be necessary and successful'. The post colonial history shows that the political architects did not go for 'either and or' option. From the very beginning, they opted for two-pronged, rather multi-pronged pathways in order to solve the issues related to poverty and unemployment.

Some efforts were made since the 1960s to improve the agricultural production, viz., Intensive Agricultural District Programme (IADP), Intensive Agricultural Areas Programme (IAAP) and the High Yielding Varieties Programme (HYVP). The high yield varieties programme which was later developed, and known as Green Revolution Technology (GRT), had actually been the most trumpeted state programme of the central government, and has still been continuing in most parts of the country as an exclusive mode of cultivation.[1] In order to get some respite from the wrath of ongoing food crisis and the subsequent peasant agitation, the Indira Gandhi government successfully adopted the GRT, thereby increasing the productivity of crops. Whether the successful implementation of GRT could resolve the crisis of food scarcity, and could curb the peasant unrest in India, is still presumably a debatable point. Large-scale quantitative data, and my ethnographic field findings that collected in two phases from 2004 to 2014, reveal that marginal peasants including the sharecroppers and landless peasants got more employment after the implementation of GRT at least for some years in terms of number of man-days. However, the success story of GRT soon ended in a tragedy with the decrease in yielding of crops coupled with adverse effects of market. I explained elsewhere (2013) about how the increase in essential inputs of production as well as the lack of remunerative price of the outputs made GRT-based farming as a loss-making enterprise which prompted many small peasants, and the farmers to leave, at least partially, cultivation. The agricultural scenario could be gauged through the narration of a solvent farmer in West Bengal. Arun Kole, a wholesale businessman of potatoes in Dhaniakhali block of the Hooghly district belonging to *Mahishya* caste, owned 3 acres of land where he grew *aman* paddy and potato by employing '*kishans*'.[2] Kole commented

> the agricultural scenario has deteriorated immensely. Due to the withdrawal of subsidies from fertilizers, the cost of cultivation has increased substantially. But the crop prices have not increased proportionately with the increase of production cost. The rate of labour wages has increased, and that seems to have some justification. But with all these, the cost of cultivation is so huge that agriculture has become increasingly unprofitable.

It is thus obvious that 'the general course of economic development' has always been an agenda in the official discourse of the Indian state as a principal way of removal of poverty throughout these long years of postcolonial period though the latter hardly ever manages to curb poverty. In fact, the governmental agenda of economic development has always been designed and hypothecated as an essential part of capitalist development or, at the very least, in the shadow of capital. Capitalist transformation, or the expansion of market, it has been thought, as I have argued earlier, would gradually resolve the problems of poverty and unemployment in its own dynamic way. But we have seen that capitalist transformation of agriculture, and the expansion of market deep into the rural fringes could actually transform a little in question of employment stability and economic prosperity. Even the successful implementation of progressive land reforms has ended in vain since its fruits are mostly counterbalanced by the accumulation of capital through exploiting the spaces of production, trade and consumption. It is thus doubtful whether, instead of corporate capital, the regional or 'non-corporate' capital could play any protective role in making the agriculture sustainable, and thereby benefit the peasants and farmers. The government itself was not buying the theory that 'the general course of economic development' would solve the problem of unemployment and poverty in India. If it did, it could have easily ignored the 'direct attack' to curb the issues of poverty and unemployment at least in the initial period of postcolonial era.[3]

Introducing the 1st Five-Year Plan in the year 1951, the government pledges (1st chapter) that 'the State shall strive to promote the welfare of the people by securing and protecting as effectively as it may a social order in which justice, social, economic and political, shall inform all the institutions of the national life', and 'a rapid rise in the standard of living of the people by efficient exploitation of the resources of the country, increasing production, and offering opportunities to all for employment in the service of the community.' Notably, as an underdeveloped country, India is always characterized by the coexistence of unutilized manpower and unexploited natural resources which subsequently creates poverty and unemployment. However, the elimination of poverty and unemployment cannot be achieved 'merely by redistributing existing wealth' or by 'aiming only at raising production'. It has been also mentioned in the same report that the existing socio-economic framework (ibid.) 'has itself to be remolded so as to enable it to accommodate progressively those fundamental urges which express themselves in the demands for the right to work'. Thus it seemed to be very clear from the very beginning that, on the one hand, the two pronged measures were to be required to curb the menace of poverty and unemployment, and on the other, the existing socio-economic structure had to be altered to accrue the fruits of these development measures. Keeping in mind all these things, along with the major policy formulations on redistributive justice, and enhancement of (agricultural) production, the policy makers had intended also at the first instance to create employment by utilizing 'the idle labour' for the purpose of development. The actual intent of this effort, however, as the planning report mentions, was to effectively mobilize 'all the available resources at minimum social cost' and, subsequently, to increase 'the productivity of labour so that larger employment can be provided at rising levels of real income'. But anticipating the possible risk of breaking down (ibid.) 'on account of excessive pressure of money incomes on available supplies', the planners emphasized on 'the need for relying as far as possible on voluntary labour, and using money mainly as a means of attracting and organizing such labour'.

In other words, the Indian government and its policy planners tried from the very beginning to consider a number of dynamic economic processes and their immediate fallout in lives and livelihoods of the rural people, and thus taking an accommodative stance in the subsequent policies. But, it is very crucial to know about the guiding principles which have all the way through been urging the respective policy makers to take certain stances towards India's development. By analysing the arguments and analyses enshrined in the Planning Commission Report, and the pathways undertaken by the policy makers, it can be said that the government, not surprisingly, has constructed its economic reasons on the very basis of capitalist expansion. This is to mean, they suppose in explicit terms that the development of capital, or the economic growth, would inevitably resolve gradually the problem of unemployment as well as poverty. However, it is evident that the problem of unemployment has far from been resolved, if not being further aggravated, as consequences of economic growth though the policy makers, at the very onset, informed us that the process would take time to come to fruition. If we just take an appraisal of these 'capital centered policies', we must see that the redistributive justice like land reforms, and the enhancement of production in agriculture i.e. the application of GRT have only made the expansion of capital and market possible, instead of resolving the issues of unemployment and poverty. Moreover, although the efforts of employment generation 'related to development' projects took an effective role in developing the agricultural sector, in terms of capital productivity, by utilizing 'the idle labour' at minimum social cost,[4] they could hardly make a significant impact on issues of employment and poverty in rural areas.[5] The question that arises is whether the governmental efforts of employment generation could in any case serve the political purposes of the respective parties.

Any possible answer to the abovementioned question regarding the achievement of political goal of the political parties both in power as well as in opposition seems very complicated, as Nayar (1960) rightly argues in his analysis of the impact of implementation of community development projects on the issues of unemployment, since some other factors also matter in the underlying political processes. We would find enough scope later to deal with this interesting question about how 'aspirations and expectations' of the rural people always outrun the accomplishments of political goal. Let us rather now take care of the question which is more significant in our context of whether these special measures undertaken by the Indira Gandhi government after the grave failure of Nehru's grand narrative of industrialization and 'top-down national planning' had been effective in curbing the extent of unemployment and poverty in the early 1970s. Dandekar (1986) informed us that the special programmes – for benefiting the poor sections of the rural people, and for the development of disadvantaged areas, undertaken amid protest movements against rising food crisis, poverty and unemployment throughout the country – had actually made a mixed impact on the issues to which it targeted. Despite the fact that the special measures could facilitate the expansion of GRT, at least to an extent, through improving the infrastructural condition along with irrigation system, it could deliver very little in terms of employment, thereby failing to curb the sufferings of poverty. Among various special programmes undertaken by the then government, the Food for Work Programme (1977), which was later restructured and renamed as National Rural Employment Programme (NREP) in 1980, was formulated for generating rural employment 'on works creating durable community assets' by utilizing mainly the surplus stock of food grains (ibid.). While more funds and food grains had been made available gradually in the subsequent plans, less had been utilized for the very purpose. Although 'the generation of additional employment' had been 'more or less as targeted',[6] the utilization of food grains and also the fund had fallen sharply since, as Dandekar (ibid., A-91) argues, 'market prices of food grains were often lower than the implied issue price on the works'. What is really important in our context is the extent of physical achievement in terms of creation of durable community assets in rural areas. This aspect is important because the very objective of these kinds of special programmes is to develop the agricultural sector by utilizing the idle labour at minimum social cost.

Although Dandekar's study analyses the special programmes of development mainly in 'per capita consumption' term, it shows that considerable efforts had been made as part of this NRE programme to develop the agricultural sector in rural areas in early 1980s. This is to say, the purpose of developing the agricultural sectors in terms of capital productivity was achieved as targeted.[7] However, it has been rarely of one's concern about who among various sections or classes of people in the rural areas are amassing the benefits of these development works. The mainstream analyses including the Planning Commission's reviews seem to presuppose that the achievements in development of agricultural sector would automatically do good to all people cutting across classes, castes and genders at the rural margin. This presumption has become, as it were, an axiom, and raising any question about its validity is generally regarded as absurd. In other words, this presumption is so dominant or, say, pervasive, in our society that even various shades of Marxists couldn't avoid to be engrossed in this ideology of capitalist growth. If one simply reviews the achievements of the Planning Commissions in the successive Plans, s/he could find an interesting phenomenon that the proportion of poor or unemployed persons remains more or less the same in rural parts of the country even after these planned efforts to develop the agricultural sector throughout the span of more than six decades. Neither has the problem of landless poor been sorted out, nor have the marginal peasants prospered. The post-GRT crisis does clearly show that despite the development of agricultural sector in terms of capital productivity, the future of agriculture for many reasons is not so shining. However, a section of cultivators having a substantial proportion of fertile land and mainly belonging to agricultural castes like *Mahishya*, as my ethnographic research shows, could utilize the GRT and GRT associated trades to make their own fortune (Roy 2013).[8]

The objective of employment generation, I suppose, and the government has also otherwise proclaimed, is actually a secondary component of these kinds of special programmes. The planning commission report categorically mentions that 'all the available resources' have to be mobilized to increase 'the productivity of labour so that larger employment can be provided at rising levels of real income'. This means, the issues of employment were not so emphasized though these special programmes are called as employment generation programmes. The planning commission instead emphasized more on the productivity of labour, or on the subsequent productivity of capital, when it called for (1st Planning Commission) 'relying as far as possible on voluntary labour and using money mainly as a means of attracting and organizing such labour'. The government didn't even fix its target who among the rural people were to be given employment for which period of time. Instead, it specified and fixed the amount of social cost which it could bear. It seems that the main aim of the government was to recreate or restructure agriculture related infrastructure by utilizing the cheap and idle labour at minimum social cost.

Hence, the outcome of analysis of the programmes like Food for Work and NREP in terms of their roles in employment generation is very simple since it (the analysis) has taken into account only one component, that is, whether the funds released by the government were being utilized. Despite having a substantial impact, as the government's evaluation says, in terms of 'stabilization of wages, containing prices of food grains, and the creation of a wide variety of community assets', the NREP programme 'has apparently lacked a direct focus on the target-group population' i.e. the landless and the poorest among the poor. In fact, the domain of policy regime has its own dynamic pathways whereby not only are the newer policies made but also are their legitimacy, coherence and strength continuously shaped. On the basis of critical discussion and reviews of the earlier policies like NREP, another new policy i.e. the Rural Landless Employment Guarantee

Programme (RLEGP) was formulated in 1983–1984 'with an object of providing employment of up to 100 days every year to at least one member of every landless household', and of creating more assets 'for strengthening the infrastructure so as to meet the growing requirements of the rural economy'. The question arises whether there is any linkage between the 'direct focus on the landless and the poorest among the poor' and the need 'for strengthening the infrastructure so as to meet the growing requirements of the rural economy'.

Although the problem of unemployment and poverty in rural areas has constantly been a concern of the government, the generation of employment on the part of the government has always been aimed at strengthening the infrastructure required for the growing rural economy. Whether, and how far, the growing rural economy and the strengthened infrastructure could set the ground for solving enduringly the problem of unemployment and poverty, and subsequently provide relief for the landless and poor people in rural areas has, though always been a question, rarely been addressed with utmost necessity. Had this question been addressed properly, the government could have kept itself away from promulgating newer policies every now and then in order to the very purpose of governance. While the leaders of the then ruling party could strengthen their party network, and mass support deep into the grass root by utilizing various policies undertaken both by the central and state government, my ethnography (Roy 2013) reveals that the same section of rural people, that is, the landless agricultural labourers belonging to the SC and ST group, are still in search of employment in most part of the year. Despite the fact that the growth in agriculture as a general course of economic development has enhanced in this period, and that the big farmers have prospered subsequently by utilizing the infrastructure, the landless labourers usually would get scope to work only for 4–5 months in a year. While Jagannath Das belonging to *Mahishya* caste having around 4 acres of land in Singur has become a prosperous farmer and a small industrialist based mainly on farming and marketing agriculture related products during the last three decades, most of the landless labourers in the same agriculturally prosperous village inform that 'they are unable to get work throughout a year, and thus having been poor' (ibid.). In fact, the policy is such an instrument in the hands of the political leaders both in government and in opposition that its very purpose often does fade into oblivion. The question is: when all these policies were almost ineffective to solve the problem of unemployment and underemployment in rural India, what prompted the government in the last decade to declare 'right to work' agenda for all rural families?

An analysis of successive reports of the Planning Commission could give us a clue about how the government's intent to curb the rate of unemployment and underemployment would evolve gradually, and about the way its ensuing vision of India's development would change based mainly on the dynamic relationship between various intrinsic and extrinsic factors operational in the country's political arena. However, it is factual, I assume, that notwithstanding the evolution of intention, and the change in vision on the part of the government, the main purpose or, say, the principles, of employment generation remains mostly unchanged throughout the expanse of various regimes. While some scholars consider 1977 as a break with the past, and the beginning of a new regime of development, I argue, as Frankel (2005, xi) did from a different perspective, that 'there is no sharp break between the trends that preceded, and followed, the 1977'. It is obvious that a new kind of discourse has begun to surface since the introduction of economic liberalization, but it could hardly introduce any new kind of basic transformation in the erstwhile governmental agenda of employment generation. It must be mentioned, however, that despite its failure to transform and renew the programmes of employment generation, the government has opted for a new kind of governance to be implemented in rural hinterland. This new regime of governance could not only suffice the government in its effort to tackle the issues of unemployment but also could provide some avenues for future respite from the negative consequences of implementation of hyper-liberal policies.

While both the governmental programmes i.e. 'the general course of economic development' and the 'direct attack' to curb the rate of unemployment could alter a little in the lives and livelihoods of the labouring people until the first two decades of the postcolonial period, as the planning commission's reports demonstrate, the three consecutive Plans (i.e. 5th to 7th Plans) would adopt gradually a revised stand to treat the issues of rural unemployment in a newer way. The programmes like Twenty Points Programmes (TPP), introduced in 1975 during the regime of Indira Gandhi, had definitely marked a beginning of a changed phase in the history of India's central planning only to be altered again significantly in the subsequent period. The objectives of the 5th Planning Commission, as declared unequivocally in the Report, are 'the removal of poverty and achievement of self-reliance' particularly in agricultural sector along with other two leading sectors. However, it was still believed that the problem of rural unemployment could effectively be curbed 'by augmenting agricultural productivity and vigorously implementing land reforms' while through due implementation of the programmes like 'Food for Work' as part of TPP aimed at development of agricultural sector, and provision of additional work for the land-poor. Upon realizing the fact that the government has only done a little thus far notwithstanding its consistent efforts as far as the issues of poverty alleviation are concerned in last 25 years, the 6th Planning Commission had launched a more direct attack on poverty and underdevelopment particularly in rural areas. While, truly, it might be a possibility that increasing growth in agriculture would strengthen the market, and subsequently broaden the extent of more economic avenues to be open, the capital or labour productivity, at the same time, might decrease, regressively, the requirement of labour at least in agricultural sector. This apart, the idea that the utilization of 'idle labour' of the land-poor who are in search of jobs so as to restructure the rural infrastructure for the sake of development is certainly nothing but an elite agenda which makes the labouring people available to serve the interest of dominant classes in the name of development. In other words, this agenda is an obvious reflection of class domination in state institution.

The reason why I propose that these kinds of development programmes are, in the main, meant for serving the interest of propertied classes is simply that the labouring class rarely get benefited in longer term by means of implementation of these programmes. The district level leader of a reputed national level NGO says candidly during my field work in the year 2006,

> the section of peasants or farmers who at least own a portion of agricultural land are getting benefited by means of implementation of these programmes since they could utilize the effects of durable assets produced in course of implementation of the same. We have not been able to generate such options for the landless poor.

The government itself perhaps didn't accept this conjecture as true that agricultural growth would accrue the benefit in regard to employment, and that implementations of development programmes would anyway aid the land-poor in their search of livelihoods. If the government could, it didn't have to frame ever larger number of policies aimed at poverty alleviation in every approaching period. Interestingly in the 6th Five-Year Plan (1981–1985), when the annual growth rate of agriculture was the highest, the government had prioritized the development measures in order to curb the rate of poverty and employment though, simultaneously, it had expected 'to see progressive reduction in the incidence of poverty and unemployment'.[9] In a democratic country like India where declared direction of planning is to achieve a number of diverse goals like 'growth, removal of poverty, modernization and achievement of self-reliance', the intention of government is clear in its endeavours to appease both sets of main classes in rural areas. The desired appeasement of two sets of classes at one and the same time through increase of growth in agriculture, and implementation of low-range poverty alleviation programme seems actually an attempt on the part of the government to maintain a status quo, if not a bias towards the rural propertied classes. While the benefit of the increase in growth of agriculture goes to the landholding class who could accrue the profit of labour productivity and mechanization of cultivation as well as land development, and to the commercial classes who could manage to amass the gains through trading agricultural inputs and crop outputs, the landless agricultural labourers, although they could get more jobs in the initial period, are mostly vulnerable to uncertainty of erratic market forces and growing mechanization. This is to mean, increase in growth as an utmost aim of the state is primarily set meant for a drive on the part of the government to enhance production mainly in the interest of landed classes. Likewise, although the implementation of poverty alleviation programmes would benefit the rural landless poor to at least some extent, in the slack period of the year the programmes would actually serve the interest of the landholding classes by means of increasing the productivity of land, labour and capital.

Given this political trajectory of planning, the government drove purportedly faster in its planned agenda to augment growth in agriculture, and to manage concurrently the issues of poverty and unemployment during the 7th Five-Year Plan. Keeping pace with the changing course of international political dynamics, the planning commission in India opted not only for an aggressive increase in growth, but also for an introduction of new sorts of political discourse. During the 1980s, when both developed and developing courtiers were going to experience 'the worst recession since the thirties' and the policy makers across the globe sought to adjust with this changing circumstances, 'the Indian economy has emerged stronger, with an acceleration in growth' (Rajiv Gandhi 1985). While the leaders of the developed countries had begun to pursue 'neo'-liberal reforms (i.e. more liberalization including privatization and foreign direct investment), the governments of the countries like India had prompted to comply with these prescriptions, and to take various measures to accelerate growth. Agricultural sector was, of course, thought to be the appropriate field by the policy makers at that moment to carry out experiments on economic growth since lot of untapped resources, both natural and human, in rural areas were still left to be explored. Simultaneously, as mentioned, a new kind of governance and of political discourse were aimed to be introduced to tackle the knock-on effect of growth on the issues related to unemployment and poverty. The conceptual framework of 7th Five-Year Plan seemed to have acted as a rehearsal episode if the 8th Plan being considered as commencement of a new phase in central planning. The 7th Plan, as it envisages, however, didn't spell out any such advancement as far as the steps regarding unemployment and poverty are concerned that we might call it a shift in general understanding. Rather, a meticulous appraisal would reveal that the chronicle is actually the reiteration of the same rhetoric of removing poverty and unemployment through the increase in growth.

The 7th Five-Year Plan invokes a hyper growth in agriculture through the application of GRT facilitated by irrigation, and more strengthened efforts for curbing unemployment and poverty, while trying to infuse new political vibes by encouraging more decentralization and people's 'meaningful participation' in rural (re)construction. The Plan highlights by mentioning a data from NSSO that the percentage of people below poverty line in rural areas has decreased from 51.2 in 1977–1978 to 40.4 in 1983–1984. The main reasons for this, it shows, not surprisingly, 'are the higher rate of economic growth and the increases in agricultural production', and thus justifies the government's consistent prescription for enhancement of economic growth. Notwithstanding the government's effort to adopt growing number of newer policies related to poverty alleviation for incorporating various sections of rural people in its purview, it has always been swayed by the ideology that the increasing growth would only solve the issues of unemployment, and so poverty. In order to accomplish this task of facilitating growth, or in other words, 'nation building activities', Singh says in the preface of that Report that, '(W) e need to tap fully the latent potential of the Panchayati Raj institutions (PRIs) for harnessing the people's energies', and also to 'exploit the creative potential offered by voluntary organisations'.[10] While the PRIs are commonly believed to have been activated for giving more power to the people, interestingly, as categorically said in the preface, it is only meant for harnessing people's energies for development works from the perspective of the government. It seems, I argue, there is no such contradiction between these two ends. Both the ends i.e. execution of development works, and provision of more power for the people, can actually be met by way of one means, that is the implementation of PRIs. The PRIs have not only been effective to manage the issues of poverty and unemployment at the level of grass roots, but have also fulfilled the task of developing rural sector required for agricultural growth.

However, nothing could remain unchanged during the period of 8th Five-Year Plan when, as the prologue of the 8th Plan construes, 'the international political and economic order is being restructured everyday' and are the policies of the government to deal with these 'changing realities'.[11] The question arises about the nature of change in reality, and the way the government has dealt with these changing realities. If the changing realities denote privatization, free trade and foreign direct investment to the greatest extent aiming at further economic growth or accumulation of capital worldwide only to recuperate the capitalist crisis in the preceding period at a higher pace, the government has to press forward more reforms and structural adjustment to deal with these changing realities. In other words, there must be a possibility in context of these changing realities to promote an enabling condition whereby the market reins as supreme, and the government would just regulate the processes. However, in the postcolonial countries like India, it might not be the case that the market would rein at the cost of the welfare provision of the government. Although 'development can best be ensured by freeing them of unnecessary controls and regulations', the then Prime Minister opines (1992, 8th Five-Year Plan), 'the growth and development of the country cannot be left entirely to the market mechanism'.

While some scholars like Bhargava (2006, 446–447) believe that the idea of neo-liberalism means the 'hyper-antistatism', the above-mentioned revelation asserts that not only can't the development but also the growth of country be taken care of entirely by the market, and thus it implies, the role of the government is indispensable. The planning is indispensable, the Prime Minister reminds us categorically (1992, 8th Five-Year Plan), 'for taking care of the poor and the downtrodden who are mostly outside the market system…. It is thus not a choice between the market mechanism and planning' but the challenge 'to effectively dovetail the two'. Does it mean, as transpired, that the role of government is essential even in strengthening the market system of postcolonial countries? I argue that the government's role is essential, and so the Indian government has intended to strengthen all the way through its policy regime the market system, i.e. the economic growth even in the course of implementation of poverty alleviation programme. Thus, Bhargava's view (2006, 446–447) that 'the public provision of public goods is meant to become scarce', and that the Indian government has been required to adopt 'New Rights agenda' even in the neoliberal period due to the very existence of democracy is actually one-sided. He seems to fail to see the fact that the government has concurrently been supporting by means of its planning and development the purpose of market mechanism. Serving the purpose of market is presumably more than obvious in the current period of 'neo'-liberalism when the planning commission (1992) says explicitly, that the challenge is to effectively fit together the market mechanism and the planning 'so that they are complementary to each other'. Hence the neoliberal development in postcolonial countries doesn't mean that the government is withdrawing itself from welfare, rather it actually means that the government involves creatively in both welfare and market mechanism in such a way that, as mentioned, both are complementary to each other.

The prologue thus created a discursive field on the basis of which the government could effortlessly justify economic reforms like privatization and structural adjustment as a best option during the course of 8th Five-Year Plan. The efforts of privatization and structural adjustment did, however, affect negatively the agricultural sector, and had the peasants and farmers become the losers in various ways. Identifying the 8th (Five-Year) Plan as a plan 'for managing the transition from centrally planned economy to market-led economy', the commission also profitably recognized the need of people's initiative for development, and had propagated this requisite widely since. This changed attitude towards the policy is significant in our context as, it seems, the government would no longer encourage the people's dependence on itself (government) for development. This is to say, as the government anticipates, the people should take initiatives for their own benefit. The 'people must operate and the government must cooperate' approach prompted the government soon creating or strengthening at various levels of rural landscape various people's institutions which have played multifarious roles in formulating and implementing the policies since. The entire country then witnessed the introduction of institution of three-tier PRIs, and the subsequent constitutional amendments for ensuring the participation of people belonging to the so-called deprived sections in their own development activities. The subsequent years saw many such legislations, policies and amendments aimed at strengthening the active participation of the people across social groups and classes in the PRIs, but their impact on the lives and livelihoods of the rural people have still been debated across the globe. Simply put, the rural has since begun to transform in every respects surrounded by the new unfolding context i.e. neoliberalism wherein the market operates hand in hand with the government based on the ideas of autonomy and efficiency. The significance of 'neo-liberalism for contemporary forms of governance', as Larner (2000) argues, is undoubtedly enormous as neoliberalism signifies 'new forms of political-economic governance premised on the extension of market relationships'.

MGNREGA: right to work!

While some scholars have analysed neoliberalism as a hegemonic class-based project (Harvey 2003), I draw from Véron (2010), and interpret neoliberal governance as constructed by a network of different actors, organizations and institutions that create and implement public policy. By examining neoliberalism as complex processes originating in and shaped through a politics of restructuration, I describe the processes in which the MGNREGA had been created and implemented by a network of different political parties, NGOs and government institutions. It seems to be important, first of all, to identify what necessitated the enactment of this kind of act in the period of hyper-liberalism. Despite the consistent attempts of the government ever since the inception of its policy regime to trade it as a truism that the expansion of employment opportunity must require high growth rate, interestingly, 'a third of our population lives in conditions of poverty' and, as the 8th Five-Year Plan says, 'the phenomenon of growing unemployment' had 'emerged as a major problem'[12] even after the achievement of high rate of growth in agriculture, and the successful implementation of various employment generation projects particularly during the last two Five-Year Plans (6th and 7th). Furthermore, it has also been recognized by the government that underemployment constitutes 'a problem of much higher dimension than unemployment' and so the rate of poverty has been always much higher than that of unemployment. However, it is certainly not tenable what the government tries to argue, that the low productivity of labour is the cause of underemployment since, as even the official statistics reveals, the enrolment of labourers on casual or informal basis, of late, becomes the employers' preferred choice.

The growth rate in employment as estimated had been very low, and its annual rate was just 0.92 per cent in rural areas (while 3 per cent for all major sectors) during the period 1977–1978 to 1987–1988 when, conversely, the growth rate in agriculture particularly in West Bengal jumped to 5.8 per cent, the highest in the last century (Swaminathan and Rawal 1998). However, another set of data indicate that in rural areas 'the usual status unemployment[13] has increased from 1.91 per cent of labour force in 1983 to 3.07 per cent in 1987–88', and although there are wide variations among different states, the unemployment rates in terms of usual status in case of West Bengal was 6.06 per cent while the all-India average was 3.77 per cent (8th Five-Year Plan). Surprisingly, the agricultural sector demonstrated a rapid decline of employment-potential in the same period, and the reason behind this overall decline of employment-potential in agriculture, as the government supposes, was the sharp deteriorating of employment potential particularly in the regions with high output growth like Punjab, Haryana and Uttar Pradesh. In these states, 'the sources of growth are now turning to be labour substituting', the planning commission rightly recognizes. In fact, the high growth rate in agriculture has never encouraged boosting the growth rate in employment. For instance, in case of West Bengal, the boom in food grain production in the decade of 1980s was enabled (Rogaly et al. 1999, 20) 'by the rapid growth of groundwater irrigation, mainly in the form of privately owned shallow tube wells (STWs)', and also through the expansion of area under the *boro* crop (Banerjee and Ghatak 1995).[14] While the introduction of *boro* crop could enable a condition thereby some kind of employment generation was possible, there emerged a possibility that the high rate of growth could advance more mechanization, thereby inducing the incidence of labour substituting. Therefore, the issues of unemployment and poverty have never been solved whatever the implications of the increasing growth in agriculture might be.

Ironically, although the government recognizes the fact that the growth in agriculture has failed to address the problem of unemployment, it has continuously been preoccupied with the rhetoric of economic growth. This is to say, the official version always prioritizes the economic growth as a means to eradicate poverty while concurrently undertaking diverse kinds of other employment generation and poverty alleviation programmes. Also, the more the government opts for acceleration of economic growth, the more these kinds of programmes of direct attack to poverty it encourages adopting. Ever since the beginning of a new era of hyper-liberalization, or neoliberalization, in 1990s, the government would attempt to up the ante with more employment generation programmes alongside upholding more privatization, free market and structural adjustment. The nineties of the last century thus saw an aggressive reign of the market even in the remotest corner of the rural, and a simultaneous rise in attempts of managing the issues of unemployment and poverty. Furthermore, this basic change that occurred in approach to deal with the issues related to by and large development after the introduction of decentralized governance has actually lessened the liability of the government for delivering public welfare simply in the name of strengthening people's initiative. Notably, these decentralization efforts don't at all minimize the hegemony of the state which we often presume; rather it strengthens the same through the ever-increasing networks of the state. The efforts of strengthening rural decentralization have transformed the rural network in such a way that the entire population in a jurisdiction being held responsible if anyone fingers the panchayat over its malfunctioning. However, it is now well known that despite the reservation of the posts with an aim to ensure the participation of various deprived sections, the representatives of dominant social groups are usually the de facto leaders of the panchayat Raj Institutions (Roy 2008). The last two decades thus saw a new kind of governance which would restructure the welfare state processes at the rural margin, I argue, as a part of governmentality. Governmentality could be a lens to analyse the implications of neoliberalism as well as restructuring of welfare state processes in all spheres of rural lives.

The question that arises whether this age of neoliberalism which calls for dramatic restructuring in regard to people's initiative would anyway entail less governance. The answer is emphatic no since, as Larner rightly argues citing the neo-Foucauldian literature (2000, 12), 'neo-liberalism may mean less government, it does not follow that there is less governance'. The plans of the government since during the 1990s in due course show that while the government relocates its roles by way of some kind of dynamic policy shifts in everyday planning, and implementation of welfare policies at the grassroots, it enhances 'forms of governance that encourage both institutions and individuals to conform the norms of market', and to take initiatives to perpetrate the tasks of their own development. In other words, the first half of 1990s seemed to have set the background of a grand play like the NITI Aayog (2015) that officially calls for a major shift in administration wherein 'the government is an enabler rather than a provider of first and last resort'.[15] While it remains ambivalent whether the major shift in administration could push the country to develop into a new kind of state, as the scholars recognize India having developed a 'new Indian state', it has no doubt that the Indian state in post-liberalization period is advancing rather than retreating or withdrawing. Can the Indian state, however, be identified as a relocated state, as Chandra (2015) argues, and Nielsen and Oskarsson (2016) endorse, for the reason of its continued entanglement with business? What I try to argue on the basis of subsequent developments in both ideational and policy level on the part of the Indian state is that, alhtough the government claims 'the role of the government as a "player" in the industrial and service sectors has to be reduced' (NITI Ayog 2015, Cabinet Resolution), the government has also continually been patronizing the private sector or the investors in their attempts to maximize profit by means of its various policy protection and bureaucratic discretions, lawfully and unlawfully. Nothing seems to have essentially altered in the deliberation of the Indian state so that we could call it as 'new Indian state'. What has transformed is actually the way the Indian state has begun to move towards desperate accumulation of capital, or toward more economic growth, by maintaining, albeit most often unsuccessfully, a balance between two conflicting interests. It has now entered into mediations between these conflicting interests by means of intervening in the domain of policies, legislations and regulations. As a result, the Indian state in post-liberalization period has enacted, on the one hand, the SEZ Act, and on the other, the MGNREGA, and thereby becoming an 'all-pervasive state' instead of a relocated state.

However, the interventions by the Indian state though being actually 'all-pervasive' have growingly been limiting otherwise by way of 'targeting' the people across all social groups and classes through bureaucratic means of enumeration and classification primarily based on some kind of demographic criteria. This is to mean, the period saw the simultaneous increase in number of policies and legislations as well as of target groups, and accordingly the entrenchment of the state system deep into the social roots. Furthermore, several new policies were always to make headway in all Five-Year Plans which were, in actuality, nothing so new but the repetition of the old one with only a few modifications and new names. For instance, in the 8th Plan, two erstwhile wage employment programmes, the NREP and the RLEGP, were merged into another wage employment programme called Jawahar Rozgar Yojana only to be altered into Sampoorna Grameen Rojgar Yojana (SGRY). Also, these wage employment programmes had increasingly been turned not only into a demand-driven but also into a target-based effort.[16] It might appear from the succession of policy initiatives toward wage employment in rural areas that the extent of government's efforts in providing wage employment to the rural poor has increased, but the truth is that, as I mentioned, the purview of wage employment programmes had actually been on the wane. Many were thus surprised at the promulgation of the NREG[17] Act (Chopra 2011, 89) 'as a complex and iterative process, which is mediated by a multiplicity of actors who operate in relation to each other'.

However, although the enactment of the MGNREGA being mediated, as Chopra (ibid., 102) argues, by a multiplicity of actors, and subsequently liable to shape the nature of the state through the very mediations and agency of the actors in course of its operation, it has not just come into being only due to the mediations of multiple actors. Rather, I argue that the act has been the obvious outcome of the state processes that operate based on its own objectives and principles in order to comply with the interests of capital and the dominant classes. While, it is undeniable that there are some drivers 'that come together at a particular point of time', and have facilitated and shaped the formulation of this act (ibid.),[18] and that the networks and inter-linkages built by the actors affiliated to both state and non-state would transcend 'the binary distinction between state and society', the essence of the said policy structure has been conceptualized as part of the dominant discursive contour of the Indian state. I have shown, and Chopra also recognizes in somewhat limited ways, the way the issues of unemployment being a persistent concern of India's development throughout the postcolonial period have been tackled with new kind of policy interventions in neoliberal context. This new kind of policy intervention does clearly pursue, on the one hand, demand-driven and rights-based approach, and on the other, (Carswell and De Neve 2014, 567–568) 'self-targeting mechanism and universal availability', and thereby ensuring 'high level of participation' and opening up spaces for more empowering processes. Whether this approach is extensive and ambitious in terms of its transformative impact is possibly not so important in our context. What is important is the way the government or the state attempts to strengthen (Barrientos and Hulme 2009, 439) 'the agency of those in poverty so their capacity to overcome their predicaments is increased'. This is to say, the 'New Rights Agenda' are just not the outcome of the mediations of the inter-linkages between the state and non-state actors, rather purposely conceived state agenda aimed at strengthening the capacity of the poor to overcome their plight in the hyper-liberal market economy.

India's New Rights Agenda have thus not been 'culminated from social activists, and activist judges working in tandem with progressive political parties', as Ruparelia (2013) tries to establish, and are not any distinct social contract either that (ibid., 570–571) 'marks a break by setting new standards for genuine social citizenship'. His argument would convincingly be refuted if one follows the trail the history of wage employment programmes formulated by the planning commission in India, and of enactment of Maharashtra Employment Guarantee Act in 1977. Let's now discuss about the way in which the 'rights' enshrined in the MGNREGA have been conceptualized, and what kind of possibilities the said act promises to enshrine in regard to employment. Actually, the MGNREGA, I argue, seems to be not so distinct from that of other erstwhile wage employment programmes as far as its scope, objective and purview are concerned. I doubt, which may cause many to be concerned, whether the MGNREGA can be considered as 'right to work' whatsoever in the context of rural India since the very enactment declares at its onset that this is (Ministry of Law and Justice 2005, 1)

> an act to provide for the enhancement of livelihood security of the households in rural areas of the country by providing at least one hundred days of guaranteed wage employment in every financial year to every household whose adult members volunteer to do unskilled manual work.

This type of guarantee of wage employment for rural adults is anything but new actually being operational as early as at least since 1980, while, as a quick analysis of the content of the act finds, it is anything but to be considered as a right to employment. Ironically, the law itself does not proclaim it as a right either. What the law proclaims unequivocally in its enactment is that the government would only enhance, though conditionally, the livelihood security of a very specific section of rural families who do not have any objection to do unskilled manual work merely for one hundred days in a year. Since the legislation contains a number of clauses and sub-clauses about who are to be entitled to get work in which circumstances and by whom, it is certainly not so simple that everyone is guaranteed to get unskilled manual work in rural areas.

The MGNREGA which aimed at enhancing livelihood security of the rural households has actually been limiting itself in many ways in terms of its employment assurance agenda. First of all, an act which has been enacted to provide for the enhancement of livelihood security is certainly not expected to create barely a single kind of work that is unskilled manual work. The question arises about the how and the why of government's intention to create unskilled manual work for all the rural jobless. How do the government and its bureaucracies conceptualize the creation of manual work in rural India as part of employment guarantee? Why do they only create unskilled manual work as employment, and consequently believe that the unskilled manual work is suitable for all of them who require employment in rural areas? The durable assets which a scheme under the MGNREGA is supposed to create in rural areas include, as the act stipulates, draught proofing, irrigation canals, land development, and renovation of traditional water bodies among many such works. All these jobs, undoubtedly, require hard manual labour, and many among rural landless as well as among marginal landholding class, particularly the youths, are not supposed to be habituated with this kind of work, leave alone among the other people belonging to small farmers' category. Anyone who is familiar a little with the rural space may be aware how the rural economy is changing and getting mechanized fast. In my field survey, several respondents would just mock the MGNREGA job as worthless, calling it 'digging the soil'[19] work. Women of the poor families belonging to Muslim communities in some places would just avoid these kinds of work as being unsuitable for them, while some other women though being involved under compulsion with such kind of schemes were visibly unable to comply with the norms of the work. In fact, it seems very clear that government has planned to create these kinds of unskilled manual work only to utilize the labouring class who have often no other option but to give their labour in public works. By utilizing their 'idle labour', the government, conversely, since the inception of planning, has been adopting various policies of economic growth, and thereby developing the agricultural sector in order to increase capital productivity. This is seemingly the last attempt on the part of the government to adopt development works meant for enhancement of capital productivity since the rural has almost been exhausted for this purpose. We see later, however, the way the labouring class is least benefited by means of continual development of agricultural sector. While the scholars construe the 'New Rights Agenda' as meant for active citizenship, the elites among the bureaucracies who have essayed the act actually consider rural unemployed as just another target group of population being intervened by the governmental technologies through various policies. This group of people thus are far from being 'citizen' and do still belong to population, the domain of policy for governmental intervention.

As a target of policy, this population group though having enjoyed recourse to negotiate with, and contest the governmental policies, often only seek to solace in engaging themselves in various governmental programmes like MGNREGA. The government, conversely, limits its own proclamation of assurance of jobs security once again, apart from the creation of unskilled manual work, by creating only 100 days a year for even not every individual but for a household in rural areas. The question arises about why the government stipulates only 100 days a year while many in rural areas managing to find work at most around for three months. My field survey in rural West Bengal manifests that the landless and marginal families usually find roughly around 100 days in agriculture along with other farm-based works. Like many landless labourers in West Bengal, Lal Kamal Bag from a village in Barddhaman district informs me that he gets jobs only for around 60 days in agriculture, and does his utmost to involve himself throughout the year in myriad kinds of non-farm works. Also, unlike the women belonging to the solvent landholding classes, the women of landless and marginal landholding families are ever ready to labour hand in hand with their counterparts. Many among these landless labourers were, therefore, surprised at the attempt of the government for providing only 100 days per annum for a family.

Ironically, in the art of modern government, while population is supposed to be the ultimate end of the government, it seems, in this case, the family still retains its place as the end of policy conservatively. As Foucault (1991, 98) explains through using the technique of genealogy, the family is 'too thin, too weak and too insubstantial' as a model so that an economy based on a model of the family is unable to respond adequately. The family-based job assurance in the MGNREGA, so to speak, instead of solving the crisis of unemployment in a rural family actually engenders diverse sorts of troubles within it. The 'One job card for one family' idea does not only miss the issue that the households belonging to the category of landless and marginal peasants are mostly two-income economies due to which, despite a meagre amount of wage, a family could at least survive, but also often prioritizes the participation of either spouses depending on specific situation. However, in either case, the payment for the job would be delivered for the default jobcard holders who being necessarily the head of families, that is to say, the husbands or the fathers. As a result, not only are the jobs being restricted to the male heads, but also are the payments for the jobs. Both jobs and payments thus revolve around issues of gender as well as seniority. For instance, a 30-year-old married man from 24 Paraganas (S) candidly says,

> I do work in 100 days project, but my father draws the entire payment for my work. I couldn't even come to know when he draws the same. I don't have any cash on my own, so I have to decide to be separated from my father's family, and start a new one thereby getting a job card for myself.

However, in many cases, it has been observed that only the women do work in 100 days project, and subsequently draw their own payment while their husbands or fathers do work and migrate to somewhere else to earn a modest and more secured wage on daily basis. In a nutshell, the act which declares to provide only 100 days of wage employment in every financial year to every household whose adult members volunteer to do unskilled manual work is clearly anything but an employment guarantee in rural areas of India.

What kind of provisions does the act, anyway, contain in regard to creation of jobs in rural areas? This aspect seems to have been fuzzily conceived in this act, and is also not very clear enough to all the stakeholders who are concerned about job creation in rural areas. The act has stipulated categorically a sequence of bureaucratic steps about the way in which a feasible scheme under MGNREGA and a subsequent job could be sanctioned and created. A variety of approvals both top down and bottom up is required for sanctioning a project/job. This is to say, while a Gram Panchayat (GP) is responsible for 'identification of the projects in a particular GP area to be taken up under a scheme as per the recommendations of the Gram Sabha', the Panchayat at the district level is in charge of finalizing and approving 'block wise shelf of projects to be taken up under a programme under the scheme' in a district. The long journey for both ways from Panchayat to district would often stall the sanction of projects particularly when the rural representatives of Panchayat being understandably not so prudent to essay a bureaucratically realistic project. The Panchayat at intermediate level i.e. the Panchayat Samiti, on the contrary, has to play a difficult role in mediating between the top and bottom for accomplishing the task. The BDOs are therefore seen very proactive even to contact directly the local representatives and 'pressurize' incessantly to realize the project at any cost. In the contemporary period of TMC rule, while many of the people's representatives from different levels are not so apt to manage the tasks, the BDOs (though being responsible 'to supervise and monitor the projects taken up at the GP') are stepping up and taking all responsibilities. It is for the reason that the government officials are liable, at the end, for failing the act which is now subject of concern to many since its successful accomplishment being the marker of good governance.

Notably, it is also by no means the fact that one's pro-action solely could succeed to make the act implemented. The state, society and the terrain of their blurry relationship – all may perhaps cause to advance or to halt the act since each and every one is legally connected to run the job guarantee programme. While the Gram Sabha is required to enlist the possible works of a particular GP, the programme officer is in charge of sanctioning it based on many scrupulous rules and the endorsement of concerned authority. For instance, at least 50 labourers 'are to be available, or enlisted', to start a new work, and the labourers who are not enlisted for any particular work can't be absorbed in any ongoing work. This is to say, the job cardholders who would expect work must have to apply for jobs in advance, and have to be notified in writing or in public notice. The process of obtaining jobs is at first instance neither effortless nor instantaneous; rather, as the act scripts, it is very troublesome and prolonged. The 'labourers' for whom the jobs are supposed to be entitled are predominantly the day labourers and, in most cases, unlettered, and thus might not be interested in complying with this kind of complicated processes. The issue of unemployment allowance seems to be another nebulous zone to be availed by the entitled people. Apart from being a prolonged process, from the GP to district office, of resolving the fate of allowance of the claimants, the matter of unemployment allowance seems to be elusive as far as its rules and regulation are concerned. First, the issue of unemployment allowance may easily be avoided on the part of the authority due to the reasons that the bureaucratic strictures could not authorize some jobs to be created. This is to mean, the authority could show in all probabilities, particularly when the state government is responsible to pay the same as it is considered its mistake, the lack of legally favourable conditions to create work. Second, very few scholars believe that the labourers in our country have enough guts to claim on their own unemployment allowance, and jobs as well, by complying with various legal norms. The same is also probably true in regard to the question of claiming either their payments in time or the compensation. The day labourers who are most often in badly need of wages on daily basis could hardly wait until the 14 days' time stipulated by the government. Hence, the MGNREGA, which is believed by many as 'New Right Agenda', does actually limit it to guarantee even manual jobs for a very short period to rural labourers' households, leave alone consigning a right to work for them.

Furthermore, no fewer than many among the scholars do often champion a campaign to promote the MGNREGA as a game changer that could revitalize the rural economy in terms of creation of durable assets. They believe that the work under the act would create durable assets in rural areas, and thereby not only accelerating the economic growth but also generating more employment. This is actually the same old rhetorical anecdote that has flowed forcefully within the bureaucratic camp since the inception of planning commission in India. Looking at the long history of these kinds of governmental wage employment programmes, there is no reason to believe these stories whatsoever as to the generation of employment for long-term perspective. However, an intensive study of such a scheme under MGNREGA could shed a light to assess the old saying. Other than this, the issue of market renewal through pumping of huge money from the government exchequer meant for both wages and materials seems also to be a bone of contention among mainly the financial commentators, though neither of two camps, the proponents and the opponents of this investment, could ignore the task of poverty alleviation. Whatever their actual contention may be, it is undeniable that, if the money gets spent, the local market becomes strengthened to an extent. The question arises about who benefits from the strengthening of market. Do the persons who benefit belong to the category of rural labourers?

Much has also been discussed about the so-called promise of governance reforms in the said act. Harriss who is though very critical of the intentions of the Indian Government in its poverty alleviation programmes since long, particularly of the MGNREGA, by considering the same as nothing but 'the management of poverty', commented that (2014, 16) 'the social audit can have a powerful impact'. Harriss asserts that the social audit aspect (ibid.) 'promises a new kind of democratic participation and a way for ordinary people to hold the state to account'. In fact, he might be correct in his assertion as, it is truism to say, the social audit must ensure democratic participation, and make the state more accountable. The point is whether the concerned people of a particular society are at all able to conduct a social audit for this purpose. Actually, the social audit is always subject to assurance of participation of the entire people. It is most unlikely in a stratified society like ours that the audit for the very purpose has ever been social in nature and essence. The issues of caste, class, religion and gender always would affect negatively on the very purpose of these kinds of efforts. For instance, one who would go through the scholarly work on the *Gram Sansad* functioning could easily gauge the importance of the operational dynamics of various inherent social barriers.[20] However, the people in larger proportions might participate in the social audit, if conducted, as part of MGNREGA since it is their concern of livelihood. Another question seems to still remain mostly untouched: the way in which this kind of enactment including the social audit could strengthen the state processes in rural areas. In other words, the point is to examine the process by which the state is changing, as Chopra (2011, 95) says, 'in and through these porous interactions between the state and society during the policy making process', and also in course of its implementation.

Summing up, tellingly, the trajectory of enactment of the MGNREGA reveals that what is enacted in the name of employment assurance is nothing new but reiterating the same age-old policies of employment generation intended for the 'idle' labourers obviously for some days in a year to create durable social assets in rural India. Also, the programmes of employment generation has been aimed to reinforce the economic growth which is actually believed by the policy makers as a remedy for all ills whatsoever in the country. What is new, however, in content in this enactment is that the government would encourage that the people should take initiatives for their own benefit instead of sitting 'idly' in expectation of the government's doles or other kinds of actions. This means, the 'people must operate' of course legally, and 'the government must cooperate' by means of own governmental technology. As a result of which, on the one hand, the government could bypass, at least to an extent, its liability to provide employment to the rural labourers, and on the other, as Scott (1998, 2) argues, 'the state's attempt to make a society legible, to arrange the population' gets achieved. In its efforts of assurance of employment, the government seems to be not so resolute while it categorically mentions in the pages of the law that the government would attempt generating employment under the so-called programme 'within the limits of its economic capacity'. This is to mean the government always seeks some dispensation from complying with its duties so far being committed, and it's failing of guarantee to create jobs in rural areas. Had employment been even recognized as a right, the scenario would have not often been changed to a great extent, as we have witnessed the fate of other acts like the Minimum Wages Act (1948). My ethnography in rural West Bengal (Roy 2013) reveals the instance of non-compliance of minimum wages for agricultural labour during both the left front and the TMC rule. Finally, the MGNREGA has very limited potential in regard to the assurance of employment generation in rural areas though this kind of enactment of guaranteeing employment could rarely initiate any political and social change in the respective terrain.

Notes

1 Not only were the peasants of all kinds including the rich peasants and the big land-holding class encouraged and supported by the government financially through subsidy

in agricultural inputs, but also the *bargadars* were provided with loans with subsidies and other facilities like the supply of minikits (this was a package containing HYV seeds, fertilizers and pesticides) free of cost.

2 *Kishan* is a local term denoting the agricultural labourer.
3 Even in the 1st Planning Commission Report, it had been declared that the steps would be taken to eradicate poverty, and to provide jobs to the rural unemployed. It was categorically written that jobs will be created in the development works.
4 There is ample evidence that a lot of development works, e.g. facilitation of irrigation, development of land, construction of roads etc., have effectively been accomplished in rural areas by utilizing the labour force in a number of projects undertaken by the government particularly in the period of 1970–1980s.
5 The governmental data show that around the same proportion of rural people still have been suffering in abject poverty and unemployment. Regarding the question of labour productivity too, a little has been done as because of the sheer fact that there is hardly any technological advancement which could enhance the labour productivity.
6 The target was to generate 300 to 400 million man days of employment in rural areas every year. See for details Dandekar (1986, A90).
7 Please see Dandekar (1986, A91) for details on the development of agricultural sector.
8 Khetra Pal and his brother, prosperous farmers of Kalipur in Hooghly district, had owned 12 bighas of land in early 1970s. By utilizing the GRT coupled with money lending and trading of agricultural produce, he has made his fortune since. Now Pal has become landed elite and owns around 60 bighas of land.
9 Indira Gandhi, the then Prime Minister of India, wrote these words in her foreword of the Report of the 6th Five-Year Plan (1981–1985).
10 ManMohan Singh was the Deputy Chairman of the Planning Commission in the period of 1985–1987.
11 The foreword and the Preface of the 8th Five-Year Plan were written by the then Prime Minister P V Narashima Rao and the Deputy Chairman of the Planning Commission Pranab Mukherjee respectively.
12 The government claims that 'a relatively higher growth of population and labour force has led to an increase in the volume of unemployment from one plan period to another'.
13 A person is considered unemployed on Usual Status (US) basis, if he/she has not been working, but is either seeking or is available for work for a relatively longer time during the reference year (as par the Report of 8th Five-Year Plan).
14 See for details Gazdar and Sengupta (1999) in Ben Rogaly et al. (1999).
15 See the Cabinet Resolution in the website of NITI Aayog. Downloadable at www. niti. gov.in
16 Jawhar Rojgar Yojona was targeted at people living below the poverty line, and preference was given to the SC and ST people, and also aimed at freeing the bonded labour. Around 30 per cent of gross employment was agreed to be provided to women under this programme. These apart, the resources for this programme were also allocated on the basis of proportion of rural poor in the state to the total rural poor in the country. See 9th Five-Year Plan Report.
17 The said act was first named as National Rural Employment Guarantee Act in 2005 only to be renamed as Mahatma Gandhi National Rural Employment Guarantee Act later in 2008.
18 By describing the story of formulation of the MGNREGA, Chopra identifies four critical drivers liable to facilitate the process:(1)the creation of network like National Advisory Committee, (2)powerful state actors like Ms. Sonia Gandhi, (3)active civil society actors like People's Action for Employment Guarantee (PAEG) and (4)political compulsion.
19 In Bengali, they call it '*maati kaata kaaj*'.
20 My own work (2013) helps to shed a light on these issues.

References

Barrientos, A. and D. Hulme. 2009. 'Social Protection for the Poor and Poorest in Developing Countries: Reflections on a Quiet Revolution.' *Oxford Development Studies* 37 (4): 439–456.

Bhargava, Rajeev. 2006. 'Indian Democracy and Well-Being: Employment as a Right.' *Public Culture* 18(3): 445–451. doi: 10.1215/08992363-2006-013

Carswell, Grace and Geert De Neve. 2014. 'MGNREGA in Tamil Nadu: A Story of Success and Transformation?' *Journal of Agrarian Change* 14(4): 564–585. doi: 10.1111/joac.12054

Chandra, Kanchan. 2015. 'The Indian State: The Relocation of Patronage in the Post-Liberalization Economy.' *Economic and Political Weekly* 50(41): 46–58.

Chopra, Deepta. 2011. 'Policy Making in India: A Dynamic Process of Statecraft.' *Pacific Affairs* 84(1): 89–107.

Dandekar, V. M. 1986. 'Agriculture, Employment and Poverty.' *Economic and Political Weekly* 21(38&39): A90–A100.

Foucault, Michel. 1991. 'Governmentality.' In *The Foucault Effect: Studies in Governmentality*, edited by Graham Burchell, Colin Gordon and Peter Miller, 87–104. Chicago: The University of Chicago Press.

Frankel, Francine R. 2005. *India's Political Economy 1947–2004: The Gradual Revolution*. New Delhi: Oxford University Press.

Gazdar, Haris and Sunil Sengupta. 1999. 'Agricultural Growth and Recent Trends in Well-Being in Rural West Bengal.' In *Sonar Bangla? Agricultural Growth and Agrarian Change in West Bengal and Bangladesh*, edited by Ben Rogaly et al. New Delhi: Sage Publication.

Harvey, David. 2003. *The New Imperialism*. New York: Oxford University Press.

Larner, Wendy. 2000. 'Neo-Liberalism: Policy, Ideology, Governmentality.' *Studies in Political Economy* 63(Autumn): 5–25.

Nayar, Baldev Raj. 1960. 'Community Development Programme: Its Political Impact.' *Economic and Political Weekly*, September 17: 1401–1410.

Nehru, Jawaharlal. 1938. *Eighteen Months in India*. Allahabad: Kitabistan.

Nielsen, Kenneth Bo and Patrik Oskarsson. 2016. 'Development Deadlocks of the New Indian State.' *Economic and Political Weekly* 51(4).

Rogaly, Ben, B. Harris-White and Sugata Bose, eds. 1999. *Sonar Bangla? Agricultural Growth and Agrarian Change in West Bengal and Bangladesh*. New Delhi: Sage Publication.

Roy, Dayabati. 2008. 'Whither the Subaltern Domain: An Ethnographic Enquiry.' *Economic and Political Weekly* 43(23): 31–38.

Roy, Dayabati. 2013. *Rural Politics in India: Political Stratification and Governance in West Bengal*. New Delhi: Cambridge University Press.

Ruparelia, Sanjay. 2013. 'India's New Rights Agenda: Genesis, Promises, Risks.' *Pacific Affairs* 86(3): 569–590.

Scott, James C. 1998. *Seeing Like a State: How Certain Schemes to Improve the Human Condition Have Failed*. New Haven: Yale University Press.

Swaminathan, Madhura and Vikash Rawal. 1998. 'Changing Trajectories: Agricultural Growth in West Bengal, 1950 to 1996.' *Economic and Political Weekly* 33(40): 2595–2602.

Véron, René. 2010. 'Small Cities, Neoliberal Governance and Sustainable Development in the Global South: A Conceptual Framework and Research Agenda.' *Sustainability* 2(9): 2833–2848.

Newspapers, magazines, reports and other media

Banerjee, Abhijit V. and Maitreesh Ghatak. 1995. 'Empowerment and Efficiency: The Economics of Tenancy Reform.' Mimeograph, Department of Economics, Harvard University.

Harriss, John. 2014. 'State of Injustice: The Indian State and Poverty.' CAS Distinguished Lecture Series, JNU, New Delhi. May 2014 CAS/DL/14-1.

Jenkins, Rob. 2014. 'What Will a Modi-Led Govt Do with MGNREGA?' *The Times of India*, April 13. Downloadable at https://timesofindia.indiatimes.com/home/sunday-times/allthat…will…/33691995.cms

Ministry of Labour and Employment. 1948. Minimum Wages Act. Downloadable at https://labour.nic.in/sites/default/files/TheMinimumWagesAct1948_0.pdf

Ministry of Law and Justice, Government of India. 2005. The National Rural Employment Guarantee Act. Downloadable at nrega.nic.in/rajaswa.pdf

NITI (National Institution of Transforming India) Aayog. 2015. Government of India. Downloadable at niti.gov.in/

Planning Commission, Government of India. 1st to 12th 5 Years Plans. Downloadable at planningcommission.nic.in/plans/planrel/fiveyr/welcome.html

Report of the Land Revenue Commission, Bengal (Floud Commission Report). 1940. Downloadable at Archive.org

3 Political parties, employment generation policies and governance

Parties, policies and the state

It is difficult to conceive of, as Hasan (2010, 241) argues, 'India's democratic system' and its apparent success 'without the crucial role played by the political parties'. However, I problematize this axiom through interrogating both 'India's democratic system' and the roles played by the political parties in it, and enquire into the way democracy fails to deliver justice in employment terms to the majority of India's people, as well as into the actions by which the political parties would attempt to resolve this issue but most often failing to do. While Frankel supposes (2005, 491) that the 'Nehruvian socialist programme of poverty alleviation and social justice … could not be redeemed within the existing structure of political and economic power' since 'the privileged dominant castes and classes were able to subvert the goals of social policy' by virtue of vibrant existence of democracy, I propose to explore the potentiality of the social policies to deliver social justice, as well as the actual character of democracy that is prevailing in the country. I argue basically that the ideological, or class, premise of the very politics of all mainstream political parties including even the left of all hues is the main culprit for which 'India's democratic system' fails to resolve the issues of unemployment. I am not sanguine that the social policies including the Nehruvian socialist programmes promulgated so far by the Indian government throughout the long postcolonial period are in itself perfect and just. I have also doubts that the programmes of poverty alleviation are 'socialist' in nature, be it the Nehruvian or the Marxist, and that these programmes are called social justice.

Very recently, Thachil (2014) argues that political parties in the global south particularly in India are essentially dominated by the elites and their policies representing elite policy interest though most often in support of the poor. The political parties in India which grew out of the nationalist struggles against British colonialism by a handful of elite representatives from among affluent classes during the late nineteenth century are definitely now well entrenched deep into the grass roots; and (Hasan 2010, 241) the 'democratic process has deepened, drawing historically disadvantaged groups into the political system'. Departing from his earlier stand (1984, xliii) that 'the arena of politics as consisting of two domains' i.e. the elite (political parties) and the subaltern, Chatterjee (2004, 39–40) proposes a concept of 'political society', drawing on perhaps from Foucault (1982), to understand the recent political formations and processes whereby these two domains of politics have been entangled more and more throughout the postcolonial period. Foucault (1982, 791) argues that 'power relations are rooted deep in the social nexus', and not reconstituted above society as 'a supplementary structure'. Which is, thus, important in our context is how far the democratic process could bring under its influence the lives of subaltern classes in India where class, caste, ethnicity, religion and gender still act as a source of unequal power at rural margin, and so matter a lot in determining the politics of the peasantry. The question would arise at this juncture about whether the political parties and their policies in India are still designated as elite.

What is meant by elite in context of politics above all? While Chatterjee (2004) believes that the elite as a domain which being organized according to the legal political principles led down by the state doesn't exist anymore since the subaltern domain as defined by him has now been closely entangled with that of the elite, Thachil (2014) strongly believes that most of the political parties in India are elite, and still in power through winning over the poor in the global south. But 'it is necessary', Thachil suggests (ibid., 3), to define the political parties (ibid.) 'on the basis of the social composition of their core constituencies (the groups most influential in providing their electoral, ideological, and financial support, and in shaping their policy profile)'. The core constituencies of elite parties, he thinks, 'are located within the upper strata of society'. The question is: whether the elite communities constitute the party's core base of support, when Hasan (2010, 252) argues that the social composition of the 'ruling political elites' has changed significantly since independence, 'both in politics and in bureaucracy' due to 'parties opening their doors to new recruits from marginalized groups' signalling 'a social revolution' 'that is giving voice to previously marginalized groups'.

Thachil's binary of elite party and poor voters is actually ontologically baffling. The expansion of the state and the political parties deep into the grass roots in India has transformed the political space in such a fashion that the binary supposition of elite party and poor voters as two different conceptual entities, or two separate ontological formations, seems hardly to be conceivable. There is no such purely elite party, so are the poor voters. The elite parties, as Thachil (2014, 4) argues, emerge out of privileged social communities, and are thus dominated by the members of these groups, and on the other, receive disproportionate though not exclusive electoral support from the same privileged groups. What is most important is that the elite parties (ibid., 5) 'seek to advance the economic and cultural interests of the elite constituencies they emerged to represent'. All three issues as proposed by Thachil while are helpful to analyse the class basis of any political party, are not exhaustive for classifying the political parties into elite and non-elite. Any political entrepreneur, be it from the 'elite' or 'non-elite' party, must attempt to win over the poor, the most potential voters these days, with an aim to incorporate them in the party. Every political party now becomes, as Hasan (2010, 247) argues, 'a pragmatic party', and 'mobilization of support using other social cleavages, which are electorally salient, tends to rise'.

Truly, each and every party is pragmatic, particularly since 1990s, in its practice devoid of any ideological urge, and so being difficult to be categorized as elite or non-elite only on the basis of above-mentioned criteria. The question of 'who these elites are' has, therefore, not only 'contextually specific answers', but the way a party is going to be organized in a specific social milieu, and subsequently framing its electoral strategies to win over different classes and social groups on its behalf is also contextually defined answers. Who are, in actuality, deciding the policies and matters in the party and, 'what economic and cultural interests the decision makers seek to advance' (Thachil, ibid.), I argue, are probably more significant to fix on whether a party is elite. However, it has been an enduring puzzle the way the parties that have an aim of absorbing each and every one would manage the interests of different classes ranging from rich to poor in order to win over them fruitfully for electoral purposes. It is also well worth interrogating how the elite classes with its policies that represent their own interests are able to dominate the so-called poor classes in and around the parties. The chapter addresses these questions from a sociological point of view in relation to the question of rural employment. I argue that the policies so far conceived and undertaken by the political parties while being fastened with a common thread, i.e. the capitalist growth, are more or less accepted as righteous by the people of all classes. Since the very beginning of policy intervention, the question of employment has mainly been discussed from the perspective of economic growth, and thus been managed politically based on supplicant modality. While the elites would usually decide the policies whatsoever within the parties, the poor have always been under the influence of those policies.

Through tracing a brief historical trajectory of the development of political parties in India, Hasan (ibid., 242), instead of concentrating on issues like the division of parties on the basis of elite-poor dichotomy, put forward a 'two-phase' theory in which she divides the postcolonial period into two broad important phases 'to understand the significance and implications of the parties' developments. While the first phase, i.e. 1950 to 1989, is marked by 'one-party dominance, moderate levels of political participation and elite consensus', the second phase, i.e. from 1989 until now, signifies 'greater democratization, and the opening up of the political system to non-elite participants'. While in the first phase, ideology characterizes the political parties, the political parties since 1989 are marked by pragmatism. What is important in our context is that Hasan's conceptualization rightly identifies the phenomenon that the political parties in contemporary period are not deemed anymore to be categorized as elite and non-elite as no party can afford these days to base itself on any single class or caste as well as any particular ideology. Being an office-seeking entity, political parties do have hardly any policies, be it elite or non-elite, to advance for any specific constituency they emerged to represent.

Upon analysing these two representative arguments regarding the political party, and its leadership, electoral strategy and policy, I argue that the elites are mostly in the helm of all concerned political parties while their policies are more or less the same in ideological terms. The strategy of all political parties is just to garner the electoral support from all sections by any means based on pragmatic consideration. While the recent period witnesses more democratization and opening up the political system to the non-elite entrants though in the wider political perspective, the grass root political system still continues to be dominated in sociological term by the elites in every context. As a result of the entrenchment of party system along with the state-led politics deep into the social fabric, while 'moderate levels of political participation and elite consensus' have altered once for all, some sorts of pervasiveness of the party politics being spread into the society at the cost of other social formations only to hegemonize the prevailing regime and its ideology. The question arises about the implication of the elites being at the helm of political parties, and the undifferentiated policy regime, or the 'no-policy regime', that guide the political parties in their effort to make policies on issues of employment in rural areas. Why did all political parties fail to puzzle out why a considerable section of rural people in India still remain unemployed or poor despite the consistent policy interventions by the government?

It's really a puzzle before the social scientists particularly who are concerned about India's development that how the elites have been in power in India's vibrant democracy despite the fact that they fail to resolve a prime problem i.e. unemployment and poverty faced by the majority of rural people. It's also a puzzle that why the unemployed, underemployed and/or the poor in rural areas would vote the elite leaders of all political parties despite the fact that they hardly benefit in terms of their lives and livelihoods by the political leaders and their policies. It is still a question mark, last of all, that why the government policies aimed at alleviating poverty, and generating employment, albeit modestly, fail consistently to improve the human condition by generating employment in rural areas. Are the political leaders who are mostly elite at all interested to solve the problem of unemployment and poverty in its fullest term? Or, do the unemployed, underemployed and/or the poor in rural areas themselves expect that the political leaders with their policies would change their fate by finding a solution of the crisis of employment opportunities? Last but not least, are the government policies aimed at alleviating poverty and generating employment potential enough to solve this basic problem of employment faced by majority section of rural people? I argue that the policies being championed by the major political parties are essentially the same and guided by a dominant ideology. What is this ideology above all?

Ideology, capital and employment

The ideology is nothing but the liberal agenda which, I argue, advocates two simultaneous processes, if one is the advancement of economic growth; another is the management of issues like unemployment and poverty. Two processes are actually counter to each other. The economic precarity of Indian rural seems to be a direct fall out of the practice of this politics. I completely agree with Gupta (2016, 2) when he argues that the biased use of farmers' suicide by different interest groups, particularly the political parties, to push their own political agenda does prevent an understanding of the causes of this epidemic, and that as farmers' suicide brings together a number of problems including the political,[1] it is difficult to analyse this epidemic from the perspective of any one discipline. It is not so important in our context the way in which victim farmers have been prompted to commit suicide or the way they could evade suicide. What are important, in fact, are the causes of farmers' suicide or agrarian crisis so as to ameliorate the disaster. However, I disagree with Gupta to the extent that he would accord primacy to the ecological circumstances over political economy as causes of the said disaster. I doubt his ecological theory in the same way as he has doubted the narrative of 'seeds of suicide' (ibid., 8).

Undoubtedly, the issues of uncertainty associated with farming have heightened as consequences of climate change everywhere. Nonetheless, the economic factor is no less responsible, if not more, for the farmers' distress. While the speculative climate is a factor to be blamed for farmers' precarity, the speculative market is, probably, the real culprit. It might not be an exaggeration if I extend my argument a little further, and say that the ecological degradation is itself an outcome of political economic process.[2] Gupta's narrative, though being innovative in its endeavour to identify the causes of crisis in farming all over India, remains an unfinished agenda to trace what is responsible. In fact, he, like many scholars and the leaders of all mainstream political parties, limits himself in tracing the causes of economic precarity in rural areas as he fails to critique the dominant liberal ideology. Had he not been confined himself to liberal thinking, he would have seen that the way the expansion of market and capital would appropriate the fruits of development, and thereby making the farming continuously a speculative activity. I want to underline that it is not the speculative climate that is causing rural unemployment or agricultural crisis, but a speculative market.

The speculative market and the exorbitant tax collection by the colonial government along with the shortage of rainfall made the Deccan cotton farmers extremely vulnerable in the nineteenth and early twentieth century (Gupta 2016). The peasants and small landholders in Bengal in the same period had witnessed the same crisis. The crisis was mainly due not to the speculative weather, but the speculative market that represented the liberal ideology wherein the British colonialists exploited the most. However, right from the very beginning of policy intervention in postcolonial India, this liberal ideology has triumphed over other ideologies, be it the 'socialist' or the Gandhian, to shape the economy and society in its own way. Nehru, though being a short-time Marxist socialist, had explained the social problem in a different way in his early political career, was quickly transformed and took liberal politics as his guiding philosophy. It is, of course, a point of contention about whether the Marxists have at all had any different vision in regard to amelioration of poverty and unemployment in context of rural India. Nehru's government, therefore, set about to intervene in rural economy more or less in the same way as the Floud Commission had suggested as recommendations to the then British colonial government in order to curb the escalating unemployment, poverty, landlessness in rural India.

Echoing the essence of the Floud Commission Report (1940), the postcolonial government prescribed a number of policies for making use of 'unutilized or underutilized man power on the one hand and of unexploited natural resources on the other' so as to over-all agricultural or rural development in India. Apart from the policies of land reforms mainly by way of abolition of zamindari system, and of granting tenancy rights to the *bargadars*, the postcolonial government like its counterpart in the colonial period had undertaken a number of plans in regard to improvement of irrigation and drainage system, to increase of yield of all crops particularly the rice in perspective of Bengal. The policy makers, however, would realize from the very outset that the elimination of poverty 'cannot be achieved merely by redistributing existing wealth' or by pursuing a programme aimed at 'raising production'. The 1st Five-Year Plan asserts that 'only a simultaneous advance along both these lines can create the conditions in which the community can put forth its best efforts for promoting development'. This is, in fact, the crux of the ideology that shapes all policies the Indian government has undertaken so far, and implemented in the social reality of rural India. The policies aimed at development and modernization, this is to say, at amelioration of poverty and unemployment, as the ruling discourse propagates, are actually the fruits of this two-line approach of the government. The government thus, I would say, from the very beginning, never forgot to take up some community development projects in conjunction with other policies.

The question arises about the way this two-line approach has been determining the destiny of both capital and labour in the specific contexts of rural India. In other words, how does this ideology, or rather the politics of the state, help capital to flourish, and impede simultaneously the rural people to find employment? Conversely, how does this ideology facilitate the rural people to find employment, and impede the capital to flourish in chorus? The history of rural India is actually the history of the confrontation between these two components, viz. the capital and the labour. Many scholars, particularly Hasan, through a quick cursory glance, attempt to divide the postcolonial period into two broad phases in terms of priority of the Indian state regarding economic policies – while the earlier phase is denoted by socialism, secularism and distributive justice, the latter phase is denoted by high growth rate, and encouragement of private investment to achieve this goal (Hasan 2010). There is a shift, as Hasan (ibid., 247) asserts, 'from a multi-class state committed to pro-poor measures to a narrow conception of the state that is more closely aligned with business, capital, and the middle classes'. I argue that notwithstanding the fact that Indian state has changed in terms of the extent of its alignment with the business class, rural India has experienced the same predicament and the same economic policies grown out of, as Chandra (2015, 57) also argues, paternalistic ideologies of development and modernization. Moreover, the rural people are to bear the brunt of the fatalistic consequences of various economic policies like withdrawal of subsidies from fertilizers emerging out of the liberalization of economies.

If we take a look longitudinally into the implications of implementation of these policy initiatives in rural areas of West Bengal, we would seem to understand the way these initiatives have been shaping the rural economy, and thereby facilitating or hindering the development of capital as well as the scope of labour and employment. The narrative of rural economy in West Bengal has been divided by the author into three phases only for the methodological purpose. While the period until 1977 since 1950 constitutes the first phase being marked mainly by the Congress rule with two united front governments for a very short period, and the thriving struggles of the oppositions particularly of the left parties, the second phase is marked by the tryst of the Left Front (LF) with their 'socialist' agenda while being in power. The third phase is obviously the recent phase though being not very recent when the rural economy has undergone a considerable change mainly in terms of crisis in employment and overall agriculture as part of particularly the so-called neoliberalization in India. What Frankel (2005) concludes in regard to rural scenario of the pan-Indian perspective that, except some small pockets of rapid growth, Indian agriculture remained mainly as subsistence sectors is perhaps quite true in case of West Bengal. There were chronic food shortage and, after the first decade of planning (ibid., 4), 'fifty to sixty per cent of the rural population' 'could not afford minimum levels of consumption' 'though available estimates for the early 1970s revealed a reduction in the proportion of the poor'. The plight of the peasants in West Bengal seemed to have become more precarious than their counterpart in other Indian state as proportions of peasants who depend on agriculture just for their subsistence was much higher.

West Bengal, unlike other Indian states, thus, had witnessed a series of peasant struggles organized mainly by the Communist parties of different hues at the rural fringes during the first three decades after India's independence. When a popular film Mother India (1957) portrayed a protagonist mother, a poverty-stricken village woman, who would struggle almost alone, and survive against the atrocities of a moneylender and all hardship including the deficit of water required for irrigation associated with farming a small piece of land her family owns, and subsequently being considered as 'mother' by her fellow villagers, the peasants in several villages of West Bengal mobilized in peasant struggles organized by the Communist parties with demands like 'land to the tiller' and 'abolition of landlordism' against the zamindars and moneylenders. When the construction of irrigation canal within the village is going to be celebrated zealously by the villagers as depicted in the said film, the peasants of West Bengal in various places are going to seize forcefully the lands held by landlords illegitimately in huge amount. In both cases, the peasants had been trying to implement the development policies the Floud Commission recommended, and the central government subsequently set for implementation in its Five-Year Plan (Planning Commission). While the protagonist mother tried converting barren land into arable one, and continuing farming despite hardships, the struggling peasants in West Bengal tried only to implement the land reform acts promulgated by the central government but kept untouched by the respective state government whatever the reasons may be. In their bid to earn a mere subsistence, however, the peasants including the *Mother* would widen the development of capitalism in rural areas by way of land productivity.

But nothing much has changed on the food crisis and the poverty front all over India, and West Bengal is not an exception. Although the peasants acquired some occupational and proprietorship rights, even if, to a very meagre amount of land, in some pockets of West Bengal where they could confiscate under the leadership of

Communist parties some *benami* land from the landlords, and subsequently distribute them, called as *khas* land, among themselves, the economic condition remained more or less the same as before since the land was to a large extent unproductive, so was the labour. Furthermore, Nehru's planned economy which was thought to be the key to the removal of poverty by means of just public enterprises in heavy industries failed completely, and the rural people in West Bengal along with the rest of India bore its brunt through experiencing an acute food shortage (Chatterjee 2010, 4). After her father's demise, Indira Gandhi as the prime minister of India, starting in 1966, had no other option but the substantial state intervention in rural economy aimed at guiding growth in order to pacify instantaneously especially the agitated peasants. How did her government embark upon toward the achievement of this goal of accelerating economic growth in rural areas? She took actually no time to forcefully realize the liberal prescription, and thus undertaking a significant governmental step which consequently transformed the rural in an effective way once for all in terms of capitalist transformation. The Indira Gandhi Government had adopted a strategy popularly known as GRT, as the saying goes, to 'curb the so-called red revolution', in order to enhance the agricultural production. The GRT, or 'input-intensive, industrial agriculture', as Gupta coins, was intended to increase the production of crops manifold through, on the one hand, providing enormous subsidies in irrigation, seed and fertilizers and, on the other, protecting farmers with minimum support price for essential food crops. The rural economy, particularly the agriculture as its mainstay, which had still maintained a low level of growth was rapidly prompted and facilitated by the state to grow at a much higher rate. The GRT did undoubtedly amplify the production of crop as well as the productivity of land; however, it did so at the cost of marketization and commercialization of all sorts of resources including natural ones, like water in rural areas. The field of livelihood or employment also began to change at greater pace since.

Although the GRT as targeted had hinged primarily on the capacities of larger landholding group and, as Chatterjee (2010, 5) argues, 'tried out in the better irrigated zones of Punjab, Haryana and western Uttar Pradesh', its West Bengal chapter, though being a delayer, tells a different story as far as the landholding class is concerned. In West Bengal, as I have described, the GRT had not taken hold rapidly for a couple of reasons. If the consistent political turmoil and the ensuing lack in governance are considered as principal reasons, the absence of a considerable proportion of large/rich farmers, and of a united move on their part in West Bengal is not any less important either. While the proportion of marginal and small landholding class has increased over the years, the proportion of large landholding class has increasingly reduced in the same period. In other words, while the large landholding class in West Bengal were busy 'protecting' their landholding from lawful seizure by protesting peasants, their counterpart in western India could rapidly utilize the GRT to make their fortune at the cost of everything in rural areas that underwent massive transformation under capitalist dynamics. My ethnography (2012) in West Bengal reveals the way the farmers did cultivate their land, and were eventually content with low-ranged production in the period of 1960s and 1970s. Only one crop was grown during the monsoon season entirely on the basis of monsoon rains, and a large stretch of land being lying fallow. In the lean season, that is, from mid-August to mid-October, the landless families who mostly belonging to Scheduled Castes had no employment and often had to face starvation. May of them used to beg from the prosperous families merely to survive (ibid., 9–10).

Everything began to change once the Left Front came to power in West Bengal in 1977. First of all, the government opted for pursuing the unfinished agenda of land reform that the left parties had promised to accomplish if they come to power, and it succeeded to an extent in this respect by utilizing the party networks down deep to the grass roots. In West Bengal, contrary to other states where the large farmers could utilize the GRT to maximize the potential of land and labour, the small peasantry along with the marginal peasants and even the sharecropper landless peasants had tried the GRT in order to meet their needs of livelihood in different parts of West Bengal. Notably, the farmers or the peasants whatever we may term them, belonging to all sections, could try only when/if their land were either irrigated at least to an extent or having some potential to be irrigated, no matter in what way it is. Therefore, we would see if we investigate, as my recent field work conducted in 18 villages in 18 districts reveals, that there are lot of variation in regard to both the adoption and the subsequent 'success' of GRT at rural hinterland. The GRT while was implemented immediately in around late 1970s in some parts of districts like Burdwan, Bankura, Nadia, Hooghly, North 24 Paraganas and Paschim Medinipore, took time to be implemented in other places of different districts like Purulia, Bankura, Jalpaiguri and Darjeeling. The reasons for variation in application and effects of GRT, however, as per my field data, are many. While the availability of irrigation is one reason, other reasons include the fertility of land, the nature of land distribution, and proximity of the respective area to the city or market.

The narrative of industrial agriculture is really a complicated story, not only is it different in different parts of the country, but also is it diverse even in different parts of a province like West Bengal. The farmers who had substantial amount of land to afford investment mainly in ground water, to purchase the high yielding variety of seeds and fertilizers could obviously take advantage to benefit from it. Actually, as the class or landholdings is important to pursue this enterprise, so is the nature of irrigation. For instance, the farmers of some parts of both Burdwan and Hooghly districts who had been since long taking use of water for irrigation of their agricultural crops from the DVC canal system don't now at all depend on water discharged by the DVC for cultivating particularly some crops like *Boro* paddy and potato. They rather try to manage it on their own either through sinking their own dug tube-wells or through purchasing water from other available pump owners. Another aspect seemed also have contributed to mark a variation in regard to the adoption of GRT in West Bengal. The GRT got expanded rapidly in those places where any traditional farming community or the cultivating castes took interest to invest in intensive agriculture by way of commercialized production. For instance, in our case, the farmers belonging to Sadgope and Mahishya castes in particularly three districts, Bankura, Burdwan and Hooghly, who since very long had been cultivating land to live on took the advantage of GRT at the first instance, and made their fortune. However, after a while, the GRT set about to spread everywhere in the state cutting across class, caste, religion and regions.

With the all-pervading spread of GRT, the rural got only markeized, commercialized and commoditized. The determinant role of capital began to shape everything including the political and the social at the rural hinterland. The natural resources like water, particularly the ground water, had seemingly been the most that got marketized and shaped in rural areas through reasons of capital. Some time ago when rural economy had been beyond the purview of the GRT, irrigation of crops was dependent upon the monsoon rains, at best upon the irrigation from local ponds and lakes, and from the rivers, and of course by manually operated channels. The scope of cultivation thus was very limited in terms of both areas and seasons. Large stretches of areas, as my informant remarks, were lying fallow simply for want of irrigation. Even the water bodies and jungles in the village were kept as idle or unutilized. The condition of large landholders was appalling since they, despite having sufficient amount of land, could not cultivate the same. Being a member of an erstwhile *zamindar* family, he still owns around 20 *bighas* of land, and candidly says, 'the gloomy look of the village has changed. All land here is now arable'. I too had realized that the village was changing, particularly when I saw the agricultural field being irrigated from lots of diesel-operated pumps. To me, those field looked like a huge industry wherein innumerable machines performing the tasks of growing crops through exhausting the treasure of water especially under the ground. The village in India which was a long time ago being regarded as a place of serenity has now become a boisterous place with lots of noises arisen out from those pump-machines. Had it been any legal system that could check the level of noise in rural areas, many of the farmers who owned pump machines would have definitely been penalized. What is, however, significant in our context is the vibrant market that surfaces surrounding agriculture right from the very beginning of its making. It is likely that the ground water market would dominate the agriculture, and not the vice versa. In other words, it seems, building the market of water is the main purpose, agriculture just remains as provider. Agriculture is now, instead of being associated with labour, the ploy of capital which determines its fate.

Any cultivator who would endeavour to cultivate land, be it his own or in lease, he must have to enter the market since there is almost no option available any more as the surface water mostly have dried out. Hence, before kicking off farming, s/he would become part of this market of water about which, particularly its fuel part, one has very little idea. When irrigation makes farming so precarious, how does the issue of seed perform its part? Seed, both as a material and a concept, has been regarded since long by the peasantry as very essential and sacrosanct. They would assume, on the one hand, all crops have the potential to be a seed, and on the other, the cultivators', or communities', right to seed are sacrosanct. Only a few decades ago, India possessed hundreds of varieties of rice that would grow throughout the country. Even a village would possess a dozen of rice varieties, as Deb, the rice scientist, asserts. These all were the local varieties, sometimes being draught-tolerant and flood-tolerant, shaped and suitable for a specific local soil, climate and taste. Earlier each family could have preserved these local varieties of seeds with conventional knowledge for generation after generation.[3] The penetration of 'high yielding crop variety' (HYV) as a governmental intervention into agriculture in India has ruined these varieties, and the concerned knowledge as well at cost of food security. The cultivators and their communities have lost not only their right to seed along with the required knowledge, but also their freedom to choose crops. They are to depend today on the market, generally a remote market located in a remote province, even for the seeds, the nature of which is unknown to them. They don't know often about what they are growing and also about the ways these seeds have to be grown. These new seeds cost more, so is the production. Most precariously, these seeds are usually not just seeds but a package, rather a concept that constitutes a new prescription for farming.

This is to say, these seeds are meant for a new way of farming which doesn't bother to respect the past, to consider the particular context or the climate, and also to recognize the communities' knowledge. These new seeds actually intend to transform the economy, the nature and the culture of a particular community. While Vandana Shiva (2013) termed these seeds as 'seeds of death', I would term it as 'seeds of development'. These seeds of development intend to homogenize not only the space of heterogeneity, but even also the time. After capturing the market of seed and water, these seeds are seizing the method of farming by introducing agrochemicals and agro-pesticides, the market of which they are rarely aware of. These seeds can't grow any further even a little extent until and unless they receive the appropriate quantity of agrochemicals, agro-pesticides and even water assigned for them. The quantity of all these requirements has genetically been determined even before the germination of seeds. The cultivators are thus required to procure agrochemicals and agro-pesticides at the time when they collect seeds. But everything seems going up in the air when the cultivators enter the market with crops they have grown painstakingly overcoming a series of hurdles.

The agricultural commodity market though operating locally even in collaboration with the local entrepreneurs who often happen to be the cultivators' kindred and brethren is actually determined by the larger or global finance conglomerates. The transactions even in local agricultural market are controlled in tune with the dealings of global market which eventually revolves around the principles of supply and demand as well as various kinds of speculations. Harriss-White, though being not at all concerned about the implications of GRT or of the reforms in production, writes: (2008, 1) 'markets for agricultural commodities have influenced, and are important determinants of the performance of agriculture in the 'state' during the last three decades of the last century. She argues that West Bengal's agricultural markets are controlled through money advances by the non-landed fractions of the business class under the patronage of the state. Had it been not controlled by the dominant agro-commercial elites, i.e. the non-landed fractions of the business class, it would have been much prosperous through protecting the agro-commercial petty bourgeoisie that was emerging in rural areas. 'The balance between returns to agro-commerce and return production', she believes (ibid., 3), 'might also have been less disadvantageous to production'.

But it is unlikely that 'the gains from trade (agricultural) would have been spread more equally' and widely, if the dominance of agro-commercial elites had been arrested. My ethnographic research (2007, 2013) amply shows that even the 'elite agricultural producers', i.e. the large landholders, have also made their for- tune during the last few decades particularly in the period of 1970–1980 through investing both in business and trade of agricultural inputs and agricultural com- modities. This is to say, this category of 'agro-commercial poor' could have taken the place of agro-commercial elites, and equally would have made their fortune depending obviously on the state patronage. However, Harriss-White's argument about agro-commercial elites and agro-commercial poor appears to echo the words of Chatterjee (2008), who put forward an idea of variation of capital i.e. corporate and non-corporate capital. Is it really possible to find two simultaneous domains of capital in a specific locality? Also, it seems to be not the fact that the cultivators have only been the victim of the dominance of agro-commercial elites in the domain of agricultural commodity market. They also fall victim equally, if not more, to the market of agricultural inputs, for instance, the agrochemicals and agro-pesticides which is mostly controlled by the big corporate MNCs. Often, as described by one of my informants, the cultivators are to purchase and sell all agricultural inputs as well as the harvest respectively from the same counter or two different counters from one trader or a group of traders.

In fact, the agricultural commodity market put the final nail in the coffin of devastating farming advanced by the GRT in India. It looks like the cultivators have been digging their own graves by adopting unequivocally this technology wherever there situations permit. It has no doubt that the cultivators would never show any resistance on their part against this process by which the new system has replaced aggressively the old one. Rather, they, like many who are concerned about the condition of agriculture, at the first instance, all things con- sidered, embraced this new technology as revolutionary one. Meanwhile, capitalist market has expanded in leaps and bounds by transforming agriculture or farming into an industry or a trade, this is to say, a speculative trade. Although everything revolves around agriculture, agriculture itself has become an appendage of a larger capitalist construction. The question is: why didn't the cultivators resist this capi- talist intervention from its very beginning? Why did they concede these transfor- mations after all? The answers of these questions are perhaps linked with the way these transformations shaped the domain of rural employment and, broadly, the domain of rural commercial capital. My research concludes, on the basis of more than one decade of field work, that the community of cultivators as a whole including the landless labourers, particularly from those districts that lying in the gangetic plains wherein the GRT was first successfully put into effect in 1970s, got some respite in terms of employment opportunities, albeit for a limited period. Although each class of cultivators had experienced the said process based mainly on their own position, the standard opinion does not differ much. Widely perceived as a life- changing initiative, the GRT, as the field data suggests, could transform the stagnant rural landscape, as stereotypically held, into a vibrant hub of production and trades. For instance, the marginal cultivators (including the sharecroppers and the lessee cultivators) and the landless labourers could get scope to obtain some more employment, at least in some proportions, in all three seasons, and could also grow more crops than earlier. The small and big farmers, conversely, had benefited enormously through maximizing their profit manifold in terms of exploiting the field of farming as well as the agro-based market that emerged as a consequence of capitalist transformation.

Hence, the application of GRT as appeared marks a new regime before which, as the villagers belonging to landless families inform me, the land-poor had to starve often. However, this thriving phase whatsoever did not continue for long. Why did the prosperousness in agriculture fail to continue? If the agro-market that flourishing simultaneously together with the GRT induced farming at huge pace stands as a real culprit for this state of agricultural dilapidation, the environmental degradation, as Gupta (2016) mentions, has also been a factor which heightens this precariousness. The government, both the central and the provincial, which had once proactively introduced the GRT by way of supporting the cultivators both in tangible terms and ideological terms, withdrew its support whatever it may be only to aid, rather encourage, the corporate finance capital in its pursuit to amass exorbitant profit from the emerging fields. As part of neoliberal restructuring, what the government did at first instance was nothing but simply liberalize the country's market so as to ease the entries of all business players irrespective of their basis of origin. Moreover, the government began to withdraw its supports since the late 1980s that it had extended so far to the farming sector in terms of subsidies to help the industries and traders keep the price of commodities low. Even the regulatory structure whatsoever that existed till then to protect the indigenous sectors and industries from the eye of large corporate house were all set for deregulation steadily as consequences of neoliberal reforms. The cultivators belonging mainly to those respective fertile areas where the GRT was first applied had then been accustomed fully to cultivate by means of this technology. In fact, making the situation murkier, the GRT had risen by then to dominance, even in the regions where it has been introduced lately, and also not so successfully, as a technology for enhancing productivity in a massive scale of crops and the land. The cultivators, therefore, everywhere in the state would fall victim to these neoliberal reforms of agricultural market by the government in favour of corporate business.

There is seemingly no dearth of macro-level figures to explain the impact of these reforms on agriculture, what is really scarce is the micro-level narrative of consequential changes in the cultivators' incomes and livelihood. I have tried to understand time and again the way these reforms going to shape the income and opportunities in livelihoods of the cultivators belonging to all sections, and also by what means the cultivators trying manage the effects whatsoever. Every time I was left confused by their responses since their income and job opportunities, what I calculate, have been anything but ever profitable and positive. All sections of the cultivators categorically mention in more or less in the same tune that this trade has increasingly been turning precarious. The cost of agricultural inputs is always more than the value of the crops they are supposed to get at any standard market rate. When asked about why they still pursuing the GRT or even farming as a whole, the cultivators respond at one, 'no other way than this'. If we classify the responses to why they continue farming on the basis of their landholding positions, we would get two different kinds of versions. While the marginal cultivators state that they obtain in any case the remuneration of their labour, the substantial farmers say without hesitation that they could at least find their food, and also could retain land as dividend in their own possession. These are actually 'diplomatic' responses; there must have some complex dimensions in regard to their lives and livelihoods which I shall try to explain in the next chapter. However, both from the macro-level data and the micro-level village data like mine, it reveals that the marginal people who possess almost no land have always been in search of employment, be it farm works or the non-farm, to make only both ends meet. Failing to get it, this section of villagers, in all 18 districts where I have conducted field-work, would migrate to anywhere in the world in search of livelihoods for even any kind of jobs. While it reveals in my earlier work (2013) that the persons belonging to the landless or marginal families in southern districts migrate less, the recent field visits unfold that there is little variation in scale of migration in respect of the regions. What is significant in our context is that the changing rural situation is, as appeared, not promising particularly in employment terms.

The question is at this moment whether the application of GRT can be considered as a failed project in context of West Bengal. The answer would be both yes and no in real term. The answer would actually vary based on the perspective from which we understand the implications of the said strategy. If we understand it from the perspective of capital, the answer must be 'no', this is to say, the GRT is not at all a failed project. Conversely, if we understand it from the perspective of labour, the answer would be 'yes' in real terms, this is to say, the GRT is a failed project, and thus the peasants 'could no longer sustain their families on the old terms', but had no viable alternative, as Li (2014, 2) argues. However, in moderate term, the answer would be either mixed or no. Why I am proposing it is actually on the basis of my fieldwork which reveals that the condition of landless labouring people has not changed in real terms. By 'real terms' I mean their actual position in context of social structure. Their position has been more or less the same as earlier in terms of social structure. Rather, their condition becomes more speculative and precarious since their livelihoods have increasingly been determined by the principles of larger market, and the ensuing accumulation of capital. On the other hand, capital has managed meanwhile to tighten its grip smoothly in the rural terrain through transforming agriculture on its own term. The natural resources which was once largely untapped has now been unbarred to be exploited, and increasingly being turned into the comfort zone of capital. Imagine, for a moment, what constitutes the zone of capital today, right from the market of diesel/kerosene required for irrigation pumps to the market of harvested crops. The entire agricultural zone also includes a flourishing market of machines and machinery tools required for mechanized farming which grown rapidly during this period.

While, after all rural developments together with steady mechanization and capitalist investment in agriculture, the growth began to slump in post-reform period, and the cultivators lost to some extent their enthusiasm to continue farming, or took it often just as (Gupta 2016, 15) 'risk endeavour' 'gambling on the weather and on global commodity prices', the government intended to scale the rural economy up further toward capitalist accumulation by way of acquisition of land for industrialization. This is, as appeared, another major step after GRT to tap the land resources of the country in much greater pace in accumulation term. Levien (2013) compares the current regime with the earlier regime afresh in terms of land dispossession for industrial development. While 'steel towns and industrial estates', he argues (ibid., 381), 'reflected a regime of land for production', the recent dispossession of land represents 'a neoliberal regime of land for the market in which "land broker states" have emerged to indiscriminately transfer land from peasants to capitalist firms'. Despite various attempts by the government to project this purpose of land acquisition as intended for the overall development of India's economy, the vast peasantry are not ready to buy the theory and, instead, organized in 'land wars'. I dispute Levien's argument particularly where he compares two periods as two different regimes of dispossession. If the earlier one has been able to achieve the ideological legitimacy, the other has failed. I argue by refuting Levien's 'two regime' theory that recent development in land acquisition, and the subsequent 'land wars' in India, actually makes no difference as far as the state's role and intention is concerned. The state's intention has been all through the same. This is to say, it is not a fact that the state in the earlier period had taken land for production, whereas the state in the current regime does it for the market. The state's intention has always been to play a positive role in promoting free market, industrialization and economic growth 'with pretensions' or without pretensions of inclusive social transformations. It is certainly significant in our context to understand the way in which the political parties have intervened in the state-led agenda of capitalist transformation in agriculture, and the subsequent conflict between capital and labour, and thereby shaped the domain of employment at the rural hinterland.

Parties, capital and labour

In her analysis of democracy in India, Banerjee (2012, 49) points out that India's democracy is 'reasonably consistent' and 'her institutions have been mostly robust', but 'it remains to be seen whether India can redistribute the fruits of its economic growth to the wider society, and thereby serve as a unique model … of combining economic democracy with the robust political one'. This means that although Banerjee believes that India's records on democracy is consistent, she has no doubt that the country somehow lacks the economic democracy which, she argues, could be achieved if India would successfully redistribute the fruits of economic growth to the people. Hers is no doubt a cliché and worn-out story both among popular and academic circle who consider that India has, first of all, to increase its economic growth to attain its prosperity, and then it needs to redistribute its fruits whatsoever to eradicate its persistent inequality. Rather, what is actually important is the way the wider society, here the peasantry, could successfully make use of the capital in their lives and livelihoods, and subsequently could tame the same so that it (capital) would remain as less powerful and controllable. Obviously, this is not an easy task to do. Whether the democracy of India, or of any country, is reasonably consistent actually would depend on the way the country could prioritize democracy i.e. the interests of the ordinary people over capital i.e. the capitalist appropriation.

We might get a reasonable answer of the aforesaid question if we are able to map the trajectories, on the basis of this formula, of the political parties which have been functional in West Bengal throughout this period. To start with, we may first analyse the roles of the Congress party (Indian National Congress) in mounting the capitalist development in rural Bengal and, afterwards, that of the Left Front in particular context of West Bengal. Being a liberal national party, the Congress has unequivocally been very clear ever since its origin about the party's political stand, and so never claims that it would undertake anti-capitalist democratic movements in the wider interest of the larger society. Although it is beyond the purview of this book the way the Congress party was formed, functioned and took its stand on various political issues, I have, at this moment, been tempted to mention a couple of lines about the 'birth of Congress'. Gandhi said on 15 September 1931, I quote Ghosh (1989, 18),[4] that it was 'a matter of the greatest pleasure to me to state that it (the Congress) was first conceived in an English brain: Allan Octavius Hume we know as the father of Congress'. Ghosh had pressed forward a pertinent question in surprise about how the Indians like Gandhi 'who collaborated with high British officials to set up the Congress' and thought 'the British officials as fathers of Congress', can be considered as the nationalists. With extensive historical research, Ghosh (ibid., 21), a partisan Marxist historian, reiterated the words pronounced by Hume that the Congress party was 'a safety valve for the escape of great and growing forces, generated by our own action, was urgently needed and no more efficacious safety-valve than our Congress movement could possibly be devised'.[5]

How did a party, whose birth and nature has been so dubious, the question arises, play its roles in agricultural reforms by making a balance between capital and democracy. If we split up the history of Congress into three phases, the first phase (i.e. the pre-independence phase) would definitely be marked as a period of consistent collaboration on the part of the Congress with the landlord class in rural India. Chatterjee (1984) brilliantly describes the way the Congress party endorsed various land policies which were mostly pro-landlord. When the ordinary *raiyats* and the under-*raiyats*, were increasingly threatened by the British revenue system, and subsequently became indebted by losing even their land, both in occupation and right terms, the landholding class armed with these land policies easily got to transfer the *raiyats'* land on their behalf. In fact, the interests of the *raiyats* and the ordinary tenants never had been represented before the Provincial Legislative Council by the leaders of the Congress party who were mostly belonging to the landlord and rentier class until the Krishak Praja party was formed. As a result of this fact, the Congress party, though for a short period of time (1922–1925) when C R Das, the leader of the Swaraj party, a new incarnation of the Congress party, attempted strategically to include in his party leadership a group of radicals as well as the leaders of peasant movements and, above all, the Muslim activists, never had become a party to which the wider peasantry across religion could support.[6]

Take the passing of the Tenancy Act, 1928, for instance, for explaining the role of the Congress party in shaping the land question in Bengal. It revealed from Chatterjee's findings (1984, 91) that the Swaraj bloc generally voted against the *bargadars* and under-*raiyats*, and obviously in favour of the landlords against the tenants. What I am trying to explain is just to exemplify that the Congress party had always been since its birth in favour of the landlord or rentier class, and been opposed to major reforms in the *zamindari* system. Despite the fact that the peasantry as a whole growingly becoming impoverished and land-poor, and the landlord class was in decline, the Congress party was not against the rentier system. The rent as the principal mode of surplus extraction, as the Marxists rightly propose, stood as a barrier to capitalist development in agriculture. After long years, in 1940, the Floud Commission eventually realized the shortfall on the part of the colonial government, and thus recommended radical reforms for overall agricultural development which I have described earlier. The landlords meanwhile could increasingly accumulate lands transferred by the immiserized peasantry in the late colonial period, but had opted for continuing the rent exploitation, instead of initiating exploitation through capitalist farming. However, we might find a different trend developing particularly in the fringes of south-western district of the state as regard to the capitalist development in agriculture during the same period. Here, the rich peasants, moneylenders and trading class combined together as a new jotedars class who had challenged the dominance of the erstwhile landlord class endeavoured to exploit the land intensively through capitalist farming. In contrast to the landlord class centred in the northern districts of the state, this class of proprietors would exploit the land in a different way, and subsequently redefined the class configuration in a new fashion which we discuss at length later in the next chapter.

The question that arises is whether the Congress party which had not been at all concerned to encourage the expansion of capital in agriculture during the colonial period had endeavoured to put agriculture to rights by way of pursuing major agricultural reforms in initial days of the postcolonial period. The question becomes more relatable when the beginning of the postcolonial period was marked, at least as claimed by the political leaders of the country, (Frankel 2005, 3) 'as a democratic pattern of socialism as a new model'. Chatterjee (1999, 17) problematizes in depth this proclamation and says that this is actually a kind of 'socialist phrasemongering in an ideology of populism which goes hand in hand with this kind of political structure'. Nehru's policies which were anything but socialist had failed to achieve its declared objectives whatsoever and had, most significantly, abandoned the agricultural sector to its destiny. His government had though, in accordance with the recommendations by the Floud Commission, passed two significant land reforms acts; it was comparatively indifferent to reform the rural front. Nehru had, however, belatedly realized during the period when the country witnessed a severe food crisis, that his government could have been taken efforts to pursue at least some agricultural reforms (Gopal 1984, 168). The question is: why did the government like India's that based on liberal democracy fail to undertake major agrarian reforms? Even after the enactment of two successive land reform acts in Nehru's era, as the historical evidences show and my own field work data in the state substantiate, that the then Congress-led government and the same ruling party in West Bengal made no efforts to implement the land enactments whereas made every efforts to acquire large chunks of land for industrialization by displacing mostly indigenous populations (Parry 1999, 112; Levien 2013, 385).[7] When the peasant masses under the leadership of the left opposition embarked on to seize the ceiling surplus land, the party in rule blatantly opposed their attempt. In fact, the leadership of the Congress party in rural areas was then almost entirely based on the landlord class, so did the bureaucrats who had 'unfettered executive power' yet during the postcolonial period.[8] There are of course some economic explanations about why the government failed to initiate agricultural reforms, but, I argue, the Indian ruling class had still been in dilemma about the way in which the agrarian question could be addressed. It was really a problem, it seemed, they had been facing to design a plan of capitalist development without hurting any class that related with land.

Nehru's government had prioritized the industrial development over agricultural reforms not because only of the fact that the regime was overpowered by the big bourgeoisies including the capitalists. The government was entirely convinced of the soundness of the policy of industrial capitalism advanced both by the government and the big bourgeoisie, be it the comprador or the national, through public enterprise and the private ownership. Why it was convinced is due actually to the sheer fact that it had at any rate wanted to increase the economic growth which, the government thought, would automatically trickle down to the rural horizon. The government had no ready-made options to take up either as far as agrarian reforms are concerned. However, from the very beginning, the government had emphasized on the increase of agricultural production. This apart, it was concerned to an extent about the issues of unemployment and poverty at the rural hinterland, and so attempted to undertake a few poverty alleviation programmes. The Nehru regime, briefly, had left no imprint in rural areas particularly in rural West Bengal other than the marks of hunger, scarcity of food and abject poverty. Nehru's liberalism had massively failed to facilitate the capital as well as the labour, particularly the rural labour. But, the regime of Indira Gandhi had compensated the earlier government's neglect of rural and made a balance, at least in the initial period, by actuating a reverse of prioritization during the earlier era. Gandhi government's practice of liberalism took successfully, at the first instance, agricultural sector in India for rapid expansion of capital, and the subsequent increase in economic growth in that sector. The GRT, which was considered as the agency behind the expansion of capital in agriculture, did, I have argued earlier, aid both the capital and labour to grow in the initial period. This new technology had turned the rural into a vibrant space wherein capital got mounting scopes to be expanded, and thereby transformed the rural India. The rural sphere, particularly in West Bengal, began to get a momentum, be it the positive or the negative in longer term, after a long period of dead stop. While, however, after a short period, the scope in employment got to shrink, the capitalist expansion took a forceful role to exploit the agricultural sector.

This is to say, the liberal agenda set by the Indira Gandhi government put the capital up in a safe room of burgeoning agricultural sector particularly since it was tied favourably with the programmes of poverty alleviation like 'Food for Work'. Based increasingly on these kinds of poverty alleviation programmes, the Rajiv Gandhi government ascended to rule, and subsequently initiated to liberalize the economy including that of the rural, after a short while, at the very juncture when the scope of labour already began to diminish. The successive governments then launched the welfare policies as vehicles to drive their main agenda of capitalist expansion. If we delve into the survey of welfare policies undertaken, and the extent of liberalization of economies particularly in rural sphere during the same period, we could get a clue about the relationship between these two agendas. The government being sympathetic towards capitalist expansion would design the welfare policies in such way that the available resources get marketized, and utilized subsequently to strengthen the productivity of capital, thereby increasing the growth. The enactment and formulation of the acts and policies by the two successive governments under the leadership of Dr. Singh, the then Prime Minister, actually have well reflected the dynamics of liberal principles. The question is at this juncture about the way the Communist Left had played its role in this grand capitalist script. Did it perform in a different way? Was it in war path against these mainstream policies? How did it deal with the issues of employment in rural areas?

First of all, I make it clear that I never attempt here to explain about whether the so-called Left parties can be called as Left anyway. I just consider them as Left since these parties are called as Left or the Communists. I restrict the purview of this discussion to the programmes and activities of the Left parties in West Bengal regarding the issues of employment. I make a split of the postcolonial period into only three phases in order to systematize my arguments regarding the changing views and roles of the Left parties in terms of rural employment. If the first phase constitutes the early years (i.e. 1949s–1976) when the Left parties in opposition organized a series of, particularly, land-related movements in the province, the second phase (1977–2006) constitutes its days in power as the rulers of West Bengal. The third phase constitutes the recent period (2006 till now) when the Left party has witnessed its deterioration in support at greater pace. The undivided CPI party and the CPI (M) party,[9] as major components of the Left Front, have, undoubtedly, been generally considered as the driving force of Left movements in India. The question arises about whether the undivided CPI and the CPI (M) party had played any different and effective role in the main script as described above in addressing the issues of unemployment and rural poverty.

The answer seems to be negative as far as the said party's documents betraying its thoughts and opinions about different governmental policies and strategies. As early as in the 1940s, at which time very little had been attempted in terms of agricultural reforms on the part of the government, the Communist leaders, for instance, Ranadive, the general secretary of the then CPI party (1948–1959) and Gopal Haldar, like in the same tune of the leaders of the Nehru-led Congress, were of the view that the large-scale industrialization could only solve the crisis of employment in India, particularly in West Bengal, which was once under the Permanent Settlement. Gopal Haldar (2002) forcefully states that 'we want employment so as to require the industries', and 'we have to establish various kinds of industries throughout India so as to eradicate unemployment'.[10] Those leaders were not at all optimistic even during the period of 1940s that agriculture could create employment any more as this sector had already been saturated.[11] 'There will at least be some solutions', Ranadive (in Biswas 2002, 343) writes, 'if the lands lying fallow are made cultivable and used for cultivation'; however, 'unless the existing agrarian situation is radically transformed, new areas are converted into arable land; there is really a very little possibility of employment generation. To employ the extra labour, we must have to turn towards industries'.[12] This is to say, the Communist Left had no plans for agricultural reform either during the initial days of postcolonial period. As the Nehru-led government had prioritized industrialization just at the cost of agricultural reforms, so did the Left. Their politics, or the ideology, went hand in hand with that of the Congress as far as the policies of agricultural reforms are concerned. The Communist Left had taken initiatives to organize the peasants' movement, particularly the sharecroppers', in a few districts of undivided Bengal, on the eve of India's independence, with a demand of 'Tebhaga', which was already proposed by the Floud Commission (1940). However, while the Tebhaga movement became widespread, and the Communist Left achieved a considerable support base among the peasant masses, the latter couldn't succeed to raise the broader question of employment as the movement was withdrawn suddenly by the Communist party. The platform of this movement could have been used by the Communist Left for pushing ahead the peasants to move beyond the recommendations of Floud Commission, and to raise issues in employment terms. But the Left had failed to do it as they hardly had any point beyond the liberal framework.

In a document published by the West Bengal State Committee, CPI, in the year 1954, it clearly says (Biswas 2004, 52),

> there is nothing bravery in ending the Permanent Settlement.... As early as in 1812, the report of the Fifth committee had seriously criticized the Permanent Settlement.... Even during the direct rule of British Colonialism, the Floud Commission had recommended the termination of Permanent Settlement.

Ironically, the ground for which the Communist Left had criticized thoroughly the then Congress are equally applicable to themselves when, we find that, they hardly ever extended any structure of demands beyond the recommendations of Floud

Commission. Not only has the Tebhaga movement, but have other land-related movements in general, with the exception of a few like the offer of compensation to the landlords regarding the estate acquisition (ibid., 61), also demonstrated that the Communist Left didn't go beyond the margin of Floud Commission. The Communist Left rightly pointed out that by granting compensation to the landlords, the government actually legalized the landlords' right to these properties, and created a situation for increasing eviction of sharecroppers. Despite they had been arguing since 1950s that the peasants should be the proprietor of the lands they had been tilling, the Communist Left took this issue as an immediate agenda not before 1967 when the Naxals, a breakaway group of the CPI (M) who would be later called as the CPI (ML) party or the radical Left, began to wage militant peasants' movement with a demand of 'land to the tillers' in West Bengal.

The CPI (M) party who had then been sharing power with other political parties mainly with Bangla Congress by forming the United Front government in West Bengal spent no time to snatch this slogan from the radicals. Subsequently, by acquiring ceiling surplus land from the landlords and *jotedars*, they began to distribute it to the sharecroppers and landless peasants. This moment was the beginning of the land reform phase in West Bengal initiated by the Left both in power and in opposition. The Communist Left afterwards reached the height of its popularity and ascended to power of the province only to stay there for more than three decades. The question we should ask now: what was their next agenda while they were in power? Had they intended to pursue capitalist development by maintaining a balance between capital and labour? Did they emphasize capital over labour, and vice versa? Let's look at what they had declared to be done in employment terms if/once they come to power in the pages of their common minimum programme.[13] This minimum programme doesn't portray any such account which is different from the mainstream narrative. In other words, the Left Front would growingly become an entity which had no different perspective. There was, thus, no question of being in war path against the mainstream policies. It has now been clear that the Left Front was in favour of capital by apparently maintaining a balance between capital and labour at the rural hinterland. When I am saying that it had performed in favour of capital by maintaining a balance between capital and labour, I mean it, actually, in governance terms. As the Left Front could maintain a status quo in terms of governance, so it could apparently maintain a balance between capital and labour. In fact, as I argue earlier in this chapter, the Communist Left had played an effective role in the expansion of capital in agriculture through the GRT introduced by the central government. In its attempt to facilitate the expansion of capital as well as the market, the Left Front has ostensibly prioritized capital over the farmers who constitute a major component of the agro-production system. The Communist parties unlike their counterparts in other states would rarely organize the farmers to put their demands to the government in order to hold back the capital at least a little in its (capital's) domination over the peasantry. The governmental left in West Bengal never pursued which it could do in its limited capacity the crisis of overall farming throughout its long regime by way of restraining the agro-commercial elites from its desperate exploitation of the agro-commodity market, that is, the market of inputs and outputs. As a result of which the farming which is considered as a small peasant economy in West Bengal has turned more and more into an unpromising sector.

Furthermore, the Left Front regime has been marked by another compromise with the issues of capital at expense of the agricultural labourers in rural areas. This research reveals that the agricultural labourers in general would barely get the minimum wages stipulated by the government. Even when a higher wage had been claimed by the labourers, the party leaders refused to revise it on ground that any further increase in wage would make the landowner cultivators non-achiever in farming. Thus the Communist Left would just play a stereotypical role, leave alone any socialist role as was portrayed by them some decades ago, in the grand narrative of capitalist development particularly in rural areas. In some cases, as my research shows, it plays even a proactive role in opposing the acts of the labourers in their move to demand an increase in wages. Are they still to be considered as Left, the Communist or the socialists? This question comes to the fore when the Left front became even more proactive in its role in capitalist accumulation in terms of industrialization. This time, during the third phase, the Left Front didn't only surpass itself, but surpassed also the so-called liberal parties of all hues, while it intended to pursue industrialization with a proactive approach. The neoliberal period which is often considered by the Left intellectuals as the period of ruthless accumulation of capital, and of subsequent dispossession and unemployment has been considered by the governmental Left as the period of golden opportunities for enhancing development.

By juxtaposing industries with agriculture, the Left Front government upheld industries as a higher stage of agriculture, and so regarded land acquisition even for private industries as public interest. Their political conviction that land has to be acquired for private industry as part of serving a public interest was so strong that they acquired by force a large patch of agricultural land from diverse kinds of cultivators in Singur of the district of Hooghly for a big private company. The peasant masses would rarely, however, buy the discourse on industrialization initiated by the Left Front government based on the dichotomy between agriculture and industries. The land acquisition in Singur and the declaration of land acquisition in Nandigram, Purba Medinipore district by the government eventually toppled the Left Front regime, the story of which is now well-known to us. The Left Front government tried, actually, to obliterate a basic historical fact from the popular psyche that the state had once accommodated both agriculture and industries in rural areas of Bengal, and thereby guaranteeing to everyone some kind of livelihood securities mainly during the pre-British period. I argue that the Left's strategies are essentially in no way different from the ideologies of liberal politics at least to the extent it believes in theories of social evolution. In theories of social evolution based on European Enlightenment, agriculture and all kinds of agro-land relations are regarded as part of pre-capitalist backward attachment. The Indian Left, the Marxists, were so engrossed in these social evolutionary thoughts that they opted for industrialization at any cost in either period whatever the consequences may be. Even Marx, in his early days, justified the colonial rule in India as he thought it would cause social evolution. He writes (1853),

> England, it is true, in causing a social revolution in Hindostan, was actuated only by the vilest interests, and was stupid in her manner of enforcing them. But that is not the question. The question is, can mankind fulfil its destiny without a fundamental revolution in the social state of Asia? If not, whatever may have been the crimes of England she was the unconscious tool of history in bringing about the revolution.[14]

It seems to be not a surprise that the Communist Left, the ardent followers of Marx, have become the champions of industrialization ever since the beginning of their voyage. Due to the strong conviction for industrialization, they were so overwhelmed by the prospect of GRT in capitalist development of agriculture that they threw all their weight around it. Later, they have even tried to justify the coercion exercised during the course of land acquisition in Singur by reasoning that whatever may have been the crimes of the state government and its police, land acquisition for industries was the unconscious tool of history in bringing about the revolution. When they are so ardent to regard social evolutionary stages as true, the disregard for class question on the part of the Communist Left is quite expectable. What we have been witnessing is thus a blatant disregard of the issues related to class on the part of the Communist Left throughout their regime both in opposition and power. Instead of being absorbed in liberal politics, they, as they pose themselves as the Left, could have rather put a critique against the liberal framework. Instead of prioritizing the capitalist development at any cost, they could have essayed an alternative politics based on the interest of labouring class. They could have prioritized labour over capital in the production system in order to strengthen democracy in India. However, their ideology has acted as a bar to them to fruitfully construct an alternative politics. The Communist Lefts are therefore to put a limit to themselves in scripting any such employment generation programmes, and in discharging their duties to implement them. But, what are their roles in formulating these kinds of policies? How do they implement them?

Parties, policies and its implementation

The Left Front who had made a general statement regarding the right to work and education in their common minimum programme as early as on 1977 had hardly attempted to do anything about it. When this issue was first asked, they state, as Ms. Talwar, an NGO activist, describes, 'We consider that this type of Act is essential; but it is beyond our capacity. Let's see what the Central Government would do'. But the question is, Ms. Talwar repeatedly asks them, 'if there could be an Act in Maharashtra, why West Bengal won't have one?' However, the Left Front seemed have played a dubious role in question of this kind of act. When, after the parliamentary elections (2004), the UPA government included this issue in their Common Minimum Programme, the Left parties who had been resisting it in West Bengal began to raise it at the central level (Roy 2011). It would really be an apt query why the enactment of a state-level act was beyond their capacity. Why did the idea of guaranteed employment that was mentioned once as a demand in the 1970s by the Left (Chopra 2011) 'lain dormant' throughout these long years? In fact, these are such questions which can be asked to all the political parties in India especially to the Left who assume themselves as the custodian of the poor and unemployed. If the Left Front had really been the custodian of the poor and the labouring class, they could definitely have gone beyond their capacity. Herein lies the real problems of the Indian Left. They do rarely indulge themselves, particularly while in power, in proactively prioritizing the issues of labour over capital or propertied class.

Leave alone the enactment of the act in favour of the poor and unemployed, it seems, they have even been reluctant to implement the act. The MGNREGA was passed in 2005, and starting on 2 February 2006, it was in effect and the state government was supposed to implement it. But, as Ms. Talwar says (Roy 2011),

> since the very beginning, we found that the state government was quite reluctant to implement the Act. In the first year itself the government wanted to suspend its implementation on the excuse of impending elections. Then we had to take up the issue with the election commission who issued a special notification stating that since it was an Act, a legal guarantee, it would not violate the election code.

Why were the Communist Lefts so reluctant to do it? Why didn't they implement the same at least for electoral purpose? In fact, each party might not benefit equally from implementation of every policy. The extent of benefits would depend on the sections and classes for which the acts and policies aimed at, and which sections and classes mainly constitute the party. Also, it also depends on the way the party leaders can successfully mediate interests among different sections of rural people, and eventually serve the party's interests. It has no doubt that the MGNREGA, though being beneficial immensely to the landholding class in terms of agricultural development, is of benefit to the agricultural labourers at least temporarily. Plus, during both regimes, as my research reveals, the land owners have generally been the custodians of the panchayats on behalf either of the party or of the panchayat representatives. Of course, the nature and degree of the mastery over the panchayats on the part of the landowners would vary according to regional and ethnographic difference. In south Bengal, for instance, the rich farmers who mostly belonging to dominate castes like *Sadgope*, *Mahishya* and *Aguri*, would enjoy huge power particularly based on the party authority to influence on the policies in their best interest. Conversely, in the districts of north Bengal, wherein there is lesser concentration of land, and having a kind of homogenous nature of land ownership, the policies or the acts take their own routes in context of local dynamics. In a village of Coochbehar district, for instance, the panchayat representatives, panchayat officials and the villagers en masse took the opportunity to vent their grievances against the upper echelon of the administration for not disbursing the required funds to continue implementation of this act.

As I mentioned, the landholding class along with other classes would benefit equally, if not more in the long run, from implementation of this act, the success of the act depends on the way the party leaders could mediate interests among different sections of rural people. The party or the party-led panchayat could effectively implement this act by way of creating work in various kinds of schemes like excavating and renovating tanks, lakes and irrigation canals; digging *hapa* meant for harvesting and conservation of rain water for irrigation purpose; constructing *bandhs* or bridges for flood control, and also building roads, and thereby maintaining a balance of interest among different sections of people. The landowners would definitely benefit from the above schemes, and the labourers as well would get work. The revised version (2011) of the act has rectified its earlier bias toward the traditional landowners by extending the act's purview, while recommending to create work for providing irrigation facility, horticulture and land development facilities also 'to the land owned by households belonging to the Scheduled Castes and Scheduled Tribes or below poverty line families or to the beneficiaries under the Indira Awas Yojona or that of the small farmers or marginal farmers'.[15] This is to mean, the government has belatedly tried to include the people of the marginal groups in the list of the beneficiaries of durable assets created through implementation of the act. Notwithstanding the fact that except the category of small farmers or marginal farmers, the aforesaid group of categories owns usually a very little amount of land, the step to include them as beneficiary is definitely an inclusive approach. However, we can doubt whether the people of the said categories could at all benefit from this provision when all power in rural areas concentrated in the hands of the parties mainly dominated by the landowning community.

Of course, this provision of positive discrimination may otherwise turn the situation more political as the persons belonging to these so-called marginal groups would try to politically pursue the party leaders for grabbing the benefits. Since the scope of creating work is supposedly very limited, the party leaders would also try to solve this issue politically in exchange of the beneficiaries' loyalty to the party. Not only, as a result of this, would the party-based benefit distribution increase, but also would it intensify the political conflict among the benefit-seekers both within a party, and between the existing parties. In a village of Maldah district, a tribal family got their land developed as part of the MGNREGA schemes by means of obvious patronage delivered by the leaders of the CPI (M) party whom the family supporting since long. But the family made it at the expense of their sociability in a small tribal hamlet. The story didn't end here; some of the 'deprived' tribal families in this hamlet expressed their grievances for not receiving anything from the party they support, and they desired to switch to the ruling party, TMC. On the other hand, a marginal peasant in Purulia district informs that, 'while 10–15 tanks are getting approved in the *Gram Sansad*, people having good connection at the political level are getting their tanks be renovated'. This is to say, the party-based discrimination that is prevalent throughout the state often hinders the smooth functioning of the act, thereby disrupting the same fulfilling its goals whatsoever.

The leaders of the political parties who in most cases come from the landowning group always try to implement the schemes under MGNREGA in the slack season when farming does not require labour. A panchayat Pradhan (2011) in the district of Birbhum candidly says,

> we cannot provide work in all instances. There are so many reasons. When labourers are required for agricultural works we should not initiate work at that time under this project. The demand for work also does not exist at that time. As agriculture is our principal means of livelihood, NREGA works need to be stopped so that agriculture does not suffer due to it.

In 2014, my field survey that conducted in a village of the Darjeeling district clearly reveals that the party leaders belonging to TMC party constantly opt for initiating work under MGNREGA during the dull season of the nearby tea industries so that the industries face no labour crisis. For this reason, no such crisis of labour has been felt on the part of the landowner employers that the labourers would choose pushing up rural wage levels. It seems that the MGNREGA in West Bengal has not produced the effects which it has produced in Tamil Nadu. In Tamil Nadu, the MGNREGA has produced, as the scholars argue (Carswell and De Neve 2014, 564), 'significant transformative outcomes for rural labourers, such as pushing up rural wage levels, enhancing low-caste workers bargaining power in the labour market, and reducing their dependency on high-caste employers'. However, the large-scale exodus of rural youth from the rural fringes in the province to anywhere in the world in recent period might produce, if any, 'significant transformative outcomes for rural labourers'.

Whenever I have visited villages in West Bengal as part of field work for this project during the span of five years from 2010 to 2015, the job-cardholders would continually complain either about non-availability of work or about the delay in wages payment. For instance, take the version of a villager in the district of Purulia (2011), 'they have arranged work for now. Then there will be no work say, for one and half months. We have to wait at least for two months to get our wages'. Another job-cardholder complains, 'we are not getting job even after putting our applications. We are to wait at least for 3–4 months after making applications. Even after informing the DM or BDO, we are unable to get work under this project'. But it seems that the political leaders knowingly mislead the villagers including their supporters. When asked about the grievances regarding malfunctioning of the act expressed by the aspiring job-seekers, the state level leader of the RSP party who claims all credit for enacting the MGNREGA says (2012),

> the NREGA project undertaken by the central government is good. The propaganda through radio is also substantial informing people what should be done to realise their rights. But I emphasise that nobody, the panchayat Pradhan, BDO or SDO, not even the DM, can provide job for the jobseekers within 15 days. Due to the faults embedded in the funding, operation, and system of the project, nobody is in a position to implement it properly.

The faults that embedded in the rule book seem have been more serious in regard to wages payment to the labourers. In fact, the guidelines of the act didn't at all mention the way the wages to be delivered to the labourers. It recommends compensation of the labourer for the delayed payment, but not the way in which the wages be delivered properly. Hence as the labourers are affected, so are the political leaders. The labourers who have laboured in the schemes under MGNREGA, and are yet to be paid often usually point their fingers to the political leaders. Although the integrity of political leaders is not beyond question, their roles in this business are not clearly defined on the pages of the act. The nexus between the leaders and the supervisors is well-known. The supervisors would hardly understand the work in spite of training, and could not maintain the papers of the project properly, as commented by an unorthodox Pradhan. He says (ibid.),

> they delay the whole process of preparing the master roll and accomplishing other related works. Usually these supervisors have some kind of hobnobbing with the party in power of the panchayat. They get appointment as supervisor after paying a lump sum of money to the party.

In fact, my findings might corroborate his view when the supervisors I interviewed, in most cases, are either the members of the ruling party or the close relatives of the Pradhans or the panchayat members. In some cases, for example in a panchayat in the district of Jalpaiguri (2014), the supervisor of the MGNREGA projects has even come from the same family. This elucidation is further ratified by the phenomenon that the supervisors who have been in position during the Left Front government have been altered with the change in government. 'This is the unofficial rule prevalent in West Bengal', a supervisor in Bankura district candidly informs. The supervisors I met as part of my field survey are all new, that means, employed in the regime of the new government.

Despite their hobnobbing with the supervisors, and the underlying corruption,[16] the panchayat representatives are apparently not comfortable with this phenomenon of late payment. They are rather confused about the process of payment of wages and sometimes try to console themselves with the thought that it's just a fall-out of sheer bureaucratic apathy. The same RSP leader explains (ibid.) that,

> after the labourers are accomplishing the work, the papers are sent to the panchayat; it takes more than 7–15 days for preparing this job. The work is delayed further by the BDO for some more days. Finally when the panchayat approves the fund for disbursement, the Panchayat Pradhan takes some more time to transfer the money from the panchayat account to the respective labourers' bank accounts. The bank officials then are not in a position to disburse the money immediately since they would fulfil a number of other responsibilities. Hence, a labourer has to lose 4–5 man-days to get payments for their work in the project. Isn't the administration responsible for this loss that incurred by the labourers?

A concerned panchayat member thus remarks helplessly,

> payments are delayed sometimes by 2–3 months, even up to 6 months. When we are asking the Pradhan or the officials in administration, all they do is to assure us for looking into the matter. Even though there was a lot of people took interest in the project initially, as payments could not be made within 15 days, and are often getting delayed by 3–4 or 6 months, people have gradually lost interests in the project.

But an important question arises at this moment especially in case of West Bengal about whether the pattern of implementation of this act has changed with the change in government resulting in its performance manifold through a more effective way in order to fulfil the goals enshrined in the act. The question becomes more significant when we address the same in West Bengal in context of new regime which is usually marked as 'the institutional decay of governmental, administrative and party institutions subsequently permeated by corruption', as Frankel (2005, XI) inscribes while to define the Indira Gandhi regime. In other words, we may ask a specific question, that is, how does an act perform in a regime of growing institutional decay in all terms? An activist of a reputed NGO, however, challenges this dominant interpretation, and disputes the question further when he says (Roy 2011) that 'the same practice continues even where the regime has changed, and a new party has come to the power'. But, what has changed owing to this change of government is perhaps in the nature of functioning of the panchayats. A panchayat member belonging to a SC group, in the district of South 24 Parganas, candidly describes about the changes the area is witnessing after TMC party ascending to power. He says (30.12.2013),

> the level of initiative on the part of the government has definitely increased. The BDOs are working now in a proactive way, and are often descending even on the spot. The local administration is, unprecedentedly, putting pressures on the panchayats for acting more actively to implement the Act which, in course of time, resulting in more outputs than earlier.

A panchayat Pradhan of the district of North 24 Parganas endorses the former's opinion when he says (04.01.14) that 'the BDOs are now very active, and try to intervene, of course in good sense, in all development works'. Most of the Pradhans and members of the panchayat I spoke with during my field visits had more or less similar views that the local administration dominating the panchayats in a proactive way so as to implement the policies, though, of course, some representatives evidently belonging to the opposition parties strongly opined that the functioning of current regime, that is, the dominance of bureaucracy over democratically elected decentralized governance, engendered a perfect environment for corruption.

The accusation of corruption interestingly reminds us an old debate initiated by a group of scholars who try to understand whether and/or in what way democratic decentralization is the answer to curb corruption associated with implementation of governmental policies. In other words, the question is whether there is any positive implication of democratic decentralization for the efforts of poverty alleviation on the part of government. Veron et al. (2006) had conducted a significant study to examine whether democratic decentralization really stands as good governance which in the process increases the state's accountability. Based on a study on the Employment Assurance scheme in rural West Bengal, their research reveals (ibid.) that 'the horizontal accountability structures between local civil society and officials can mutate into networks of corruption' in the absence of vertical accountabilities. It seems to be important in our context to understand the dynamics of corruption when the panchayat representatives in opposition are being consistent in their reaction that there is a wide-spread corruption in implementation of MGNREGA schemes. Although my research does not intend to focus examining whether the local structure mutates in network of corruption, and the way in which it manifests in the society, I am tempted to explain in line of arguments put forward by the scholars about why there remains a possibility to be corrupted on the part of the persons associated with local structures. First of all, the MGNREGA is structured in such a way that the entire process from planning of work to disbursement of wages to the beneficiaries requires some kinds of vertical endorsement whatsoever, upward or downward. The process of implementation of this act is in actuality bureaucratically burdensome for which the concerned people often complain that they often get frustrated to comply all the rules that required doing. This means, there is apparently little scope of corruption if all stakeholders obey the rules enshrined in the act.

During the previous regime, as Ms. Talwar's states, despite the dynamic presence of democratic decentralization, and some kinds of vertical accountabilities both on the part of the government and the party, there was some accusation of corruption below the surface on the part of the supervisors in connivance with the panchayat officials by way of fabricating the master rolls, purchasing the job cards in lieu of some amount of money, and also illegitimate payment of wages without proper work done. However, it seems, as my field survey reveals, that the custodians of the current regime would often implement the schemes under MGNREGA through bypassing democratically elected local self-governments, and thereby hindering the possibility of vertical accountabilities. It is evident that there exists an underlying pressure although among different layers of the administration to utilize the fund allocated for implementing this act, and to produce necessary statistics about the achievements of the government. In its bid to do it, the administration would even ignore to conform to transparency rules. Whether the horizontal networks between the BDOs and the panchayat representatives could at all take responsibility for the accountability is certainly a larger question to be explored. But the fact is that the activities of the panchayat representatives are generally regarded with suspicion by the rural public at large. There are certainly some grounds for their suspicion when it has been revealed from my field survey that the panchayat representatives are investing money on their own to procure the votes of villagers. For instance, take the case of a panchayat in South 24 Parganas, a panchayat member elected on behalf of a Left party candidly informs,

> we are to purchase votes from villagers; some candidates are able to 'earn' the amount s/he spent to win the elections, some are unable to do the same. The rural electorates are now demanding money in lieu of their votes. The candidates for the post of a Pradhan would even spend 0.5 million.

The Pradhan of the same panchayat, a solvent housewife, endorses the aforesaid statement of her counterpart, and says (ibid.),

> we had to spend around 0.2 million to purchase the votes. The poor villagers are more enthusiastic to demand money. We, the panchayat representatives, are discussing it among ourselves, since all candidates have spent money to win the elections.

The question arises about the way the vote-purchaser representatives could compensate their outlay while being in power. Is the fund allotted for the MGNRGA a good source to compensate the money they put into purchase the votes? The question remains to be unanswered at least for the moment.

It is evident, however, that the parties in power, be it the Left or the Right, would implement the policies whatsoever usually not with a view to serving any class issue. Rather, all the parties would formulate and implement the policies with a view to electoral purpose to win votes. But there is no doubt that the propertied class who constitutes, in general, most part of the rural leadership always shows a lack of enthusiasm on their behalf in implementing the policies and acts, especially those which hindering their interests. Even the Left who are supposed hypothetically to go against the capitalist domination for serving the interests of the labouring class are also not making any difference. They are failing to implement even the schemes under the MGNREGA, let alone attempting to pursue for scripting a more progressive act which would grant the labouring class some kind of equal rights. Although the statutory structure of MGNREGA has been conceived in such way that the rural capital or the rural propertied class would never be deprived of their interest, the political parties wouldn't take even a minimal risk to cause a pitfall to the rural propertied class in the interest of labouring class whenever they get a scope in course of implementation of this act. I have discussed about the way the party leadership chose the time while they creating work in interest of the propertied class. Chatterjee (2004) might justify this strategy of the political parties as for the benefit of non-corporate capital on which I discuss in the next chapter. All the political parties would deliberately make use of this act for their own electoral purpose, while they know that the act in itself has lots of limitations in fulfilling its stated aims. The limitations lie not only in the bureaucratic rules, as argued by Gupta (2012, 22–23), who even came to a conclusion that 'the very procedures of bureaucracy' are the main culprit for subverting the government's 'overt goal of helping' poor, but also in empirical reality. The panchayat representatives and the local administration repeatedly remind us the fact that there is dearth of land resources in West Bengal where employment could be created on the long-term basis. Hence, there is little to distinguish this act from other policies since not only the former has many limitations in terms of employment guarantee terms, but also both the former and the latter are premised on the same assumption that capitalist growth in agriculture would ensure rural employment.

Notes

1　Although Gupta didn't mention the political problem, I would like to add here the per-spective of political economy to understand the farmers' suicide in a better way.
2　Currently, the debate initiated by the Anthropocene group which is proposing to desig-nate a new geological epoch to reflect the changes that *Homo sapiens* have wrought, is gaining ground. See for details the issues of *Athropocene Journal*. And see also Harari (2011) for information about how agriculture has altered the planet.
3　See John Vidal (2014), *The Guardian*, 17 March 2014. See also the website www. seedsoffreedom.info/dr-debal-deb-indias-rice-warrior/
4　Ghosh refers to CWG, XLVIII, 15; also XLV, 398.
5　Ghosh (1989) quotes from Wedderburn, op cit. 77; quoted Palme Dutt, op cit, 261.
6　See for details Chatterjee (1984, 63).
7　To make way for Bhilai Steel plant, Chhattisgarh, and Durgapur Steel Plant, in West Bengal, land from 96 villages and 37 villages respectively was compulsorily purchased by the government. See Levien (2013, 385) and Parry (1999, 112).
8　See for details Chatterjee (1999, 18).
9　The erstwhile CPI party was split into two parties on 1964, namely the CPI party and CPI (M) party.
10　See Gopal Haldar's piece titled 'Why is unemployment?' in *Bnaglar Communist Ando-lon: Dalil o Prasangik tathyo* edited by Anil Biswas (2002).
11　The leaders of the CPI (M) party calculated that around 10.5 million people of West Bengal depended on 10.1 millions of acres of land.
12　See B T Ranadive's article titled 'Employment to all' in *Banglar Communist Andolon: Dalil o Prasangik tathyo* edited by Anil Biswas (2002).
13　The CPI (M) party led Left Front declared a list of common minimum programmes by issuing a pamphlet called 'Common Minimum Programmes of the Left Front' on 19 May 1977. See also Documents Collection Vol. 5, 2006.
14　See Marx's article 'The British rule in India', written on 10 June 1853, published in the *New York Daily Tribune* (June 25:1853). The electronic version is downloadable at www.marxists.org/archive/marx/works/1853/06/25.
15　The act clearly mentions that the small and marginal farmers as defined in the Agricul-ture Debt Waiver and Debt Relief Scheme, 2008.
16　Ms. Talwar (2011) informs,

> We have seen from our experience that the labourers would give their job cards to the supervisor or the panchayat President with an understanding that without any work being done the latter would withdraw money on their behalf; they will be paid half the amount or, say, Rs.1000. Another practice we are witnessing ram-pant in West Medinipur where the work done is not verified, and wages are paid on a daily basis. There is a tacit agreement with the supervisor and the panchayat President that some persons will get their wages without putting any labour. Such is the level of corruption prevailing at the grass root.

References

Biswas, Anil. 2002. *Banglar Communist Andolon: Dalil O Prasangik Tathya*, Pratham Khanda (In Bangla). Kolkata: National Book Agency.

Biswas, Anil. 2004. *Banglar Communist Andolon: Dalil O Prasangik Tathya*, Tritiya Khanda (In Bangla). Kolkata: National Book Agency.

Carswell, Grace and Geert De Neve. 2014. 'MGNREGA in Tamil Nadu: A Story of Success and Transformation?' *Journal of Agrarian Change* 14(4): 564–585. doi: 10.1111/joac.12054

Chandra, Kanchan. 2015. 'The New Indian State: The Relocation of Patronage in the Post-Liberalization Economy.' *Economic and Political Weekly* 50(41): 46–58.

Chatterjee, Partha. 1984. *Bengal: 1920–1947: Land Question*. Calcutta: K P Bagchi.

Chatterjee, Partha. 1999. *The Partha Chatterjee Omnibus: Comprising Nationalist Thought and the Colonial World, the Nation and Its Fragments and a Possible India*. New Delhi: Oxford University Press.

Chatterjee, Partha. 2004. *The Politics of the Governed: Reflections on Popular Politics in Most of the World*. New Delhi: Permanent Black.

Chatterjee, Partha. 2008. 'Democracy and Economic Transformation in India.' *Economic and Political Weekly* 43(16): 53–62.

Chatterjee, Partha. 2010. 'The State.' In *The Oxford Companion to Politics in India*, edited by Niraja Gopal Jayal and Pratap Bhanu Mehta. New Delhi: Oxford University Press.

Chopra, Deepta. 2011. 'Mediation in India's Policy Spaces.' Chapter 6. Downloadable at http://epress.utsc.utoronto.ca/cord/wp-content/uploads/sites/82/2014/05/Chapter-6 Chopra.pdf

Foucault, Michel. 1982. 'The Subject and Power.' *Critical Inquiry* 8(4): 777–795.

Frankel, Francine R. 2005. *India's Political Economy 1947–2004: The Gradual Revolution*. New Delhi: Oxford University Press.

Ghosh, Suniti Kumar. 1989. *India and the Raj, 119–1947: Glory, Shame and Bondage*. Calcutta: Subarnarekha.

Gopal, S.1984. *Jawaharlal Nehru: A Biography, 1956–1964*, Vol. 3. Great Britain: Harvard University Press.

Gupta, Akhil. 2012. *Red Tape: Bureaucracy, Structural Violence, and Poverty in India*. Durham, NC: Duke University Press.

Haldar, Gopal. 2002. 'Why Is Unemployment?' In *Bnaglar Communist Andolon: Dalil o Prasangik tathyo*, edited by Anil Biswas. Kolkata: National Book Agency.

Harari, Yuval Noah. 2011. *Sapiens: A Brief History of Humankind*. London: Vintage Books.

Harriss-White, Barbara. 2008. *Rural Commercial Capital: Agricultural Markets in West Bengal*. New Delhi: Oxford University Press.

Hasan, Zoya. 2010. 'Political Parties.' In *The Oxford Companion to Politics in India*, edited by Niraja Gopal Jayal and Pratap Bhanu Mehta, 241–253. New Delhi: Oxford University Press.

Levien, Michael. 2013. 'Regimes of Dispossession: From Steel Towns to Special Economic Zones.' *Development and Change* 44(2): 381–407. doi: 10.1111/dech.12012

Li, Tania Murray. 2014. *Land's End: Capitalist Relations on an Indigenous Frontier*. Durham, NC: Duke University Press.

Parry, Jonathan P.1999. 'Lords of Labour: Working and Shirking in Bhilai.' *Contribution to Indian Sociology* 33(1&2): 107–140.

Roy, Dayabati. 2007. 'Politics at the Margin: A Tale of Two Villages.' *Economic and Political Weekly* 42(32): 3323–3329.

Roy, Dayabati. 2012. 'Political Transformation and Social Mobility in West Bengal.' In *Contemporary Politics in West Bengal: Glimpses from the Left Front Regime*, edited by Dayabati Roy and Partha Sarathi Banerjee, 7–38. Kolkata: Purbalok Publication.

Roy, Dayabati. 2013. *Rural Politics in India: Political Stratification and Governance in West Bengal*. New Delhi: Cambridge University Press.

Shiva, Vandana. 2013. 'Seeds of Death.' *Ecologist*, November 19.

Thachil, Tariq. 2014. *Elite Parties, Poor Voters: How Social Services Win Votes in India*. New York: Cambridge University Press.

Veron, Rene, Glyn Williams, Stuart Corbridge and Manoj Srivastava. 2006. 'Decentralized Corruption or Corrupt Decentralization? Community Monitoring of Poverty-Alleviation Schemes in Eastern India.' *World Development* 34(11): 1922–1941.

Newspapers, magazines, reports and other media

Banerjee, Mukulika. 2012. 'India: The Next Superpower? Democracy.' In *IDEAS Reports–Special Reports*, edited by Nicholas Kitchen, SR010. London, UK: LSE IDEAS, London School of Economics and Political Science.

Gupta, Akhil. 2016. Farming as a Speculative Activity: The Ecological Basis of Farmers. Downloadable at www.academia.edu/Farming_as_a_Speculative_Activity_The_Ecological_Basis_of.Farmers

Marx, Karl. 1853. 'The British Rule in India.' *New York Herald Tribune*, June 25. Downloadable at www.marxists.org/archive/marx/works/1853/06/25.htm

Mother India. 1957. Directed by Mehboob Khan.

Planning Commission, Government of India. 1st 5 Years Plans. Downloadable at planningcommission.nic.in/plans/planrel/fiveyr/welcome.html

Report of the Land Revenue Commission, Bengal (Floud Commission Report). 1940. Downloadable at Archive.org

Roy, Dayabati, director. 2011. *Hundred Days*. Documentary Film.

Vidal, John. 2014. 'India's Rice Warrior Battles to Build Living Seed Bank as Climate Chaos Looms.' *The Guardian*, March 8. Downloadable at www.theguardian.com/global-development/2014/mar/18/india-rice-warrior-living-seed-bank

4 Caste, class and rural employment

At the outset, it is better to acknowledge a significant point that I do not, in any way, use class as an analytical category as put into practice in Marxian school of thought. I use the term *class* only to mean the social categories that have been differentiated mainly on the basis of landed property and employment in rural areas. This chapter aims to understand the state of employment in rural West Bengal, and its dynamic relations with the aspects of class and especially of caste. In other words, it attempts to understand the role of caste and class in determining the nature and extent of employment and unemployment in a particular rural setting. As in the Indian case, Damodaran (2008, 1) correctly states, 'economic behaviour is embedded in concrete social relations'; the analysis of employment issues in context of caste might yield fruitful results so as to understand the problem more insightfully. As capitalism develops, 'through a number of business communities rather than an integrated business class' (ibid., 2), the issues of employment also tend to revolve around more through the dynamics of caste relations rather than through the dynamics of class. By mapping the trajectories of changing dynamics in opportunities of employment in both colonial and postcolonial periods, the chapter tries to understand the way the land and other resources would matter and determine the issues of employment and unemployment in rural hinterland of West Bengal. Most of all, it explores the role of rural classes and castes in shaping state policies aimed at employment generation, and vice versa. More specifically, it examines the role of the state and its policies in shaping the issues of employment and unemployment in the postcolonial period with an emphasis on the current policy interventions on the part of government in terms of 'rights-based agendas' in employment generation.

This chapter reveals, first, the issues of employment and unemployment are, in fact, politically constructed through a complex process of dynamic interaction between class, caste and the capital. Second, the way the state and its policies would intervene in this complex process in order to shape the issues of employment and unemployment in rural areas has actually been complicating the matter further by way of privileging the capital, and so the landed class belonging certainly to higher castes at expense of the labouring class belonging to subordinate caste groups. The first section of this chapter explores, on the one hand, the trajectory of transformations in land relations, and the role of upper caste landholding group in shaping the phenomenon of landlessness, and on the other, the implications of the policy interventions on the part of the government on all rural classes and groups, particularly the subordinate land-poor groups, in employment terms. The second section explains the social dynamics of ascendancy of the rich peasantry to power in rural West Bengal by means of land ownership and authority over labour, and its politics within the state domain and beyond in shaping the condition of unemployment confronted particularly by the landless subordinate caste groups. The third section examines the way the people from the subordinate labouring class in rural West Bengal cope with the predicament of their landlessness and unemployment, and subsequently constructing their politics in order to shape, on the one hand, the dynamic consequences of unemployment, and on the other, the state policies aimed at generating employment. The last section concludes that owing to the determinant role of capital whatsoever in agriculture the state of rural economy of India, particularly of West Bengal, has deteriorated, transforming the class configuration and the rural economy further by means of marketization of farming and other occupations. The government's attempts that aimed at supporting the rural labour through various kinds of policies would complicate the issue further. All sections of people are more or less bearing the brunt of the negative implication of these developments in the domain of employment except only a small section of privileged folk across castes who could make their fortune through exploiting favourably the rural market by means of entrepreneurship, be it economic or the political.

Caste, landed class and land

Does caste overlap with class in rural areas of West Bengal? Do the upper castes own highest proportion of land, and then constitute the landed class at the rural fringes? If yes, how do the upper castes who owning larger proportion of land determine the politics in rural areas? How do they shape the phenomenon of rural unemployment? Do they have any role in determining the governmental policies that aim at curbing the rate of unemployment? These questions become pertinent in our context when there is a long-held supposition, particularly among those scholars who are concerned about caste in West Bengal, that each and every field of public life, i.e. economic, political and social-cultural in West Bengal, has continually been dominated by the upper castes since the colonial period. Furthermore, significantly, the proprietorship of land had been one of the major bases at least at the initial period ever since the domination of the upper castes in both economy and politics in West Bengal. By navigating the colonial and postcolonial terrain of history, Chatterjee (1997, 69–70) states that Bengali society and polity 'has concerned the phenomenon of upper caste domination'. History shows, he argues (ibid.),

> that the new opportunities opened up by the European trade in the eighteenth century, and later by the Permanent Settlement of landownership and expanding network of bureaucracy and profession, were avidly seized upon by the Hindu upper castes, and by the second half of the nineteenth century, the ubiquitous *bhadralok*

had established unchallenged command over virtually every field of public life in the province.[1] In fact, as I have argued elsewhere (2012, 952): 'landownership has always remained as a pillar of caste division in the society'. The Anthropological Survey of India has recorded similar observations through its study of 4,635 communities/castes in India that (Singh 1993, 79) 'better control over land and other resources' as one of the characteristic features of higher castes in India.

This is to say, it is pretty obvious that caste and class are actually overlapping categories in rural areas of West Bengal since the beginning of the colonial period, and the upper castes people who have had the highest proportion of land in their possession, by ignoring the restrictions of mobility whatever it may be between one occupation and another,[2] ably could capture new opportunities opened up whatsoever in the subsequent period, and thereby established their command gradually more over every field of public life. This narrative of Bengal has been substantiated by Chatterjee (1995, 4–14) who also describes vividly the way the upper castes were compelled to take enthusiastically to the new western education, including English, to grab new opportunities in the bureaucracy and trade after the rentier economy began to stagnate towards the end of the nineteenth century. I endeavour an entry into this argument, and raise questions about why the rentier economy began to stagnate towards the end of the nineteenth century, and whether the upper castes had any roles in ruination of the rentier economy. We might find an answer of the above question if we try to understand the trajectory of transformations in land relations, and the role of the upper caste landholding group in shaping the phenomenon of both landlessness and unemployment. It can be said that the changing pattern of land relations while affecting more or less each of the rural classes negatively in employment terms, at least at different points in time, has actually turned the marginal peasants at their worst. The land relations, i.e. the land-based classes in Bengal, would never cease to change and so never take a concrete shape throughout the long history of more than around five centuries. The subjects' relation with the ruling power, be it the Mughal, the Company, or the colonial government, has changed continuously over time, so has the land relation. The nature and extent of revenue collection on the part of the ruling power would actually determine the fate of what kind of relations the peasants or *raiyats* can have with the land. However, before the East India Company was granted the Dewani of Bengal, Bihar and Orissa in 1765, the *raiyats* would always possess some amount of land from which they could at least earn their subsistence, of course, in return for rent or revenue while often been determined customarily.[3]

I have described in the previous chapters a brief account of consequences of the grant of *Dewani* to the East India Company, and the subsequent enactment of Permanent Settlement on the livelihoods of the peasantry as well as the *zamindars* in rural areas of Bengal. There were lots of dimensions existed regarding the issues of proprietorship and occupation of land throughout this period. However, it does not need mention that (Chatterjee 1984, 6) 'the primary and abiding interest of the colonial government' in Bengal 'was the extraction of a part of the surplus in the form of land revenue'. In its attempt to carry on the extraction of surplus 'productively' either, broadly, from land or agriculture, the colonial government had undertaken several try-outs in vain before permanently being settled with the Permanent Settlement. Although it never explained the reasons why the British colonialists needed to extract the surplus from India's agriculture, the Floud Commission, while recommending the abolition of Permanent Settlement in the year 1940, justified the enactment of *zamindari* settlement on 1793 on the grounds that what the protagonists of the Permanent Settlement wanted to legalize were already customarily prevailed at that point of time. The Floud Commission attempted to summarize the rights of three stakeholders; the state, the *zamindars* and the *raiyats* by taking a thorough look into the evolution of land relations in India just before the end of the British rule. While the state's claim as 'the supreme owner of land' is nothing unusual according to the commission, and 'has been limited to a share of the produce', the *zamindars* had never any absolute right of property, 'nor were it intended to give them such rights by the Permanent Settlement. The rights of the *raiyats*, the Commission states, were primarily the rights to cultivate, and 'they could be evicted for failing to cultivate properly' in the earlier period. Under the regime of Permanent Settlement (Floud Commission 1940, 43), 'their holdings were heritable', and 'their rate of rent was limited by a customary pargana rates', and as earlier 'they could be evicted for failing to pay their dues'. What the colonialists actually did was, as the Commission argues, to endorse the continuation of earlier system of revenue collection.

From the beginning of the age of policy intervention, it was felt that the laws were bound to be complicated and 'filled with ambiguities' (Nielsen and Oskarsson 2016, 69) due to the very fact that the empirical reality even within a province was highly variegated in terms not only of economic relations, but also of regional specificities and ethnic traditions. For instance, take the issues of different classes of *zamindars* mentioned in the Report of the Floud Commission. It would reveal evidently what a difficult task it was to address different classes of *zamindars* with a single enactment. There were at least four classes of *zamindars* in terms of nature and level of revenue collection before the Permanent Settlement was enacted. These classes of *zamindars* included the 'original independent chiefs', the 'old established landholding families', the 'collectors of revenues' and the 'farmers'. The titles of the *zamindars* signify the extent of disparity existed then among them as far as the assets, control and the status are concerned. Undoubtedly, as the Commission observes, the effect of Permanent Settlement 'was to level all classes under the same denomination' resulting in different outcomes in case of different sections of *zamindars*. While one section i.e. the 'farmers', could obtain some rights as proprietors, another section had to lose some privileges.

The *zamindars* as a category were really variegated, so were the *raiyats*. Despite the execution of the Permanent Settlement, the primary interest of the colonial government in Bengal, the extraction of the surplus in the form of land revenue, did not go well for long. This institutional form of revenue collection could never knit the interests of three stakeholders together in a fruitful way so that each of them would benefit. What is of our interest is the fact that these three stakeholders the commission mentioned, the state, the *zamindars* and the *raiyats*, were always in a conflict, and the state of their economy had weakened since. Whereas the colonial government tries to squeeze maximum amount of profit both in terms of revenue, and from trading in agriculture and industries, the *zamindars* tried to amass profit in having it both ways, being the 'proprietors' and the collectors of revenue, and the payers of revenue to the government. The *raiyats* were the worst victims and got fragmented into different classes or segments in rural areas. Was it ever possible to achieve success in fitting together the conflicting interests of different stakeholders with a single piece of legislation? The answer is an emphatic *no*. Actually, the trajectory of revenue collection under the Permanent Settlement brought into being such a situation in which the class relations in rural Bengal did not only begin to change but also did it become more incompatible with each other. The interests of the classes are irreconcilable so much so that the small peasant economy had become almost unviable.

Most historical narratives written about the experiences of the Permanent Settlement in Bengal reveal more or less the same story that the economy of the province ceased to prosper anymore, rather decaying every now and then, despite the repeated attempts of reviewing the situation and the subsequent policy intervention, be it new or revised form, by the colonial government. Diverse kinds of interests articulated by several numbers of classes, sections and groups thus came to the fore with their own ambiguous rights, identities and demands as consequences of, particularly, the intervention of the organized domain of politics therein. The issues of ethnicity, regional specificities and economic diversities complicated further the ways in which their articulations of demands began to take shapes at the rural margin. In contrast to the interests of the British colonial state which was imagined as the 'sovereign authority' of all revenues, three categories of main classes made their appearance with their overlapping – sometimes conflictual, sometimes cooperative – demands and interests in the 'political drama' performed in colonial Bengal during the last three decades. While the colonial state which being ever threatened with its exchequer becoming empty in want of revenues had intervened with a number of successive policies to resolve irreconcilable interests of different stakeholders in rural economy, the classes in the rural soil got entangled with organized domain of politics based mainly on the nature of interests that the classes in question could as far articulate. At least, at that point in time, as Chatterjee (1984) identifies, there were three main classes that had emerged through the evolution of agrarian structure of Bengal.

First, the class at the top of agrarian structure was the *zamindars*, the proprietors of the soil. The folks mainly from the upper castes constituted this category by utilizing the opportunities opened by the Permanent Settlement. Apart from being the old established landholding families, many others from among the upper castes took the opportunities to become either the 'collectors of revenues' or the privileged 'farmers', and later in due course transformed into a *zamindar* class. Sarkar (2016) rightly argues that even the businessmen who were once prosperous had become *zamindars* afterwards. The affluent section of professionals who made their fortunes by way of practising law and medicines had also invested their surplus money either to buy the company's newspapers or the '*zamindari*' (ibid., 59). He attributes this trend to the lack of interest on the part of Bengali people in business. However, I argue, the affluent Bengali persons were tempted to buy the *zamindari* because, on the one hand, the *zamindari* was very lucrative i.e. prosperous at that time, and on the other, the businesses and trades were then progressively turned into loss-making sectors due to the invasion of British imperialist capital. Nonetheless, Sarkar's narrative depicts clearly the trend that many people, mostly the upper castes,[4] who were already settled in other sectors had conveniently become the *zamindars* owing to the facilitating arrangement provided by the Permanent Settlement. But their days were not stable and began to evaporate since, particularly, the beginning of the twentieth century. Now they were in decline, and they began to venture towards cities and urban areas to grab all new opportunities in the bureaucracy and trade after the scope of rentier economy began to vanish. This category of landed class faced a two-pronged challenge, on the one hand, from the mass of peasantry, and on the other, from a new class of rich peasant-moneylender-traders. We may say, if we read it on caste term, that the upper castes began to face challenges both from the lower castes and the middle castes as far as land is concerned.

Second, by utilizing the growing land market, commercial farming and farm-related trading, and, of course, the scope of expansion of agriculture in newer stretches of lands, a new class of people had emerged during the period of late colonialism. This new class can be called as the 'rich peasant-moneylender-trader' class. The people of this class had in the main come from the middle and lower castes as indicated by Chatterjee (1984, 1997) and Sanyal (1981), and become prosperous gradually through cultivating new land either by purchasing from the debt-trapped peasantry or from the decaying zamindar class who already began to leave the soil of rural Bengal. Considering the case of West Bengal, the castes like *Sadgope*, *Mahishya*, *Ugrakshatriya* among middle castes, and *Poundra Kshatriya* and *Rajbanshi* among Scheduled Castes would constitute this new class. We would also find that a considerable section of Muslim peasants fall in this class inhabited mainly in Bangladesh, and in some parts of the northern region of West Bengal. The history of emergence of this class is thus not so old. Hence, the narrative of this class seems to be important since it has established its (Chatterjee 1984, 62) 'control over the land and the produce of the peasantry' by 'challenging the erstwhile dominance of the landed proprietor'.

The third category is actually the mass of peasantry in rural West Bengal. The people of this category were struck hardest by the breakdown of small peasant economy in Bengal during the period of late colonialism. The peasantry at large who were once mostly the rent payee *raiyats* became marginal in terms of their dismal economic condition. Due to the stress exerted both from the upper caste proprietors and the colonial state, many of them were forced to lose their land, and subsequently became poor peasants. They were turned into either the share-croppers by losing ownership rights or agricultural labours by losing even the occupancy rights to land. The category of marginal peasants includes the poor peasants, the sharecroppers[5] and the *raiyats* (also under-*raiyats*). A fierce conflict between the uppercaste proprietors and the mass of peasantry actually had torn the eastern part of undivided Bengal apart. The organized domain of politics began to spring up at this very moment and was widespread rapidly in the politically fertile soil of Bengal. The lower and middle castes, the Scheduled castes as well as the Scheduled tribes had constituted this category for which most of the government policies are aimed at, and the politics has become so vibrant in rural areas.

If we take stock of the current status of these classes/castes, we find an interesting trajectory of class/caste dynamics at the grassroots of Bengal. My earlier (2013) as well as present research reveals that most of the local *zamindars* belonging to the upper castes have eventually fled from their ancestral villages owing to the resistance of the peasantry belonging mainly to the SC and ST, and also in some occasions to the middle caste *Mahishya* under the leadership of Communist Left during the period of the 1960s and 1970s. The upper caste families have either sold off their land or still have kept it in their possession. In the latter case, they are to engage sharecroppers for cultivating their land. Most of them have actually taken modern professions and have settled in cities like Kolkata. In my recent field survey, I find that there is no noticeable trace of upper castes in as more as 12 villages out of 18 villages. In six villages they are present with their strong charisma. First of all, they could boost up their agriculture-based incomes by taking up new modern professions like, in most cases, teaching jobs. This apart, the families of these upper castes are involved in local level party politics and hold leadership positions in different political parties. Whatever their political leanings may be, they all enjoy some kinds of socio-political power based on their incomes from modern professions, and their positions in political parties and in panchayats.

The question arises about the roles of the upper castes in shaping the policies aimed at employment generation in rural areas. The roles of the upper castes would count much as, evidently, most of the positions in 'expanding network of bureaucracy and profession' as well as in the well-entrenched political parties have been thoroughly captured by the upper castes. It is perhaps unlikely in West Bengal, as Frankel and Rao argue (1990), that the upper castes could protect their privileges only in the public institutions i.e. the bureaucracies and industries, and the lower caste groups could cling to their power in the political institutions i.e. the political parties and legislatures. As revealed, upper castes in West Bengal unlike their counterparts in other states could seize and retain their rein in both decision-making institutions. The roles of upper castes are thus more influential here in determining the birth and the fate of all social policies. This apart, the roles of upper castes in policy making would also be important, if we analyse the process, from the perspective of theories of passive revolution (Bardhan 1984; Kaviraj 1989; Vanaik 1990). As maintained by the passive revolution theories, the bureaucracy constitutes a part of the coalition of dominant classes in India. This is to mean, along with the capitalist class and the landed elites or, arguably, the rich peasantry, the bureaucracy is supposed to have a decisive role in matter of state. And, we know now that the bureaucracy has been influenced by the upper castes and classes. Hence, the upper castes and classes as custodians of bureaucracy, I argue, is a constitutive element of the coalition of dominant classes.

The theories of passive revolution (though being somewhat ambiguous, particularly, in question of bureaucracy which has been considered as a constitutive part of the coalition of dominant classes) would provide a handy tool to understand the power dynamics in relation to state in India. How does the state possess a relative autonomy, if the bureaucracy is a constitutive part of the coalition of dominant classes? Is the bureaucracy not, at the same time, constitutive part of the state too? Whatever it may be, it has always been the fact that the bureaucracy has a decisive role to play in state matters, so has the upper castes. We have already seen the effects of policy consequences in rural areas of West Bengal. Leaving out the first three decades ruled mainly by the Congress and, under the circumstances, the state had not been so entrenched into the rural grass roots, more than three decades long rule by the Left Front would mark no difference in terms of employment. Despite the mention of just 'employment to all' in their 'common minimum programme', it never emphasized the issue while being in power for 34 years. On only one occasion, the state has witnessed the proactive roles of the Left Front government and its constitutive parties, that is, of the upper castes in implementing and, to some extent, improvising the land reform policies in rural West Bengal. In so doing, the upper castes who had once been the proprietors of land and the perpetrators of rural distress attempted to cut down to size the power of their erstwhile rival, the class of rich peasant-moneylender-traders, and thereby establishing their base among the poor peasantry. Do their roles in that case indicate any antagonism between two dominant classes, as suggested by the theorists of passive revolution? In other words, is this a class contradiction between two classes i.e. the landed elites or rich peasantry, on the one hand, and the bureaucracy i.e. the upper castes, on the other?

Whether this effort of the Left front is a manifestation of perpetual class antagonism between two dominant classes is actually not a factor here to influence the role of upper castes in policy making on employment front. Being Communist (Marxist), the members of these parties could never cross beyond their class boundary, and so have hardly left any imprints, in good sense, in rural areas to turn the situation upside down. What these upper castes have done is actually the same as their counterparts in other states intended to do. This is to mean that a closer look would easily reveal that what the erstwhile proprietors of land have scripted is nothing but the end-products of their caste-class ideologies. The employment generation programmes are not meant for the absolute benefit of unemployed in long term, instead are devised keeping in mind the case of the labouring class. This means, the issues of unemployment are not here prioritized. Instead, it seems that the aim of the employment generation policies is to at best reduce the rate of poverty. The causes of unemployment are reasoned from the standpoint of the upper echelon of the society in class and caste terms, so are the measures of employment generation. Their strategy to create work only in the sphere of hard manual labour amply corroborates this statement. This is actually the strategy of the *bhadralok* – those who are educated and refrained from carrying out any manual labour – to create work for the *chhotoloks* – who are supposed to be involved in low-paid manual jobs. Hence the question arises: does the MGNREGA seek 'to strengthen the sense of citizenship through logic of right-based entitlement', as Ruud argues (2014)? The answer is obviously no. There is thus no expectation in this *bhadralok* regime that the implementation of this act would (ibid., 205) 'create capable citizen able to demand entitlements from the state'.

Peasantry, land and the dominant caste

It is really a query for exploration how far the *bhadralok* regime has been able to secure their dominance in rural areas where the category of rich peasant-moneylender-traders has supposedly been dominant in local setting. Furthermore, how did the category of rich peasant-moneylender-traders which began to emerge at the onset of the twentieth century manage to get on in terms of employment in rural areas? Does it have any role in influencing the state policies, particularly, the employment-related policies in West Bengal? What are their roles in implementing employment generation policies in rural areas? Before setting about to explore these questions, we enquire about who constitute this category of rich peasantry in caste terms? Notwithstanding the fact that there are various sets of data regarding the evolution of landholding structures in West Bengal, the data on caste-specific landholding structure is sparse. I divide the peasantry purposefully into two categories, the rich peasantry and the poor peasantry. Ignoring the consistent debates and confusions regarding different contradictory sets of data, I reiterate the conventional supposition that the rich peasantry in general represents the lower or middle castes particularly in south-western part of Bengal and, partially, two Scheduled castes *Poundra kshatriya* and *Rajbanshi* in southern and northern part of West Bengal respectively.[6] The question is why any of these castes, be it the middle or the lower, or, in class term, the rich peasantry, though being dominant locally, have not been able to be a dominant caste-class in the state level. My ethnographic fieldwork (2003–2015) found that the farmers, particularly the rich peasants,[7] belonging to two numerically dominant middle castes, *Mahishya* and *Sadgope*, though they are able to exercise control over other lower castes, most of whom constitute the labouring class, remain perplexed in the question of their political allegiance to the erstwhile ruling party. While the middle castes, which are locally dominant, usually have many grievances against the ruling party regarding its domination and anti-farmer roles, they support the party in power in order to exercise dominance in local arena particularly with an aim to control the labouring sections belonging to the SCs and the STs. This is to mean, on the one hand, they are left with limited options as the dominant commercial capital is protected by the politicized arrangements of the state government, and on the other, these petty cultivators and petty traders, belonging to the middle castes, have to come to certain terms with the ruling party to resolve their own livelihood problems with the labouring class (Roy 2013).

In other words, despite their difference in question of state policies, and their subordination to state level political leaders belonging to the upper castes, the rich peasantry from middle castes would maintain a congruity by sharing power in local echelon. In fact, throughout the history of institutional politics, not only in the colonial periods, as Chatterjee (1997, 80) argues, in terms of castes, probably all the political parties in Bengal, including the Communists, have continued to contain 'the full complement of castes, with the upper-castes intelligentsia in leadership positions at different levels, and various middle and lower castes among both leadership and rank-and-file in the local areas'. Simply put, caste, and its hierarchy, has remained strong, if not stronger in social reality of West Bengal, by adapting the modern democratic forces, and has thus manifested, as Ambedkar (1945) argues and Vasavi (2014) reinterpreted, a kind of 'graded inequality' functioning at both micro and macro levels to reproduce new forms of inequality. The people of middle castes, including the OBCs that are entitled for reservation, who are being, as I discussed elsewhere (2017), deprived and discriminated through various means by the upper castes in regard to access to power in the public sphere of cities and urban areas, are, conversely, privileged to perpetrate their domination over subordinate caste groups in rural areas. The exercise of domination here is relational in caste term, that is, each caste is relatively unequal to the next higher caste in caste hierarchy. We might observe the same phenomenon in context of class. The rich peasant – middle castes thus have been experiencing subordination while at the same time exercising domination in terms of power relations. For middle castes, the acts of subordination and domination instead of being spatially compartmentalized seem very much entangled with each other in both the spaces with the hierarchy kept intact. The nature of politics of the middle castes thus in Bengal is multi-dimensional, complex and essentially fragmented.

The middle or intermediary castes, together with OBCs (17.5 per cent), as computed by Chatterjee (1997), constitutes at present around 35 per cent of the total population in West Bengal, while (Mishra 2010) 'they have remained a weak presence in the state assembly, fluctuating between 4.6 per cent in 1952, and 6.1 per cent in 2001, peaking at 9.5 per cent in 1977'. In contrast, as Lama-Rewal (2009) argues,

> even though the importance of upper castes in the West Bengal Legislative Assembly fluctuates between 37.5 per cent in 1972, and 50 per cent in 1957 of all MLAs (peaking at 81.8 per cent in 1982), it remains consistently out of proportion with their demographic proportion (10 per cent).

While Ghosh (2001, 4) attributes this disproportionate access to power of the middle castes in the Legislative Assembly to middle castes' 'localized presence, lack of English education and professional advancement', I argue that the domination of upper castes through organized state politics is perhaps the most important factor affecting consistently the middles castes' inability to pose a challenge to *bhadralok* hegemony. Owing to the well-entrenched state-centric organized politics, the middle castes would not only fail to be united among themselves, but also would fall short to win over other subordinate castes into their fold to counter the *bhadralok* hegemony.

Long before the penetration of organized state politics, as Sanyal's study (1981) reveals, two numerically significant middle castes, *Sadgope* and *Mahishya*,[8] in southern West Bengal had broken away from their parent body known as *Gope* (a pastoral group) and *Chasi Kaibartas* (a fishing community) respectively, and shifted steadily to agriculture as their new profession. Within a short period of time, they would become prosperous cultivators as well as substantial landowners, thereby establishing themselves as a political power in this vast region. The amalgamation of economic power in terms of land occupation and ownership, and political power helped these castes to achieve cultural superiority by means of instituting social services like temple building, and offering lucrative grants, such as rent-free land, to the Brahmans. Since then, these two castes have been enjoying cultural superiority, posing as dominant castes until recently in the vast tracts of southern West Bengal. Recent ethnographies by the author on these two castes show the way the *Sadgope* and the *Mahishya* endeavour to continue their domination, cultural, economic and political, in everyday lives of rural people. The relationship between dominant castes and subordinate castes (the SCs) in this region has not only been hierarchical but also a source of severe discrimination in regard to various socio-economic aspects. The hierarchy or discrimination is such that the people of these dominant middle castes are often called *bhadralok* and that of the subordinate castes are called *chhotoloks*.

The middle castes in south-western part of West Bengal could not succeed in achieving unity among themselves and with lower castes, as happened in Karnataka in both *jati* terms as well as *jati* clusters terms in case of *Vokkaligas* and *Lingayats* (Manor 2010, xxxv),[9] since they themselves have been operating like a powerful dominant category, and depriving the subordinate castes in terms of caste and class issues. The upper castes which have no landed interest could successfully make a rift by dynamic political strategies between dominant middle castes and lower castes who labour in dominant peasant castes' land. In other words, the upper castes would always endeavour to maintain equilibrium among different castes by absorbing representatives from middle castes into the party, and establishing a strong base among subordinate castes. As a result, the middle and lower castes in rural areas rarely have any strong feeling of external domination on basis of which they could achieve an essential unity to pose a challenge to the *bhadralok* hegemony.

Although the economy of rich peasants-moneylenders-traders could maintain thoroughly a steep rise in the first half of postcolonial period, it began to collapse gradually in recent period. The GRT, as discussed earlier, had brought advantage to this category in the initial period, but tended to disadvantage them mainly due to the government's apathy to the distress call of the peasantry. While the peasantry have consistently been distressed due to the determinant role of the unfavourable market, the government instead of protecting them by way of reducing the onslaught of 'elite' commercial and capitalist classes would actually aid the latter in their venture of profit accumulation. Victimized both in the field of production, and in the field of marketing, the peasantry at large, particularly, the rich peasantry would rarely embrace a solvent position so that they could pose a challenge to the dominance of the upper castes. Although a small group of rich farmers could make their fortune even until recently through exploiting the scope of profit making by means of hording crops coupled with farming,[10] they could barely succeed in politics. While managing electoral support for the urban dominant categories, the rural dominant categories would hardly assume adequate power in terms of decision making. The rich peasantry has, therefore, been unable to be a part of the coalition of dominant classes, as the theorists of passive revolution argue, as far as the politics of West Bengal is concerned. Rather, the upper castes/classes, or the bureaucracy, as the situation betrays, allied with capitalist classes has been dominating the politics of West Bengal often at the expense of interests of the peasantry. The rich peasantry or 'the dominant castes' would hardly play any role in formulation of policies and acts that aimed at alleviating rural distress.

The main reason behind this phenomenon seems to be, I argue, the rich peasants' lack in economic power and political power in the field of political institutions and legislatures in the state. Unlike their counterparts in other states, they can't even decide the policies that affect their own issues within and outside the parties and mass organizations since the leadership was captured mainly by the upper strata. The proportion of 'agriculturists' in all party terms in Parliament had increased from 22.4 per cent in 1952 to 31.1 per cent in 1967,[11] while the proportion of professionals, particularly, the lawyers who were more active in the party during the pre-independence period was in decline. The increasing proportion of agriculturalists or 'large landlords' in Parliament might indicate the fact that the political power of the said class has increased substantially to influence at least numerically the policies and acts meant for rural and agricultural issues. Chatterjee (1999, 53) rightly states that the legislature of the states like Punjab and Haryana has, therefore, been witnessing the fiery debates 'on land ceilings or the procurement price of food grains'.

The question is whether West Bengal has witnessed any such stormy debate on the issues mentioned above at the political arena, be it the legislature or the political parties. The answer is perhaps no. The list of the MPs elected in West Bengal, whatever their party identities may be, clearly reveals that not even a single MP in West Bengal belongs to the rich peasantry at least as far as their profession is concerned. It might be the case that although at least a few MPs have been elected from the rural seats (and belong to the rich peasantry class), they may have preferred to mention business or social work as their profession to farming, whatever the reasons may be. In no case, however, the representation of rich peasants in the political arena doesn't count much, so do the issues of rich peasants. I find that the rich peasants, especially in the Hooghly district, instantly vent their grievances against the government for its failure to aid them in their acute distress. A rich farmer asserts,

> we don't have our own party or platform on behalf of which we can negotiate our issues or requirements with the government. In other states, the farmers are organized, and so succeed to garner the benefits regarding farming in a united way. For instance, the farmers of other states have largely benefited by way of subsidization in tariff for electric pumps.[12]

It is easily discernible at this stage how far the rich farmers could obtain capacity to influence the governmental policies, especially the policies aimed at employment generation in rural areas while they themselves are in want of scope to place their own demands on the government. Hence, if the legislature has spotted any such influence on its policies on the part of rich farmers or big landholding class, it has definitely received the same from the farmers of other states in India except West Bengal.

The rich peasants are, however, not in need of scope to exert their influence in shaping the nature of outcomes of the governmental policies when the latter are moving downwards for implementation to the rural grass roots. The dominant classes in rural West Bengal would, therefore, become the custodians of governmental policies, and make every effort to determine its fate, of course in collaborating with the upper castes-classes in urban areas. The top political leaders as well as the bureaucracy, most of whom belonging to the upper castes/class would seem agree to an extent to compromise on some issues proposed by the rural dominant class. Presumably, due to this very reason, the Left Front leaders, as we have seen, who were very active in formulating the MGNREGA at the centre had visibly been reluctant initially to implement this act in the state in 2006. Whenever I get scope to interact with the political leaders, I observe that issues of identities like castes and classes of the leaders of the party, be it the Left or the TMC, and the panchayats would matter a lot in determining the nature and outcome of delivery of governmental services. The rural leaders of both the party and the panchayat especially who belong to the landowning higher castes would usually interpret their tasks of implementing the act in terms of supplicant modality, particularly if and when the benefit seekers would belong to the landless subordinate groups. As there are hordes of uncertainty prevailed in every step of implementation of the programme ranging from creation of works to payment of wages, the beneficiaries are seen to be immensely depended on the leaders of respective fields, and so eventually become supplicant for even small things to be done. However, castes seem to provide more signifying terms than class through which social relations and the subsequent supplicant modality are perceived. For instance, take two cases of party leaders both belonging to the same TMC party in two districts: Paschim Midnapore and Cooch Behar.

In the district of Pashchim Midnapore, Subinoy Patra, the leader of the party core committee,[13] the de facto panchayat supervisor, has been very active in implementing the welfare policies initiated by the panchayat. Being a member of the erstwhile *zamindar* ancestor, his family now owns 10 *bighas* of land. Patra who belongs to the *Sadgope* caste has taken 'supplier' business as profession to supplement his family's income earned from cultivation. He poses like an employer and seems to be very proud to supervise the schemes under MGNREGA. It appears from his gesture that he is the provider of jobs to the villagers who mostly belong to the SC and ST categories. It seems that he considers these villagers 'clients' who have been labouring since time immemorial on their family lands. The traditional caste-class dynamics seems to be still reflected at rural margin even in course of implementation of the act for employment guarantee. In Cooch Behar, the party leader belonging to the SC (*Rajbanshi*) community would 'supervise' the panchayat in the same fashion as the former does. However, his attitude seems have been different from Patra's. The region is fairly culturally homogenous since it is numerically dominated by one caste, i.e. the *Rajbanshi*. Being a leader of this region, Shyamal Roy doesn't pose that by virtue of his position in the party he occupies a place which is higher than the villagers. Hence, when I enter his village to enquire about the way the policies are being implemented, and the way the schemes under the MGNREGA are understood by the villages, his position is not immediately clear. Neither do the villagers believe that the work has been delivered at the behest of the party leaders or the government, nor does the leader. Though it is not at all the case that the community is homogenous in economic terms, and that the members of the landless families would not labour on lands of the landowners belonging to the same caste, the hierarchical relations that exist between the landowners and the landless are not often reflected in the same way as occurred in case of the former. Rather, there is a widespread perception among villagers that the northern region of the state has been deprived in all respects including the downward flow of funds due to the sheer negligence of the state government which is dominated by the privileged classes.

After a brief while, however, the rich peasantry could realize the fact that implementation of this act would not likely pose a threat against their landed interest as they initially apprehended. Whatever guarantees of employments the state provided in legal terms in the said act, these are not going to be possible realistically on a long-term basis in context of West Bengal. Neither is it possible to create work in the long run owing to the dearth of land, nor is it possible to achieve the labourers' trust in it as the law itself carries a number of inherent hindrances. We have seen earlier the way the party leaders, most of whom belonging to the land-owning class, whatever their castes may be, are strategically fixing the timing of work under the MGNREGA at their convenience. This is to say, the landowners would enjoy every opportunity to mould the situation so that their interests are not hampered in terms of availability of labourers. The labourers, most of whom would often hang around for work, are also sufficiently convinced, perhaps in right ways, of this arrangement of creating employments under MGNREGA when there is little scope of getting jobs from agriculture. They would certainly need employments during the dull season of farming when opportunities available in local setting becoming dried out. As a result of this phenomenon, the people who belong to rich peasantry seem rarely threatened by way of wage increase, and non-availability of labourers. Due to seasonality in agriculture, all are most often aware of the seasons of work, and so the clashes of dates in MGNREGA work are easily avoided. However, if/when the dates of jobs under MGNREGA are clashed with the dates of agriculture; the labourers give priority on agricultural works as, they argue, 'the MGNREGA jobs are not at all dependable, nobody gives us the guarantee that we would get jobs under this Act for ever'.

It reveals that the rich peasants in West Bengal have hardly faced any labour crisis and any such threat of increase in wages as consequences of implementation of the MGNREGA. May we, therefore, conclude that the rich peasants in West Bengal still remain in a safe paradise as far as the threats on the part of the labourers are concerned? It is not likely that the landowners would rarely face any problem in regard to the non-availability of labourers and the increase in wages. During the last decade, the trend of migration of, particularly, the male members of the labourers' families from rural areas of West Bengal to any place wherever they find opportunities, is rampant. This flight of the labourers from rural fringes would really cause a tension among the rich peasantry in their efforts to manage labourers required for farming. From the northern part of West Bengal to the fringes of southern part of the state, the same situation seems to prevail on the labour front. The rich peasants are thus seen to say, 'what a sorry state it is. We are desperately in search of labourers. Scores of labourers are leaving the villages for alternative work in faraway places. It seems that we have to stop cultivation'. The field work findings provide interesting clues to the way they are going to solve the crisis that arising due to dearth of labourers. Farming in West Bengal has always been labour intensive owing to the existence of small peasant economy and to the abundance of agricultural labourers. But, this phenomenon might begin to change growingly since a section of peasants opting for mechanization and alternative crops as a remedy against labour crisis. There seems to be emerging a trend in augmenting mechanization, and in switching the existing cropping pattern to another that requires fewer labourers.

Take mechanization, for instance, as a measure pursued by several farmers so as to recuperate from growing crisis arisen out of shortage of labourers. The first case is a rich farmer of an agriculturally prosperous village situated just beside the Bankura–Burdwan border. His family, belonging to Sadgope caste, owns 6–7 acres of fertile land that has since long been cultivated by the labourers hired from within the village. However, his family have been facing a severe crisis in obtaining labourers as and when required during the last five years. He says,

> the labourers, particularly, who are in their young age are desperately leaving villages for various works whatsoever causing a serious threat to agriculture. I could not find any suitable way to solve this problem. Recently, however, I have begun to borrow harvester for harvesting *boro* paddy cultivated in 8 *bighas* of land. The harvester seems to be beneficial and cost-effective particularly in a labour-deficit situation. Although no one from our village has yet purchased it, it is required to purchase soon. I would buy a harvester not only for using it in cultivation but also for renting it out commercially.

The second case is a rich farmer from Uttar Dinajpur district. He owns 5 acres of land along with one tractor, one harvester and two pump sets (diesel run). He would rent out all his agricultural implements with profitable rates, and, it seems, the rent has become his family's primary income. He says, 'the people are now aggressively choosing the option of using machines in cultivation. We are expecting to buy another harvester in next year'. This narrative of mechanization in two villages of two diverse patterns of districts indicates a trend that capitalist investment in agriculture is undoubtedly gaining strength these days in West Bengal though in a variegated way based mainly on the nature of class configuration in respective areas. Ironically, the dynamics of mechanization in these two cases might reverse a prevailing reckoning that agricultural labourers are displaced due to mechanization in agriculture. This is to say, the exodus of labourers from rural areas has perhaps created a favourable situation for capitalist investment.

The question arises about whether this process of mechanization would increase the growth in agriculture. The growth in agriculture, as my findings betray, seems hardly to be rising by way of mechanization. What is expected to increase is probably the accumulation of capital in terms of extracting the profit through mechanization by utilizing the space left by the labourers. The brunt of mechanization would probably be felt by the labourers when they would return as a consequence of reverse migration owing to the pull factors whatsoever are dried out. The machines, which acted once as relievers as far as the distress of landowners is concerned, would bar the entry of labourers in agriculture. Hence, the effects of mechanization in agriculture on the agricultural labourers are vast. However, the extent of these effects would increase manifold if the landowners opt increasingly for cultivation of capital intensive cash crops. In that case, the labourers would, presumably, be at their worst. However, rural areas all over West Bengal have been witnessing a growing phenomenon of lease-in land for the purpose of cultivation of, generally, one crop in exchange of fixed cash. A huge amount of money has been exchanged around land among different types of peasants every year. It reveals that there is hardly any hard and fast rule to determine the rate of lease-in rent per year. Although the rate is mostly region specific, it varies depending on the nature of land, its access to irrigation, and the parties' discretion who are going to contract in agreement. The amount of rent varies ranging from INR 1500 to INR 3000 per *bigha* per year. The mortgage of land in lieu of lump sum money has also often been prevalent. Land has thus become a highly exchangeable commodity for making money. Instead of just being an immovable property, land is now a commodity for earning easy money. Notably, all sections of the peasantry seem get the benefits out of this practice, while the marginal peasants, particularly, even the landless families in some cases, as observed, try to seize this opportunity depending mainly on the usage of their labour. This leasing practice has evidently transformed the old pattern of land use and land rights, be it occupancy or proprietary, into a capitalist kind of utilization of land determined mostly by the market logic. It would, of course, be the task of the future researchers to study the implication of this capitalist use of land on the livelihoods of villagers.

It can be said that, whatever other implications may be, the leasing in land has undoubtedly been beneficial to the marginal peasants in creating an option for self-employment and subsistence. But, there seems to be every doubt that the implementation of MGNREGA has been creating productive assets which in due course would recreate employments for the job-seekers in rural areas. Carswell and De Neve (2014) show us that the works under the MGNREGA have more or less been very successful as far as the objectives it declares. While it has even produced (ibid., 582) 'significant transformative outcomes for rural labourers', the MGNREGA, as their evidences suggest, 'is far less encouraging' in question of strengthening the natural resource base of rural livelihoods, and its role as a 'growth engine of the agricultural economy'. Are all these works like 'road works' and 'clearing of canals and ponds' 'aesthetic rather than productive'? The scholars have not, however, explained why these works would not be considered as productive. I argue that these works which have been mentioned by two scholars would definitely be considered as productive assets in villages. The landowning class could utilize these works in various fruitful ways to support their economy. In instances of earlier 'Food for Work' programmes, and in recent instances of MGNREGA programmes, the produced assets have definitely been productive in its role as a growth engine of the agricultural economy. The clearing of canals and field channels, excavation and renovation of new and old ponds respectively, and the road works must eventually strengthen the agricultural economy. But the question is: which classes are going to accrue the fruits of these works?

Considering all aspects, I suggest that the people of all classes can garner at least some benefits from the durable assets created under this act with a definite skew to the landowning class. As mentioned, the political leaders, I mean the landowning class in our context, after initial reluctance, had begun to take initiative to implement the act in their respective regions. In a village of Hooghly district, for example, the party leaders, at first instance, have renovated under this act the old DVC canal and its field channels flowing within the village aiming at facilitating irrigation in that area. The peasantry at large, particularly the landowners, had lots of grievances against the erstwhile state government regarding its negligence in sorting out the matters concerning canal irrigation for the interests of the farmers. But, don't the marginal and landless peasants also benefit from this endeavour of canal renovation? The response would depend on whether, and to what extent these sections of peasants could utilize the fruits of this programme to strengthen and support their livelihoods. Is there any trickledown effect of this work on the livelihoods of these peasants? There seems to be no clear-cut answer; the processes are rather highly nuanced. Besides, there are several works done under this act, such as road works, flood control channels, bridges and soil conservation, from which almost all the classes more or less could benefit though not equally in terms of livelihood opportunities. However, it has no doubt that these kinds of works may often have some indirect effects on creating supportive livelihood opportunities for landless peasants. For instance, the landless families could utilize well the renovated canal for rearing their livestock as a supplement of primary livelihood. But the act has scripted some other provisions to benefit directly the marginal peasants i.e. the sharecroppers as well as other deprived sections like SC and ST people in terms of creating durable assets. Let's take stock of the situation of marginal and poor peasants on the employment front.

Landlessness, employment and subordinate castes

It is the mass of peasantry who have been the worst victims of economic exploitation of land and labour in both the colonial and postcolonial period. I have described the way this category of peasants, most of whom belonging to lower castes particularly the Scheduled castes[14] in West Bengal, have become increasingly poor, and so have become the target of various governmental policies ever since the colonial period. As far as its political aspect is concerned, the category of poor peasants belonging mainly to the Scheduled caste groups remain always allied in a dual relationship barring an exception with the higher and middle castes constituting the landowning class since the advent of organized state politics in Bengal. Upon analysing the nature and dynamic processes of alliances between the Scheduled castes and the higher castes, and its role in shaping the domain of livelihood related policies, this research identifies a few trends of political mobilizations towards social justices. First, although the Scheduled castes intend to make coalition with the higher castes through participating in party politics and in other state institutions, the coalition usually maintains a vertical integration of castes. In other words, the Scheduled castes, the poor peasants, instead of pursuing horizontal bonding, typically dwell at the lower ranks both in and outside the party and other state institutions betraying the traditional caste/class hierarchy. Second, various *jatis* belonging to the Scheduled castes in West Bengal, however, pursue the path of upward social mobility not only by emulating the principles of purity and pollution practised by the upper castes, but also by political assertion against the dominance of higher castes with the intervention of the organized domain of politics. Third, despite the rigid hierarchy existing in caste relations in West Bengal, the Scheduled castes have never been successful in launching caste/class-based political party in the state. Rather, each caste group or, broadly, the poor peasantry, prefer to manoeuvre between different political parties or in other sense, between different layers of higher castes, in order to garner more benefits for themselves or for their own 'jati' by caste mobilization in the form of 'en-bloc voting' in the electoral politics.

Due to this very fact, the poor peasantry that includes Scheduled castes comprising around 23 per cent of total population in West Bengal actually remain today as one of the most vibrant sections in terms of electoral politics. Particularly in rural areas, the political parties today (Dasgupta 2000, 455) 'are using castes as an important political idiom in gaining support', and the Scheduled castes are seemingly one of the key sections except Muslims as religion to determine the results of all elections in the multi-caste villages since they take part more in elections, and they cast their vote en bloc. This trend becomes more so after the enactment and implementation of 73rd Constitutional amendments whereby proportions of panchayat seats are reserved for the deprived sections like Scheduled Castes. However, as my research (2013, 2017) explains, the representatives from the *Bagdi* community, who hold the panchayat posts either as panchayat member or as panchayat pradhan, often are reduced to dummy roles, while the party leaders belonging to higher castes de facto manage all the panchayat affairs. While the *Mahishyas*, the dominant caste, would justify their de facto roles by arguing that the SCs being the labouring class are just 'worthless' and not eligible for these kinds of jobs, the *Bagdis* feel that (Roy 2008, 32) 'both the party and the government belong to the rich'. This phenomenon seems to be true for any multi-caste village, and for any political party in West Bengal. But it seems not true that the SC community would act only as a vote bank, as Dasgupta argues (2000), during both the regimes of the Congress and the Left Front, in which the *bhadraloks* were at the helm of power. Rather, as the recent researches reveal, while serving the role of vote bank, the SCs always enjoy some scope in social, economic and political spheres to utilize the political parties in their struggle against the landed higher castes.

On the other hand, all things considered, the people of the upper castes who hold most of the posts of upper echelon of almost all the parties as well as the government would resort to manoeuvre between the two contending caste groups, middle and lower, for maintaining equilibrium in rural areas. The upper caste leadership, first, tries to retain an antagonistic relationship between the two caste groups in such a way that would prevent formation of their horizontal unity against the leadership of the upper castes. Second, it always endeavours to ensure vote bank by pacifying both the contending caste groups through adopting various tactics suitable in each particular case. But, how is it possible to find such a solution without causing a conflict between them on the surface? For instance, consider the issue of wage rate of the agricultural labourers belonging mostly to the SC group in the village Kalipur. The party leaders, on the one hand, would keep the middle castes under consistent concern about the impending wage increase so that they remain docile to the party and, on the other, try to manage the labourers by just implementing a token wage increase annually. This strategic politics of minimizing the contention between two contending castes facilitates maintaining a status quo which appears perhaps as a pro-labourer stance but actually depriving the SC labourers even the minimum wages for the agricultural labourers stipulated by the government.[15]

But the Singur land movement that surged in 2006 witnessed a kind of horizontal unity between these two contending castes against the land acquisition move of the government, and of the ruling Left Front leadership in West Bengal. The initial unity between the *Mahishyas*, the *Bagdis* and the *Goalas* had clicked an influential movement which shook not only the popular conscience about injustice meted out in terms of acquisition of agricultural land meant for industrialization, but also threw a challenge against the top leadership of the party who were having hardly (Chatterjee 1997, 81) 'any ties of material interest with the land', for the first time in the history of Left Front regime. However, the crucial unity between these two subordinate caste groups didn't continue for long, and soon disintegrated due to the inherent contradiction between two categories of castes. In course of the movement, interestingly, the state's organized politics seemed to be not the sole culprit to make a divide among the struggling peasants, some other caste- or class-based issues were also liable for undoing the unity. The narrative of the Singur peasant movement (Roy 2012, 2017) explains vividly about how each participant caste would criticize the other for the failure of the movement, and the way the leaders coming from middle caste *Mahishyas* eventually took hold of the movement, and were later co-opted by the TMC, the then opposition party. The question arises in what way the people of the poor peasantry, the Scheduled caste groups, have intended to be mobilized to shape the question of their livelihood and their subsequent economy. How do they construct their politics to determine the nature and scope of the policies aimed at employment generation? Do they benefit from the implementation of these policies?

The socio-political perspective as discussed above clearly betrays the fact that a little has been done as far as the livelihoods of poor peasantry are concerned. The poor peasantry i.e. the landless peasants, the sharecroppers and the marginal land owners could hardy improve considerably their income throughout these years. Many people from this category seem remain unemployed or underemployed during most part of the year all over the state. If we gauge the extent of their predicament in terms of poverty discourse, it may appear that their economic condition has considerably improved. But, an ethnographic enquiry into their joblessness would soon make us disillusioned, and we would find that a particular section of people in every village is consistently in search of employment. This is the section which neither flourishes in economic terms, nor 'advances' in social position. This is the section which always remains as a basis of rural politics, since the people of this section aspire most from the state and its policies. Moreover, this is the section in rural areas which identifies that land and land relations are the basis for all of their problems in regard to employment. We might know the way in which this section of peasantry would mobilize in late colonial period under the banner of political parties taking the issues of land. However, it has also elucidated that the penetration of the state in matter of land and land-related issues has only complicated the same by rendering a section of peasantry increasingly vulnerable by way of making them either landless or sharecropper.

From the Permanent Settlement to various kinds of land reform acts that passed in postcolonial India including the West Bengal government's tenancy reforms (late 1970), the predicament of the section of people has essentially hardly changed. The people of this section have administratively been identified since long in terms of proprietary and occupancy rights as the *raiyats*, under *raiyats*, tenants, sharecroppers, *bargadars* and etc., while the forms of precarity that associated with their livelihoods has remained the same. A longitudinal survey of social policies might reveal that most of the policies and the acts in rural areas are meant for the benefit of this section of people. Why does the state fail to deliver justice to this section of people notwithstanding its consistent efforts by way of its policy intervention into the latter? Failing to identify properly the reasons why the erstwhile policies would fail to deliver justice may have debarred us to be aware of the actual extent of promises or limitations inherent in the acts that guarantee employment to the rural people. The belief that the state is neutral, and maintaining a balance among various classes and categories, seems to have been a real culprit in making our understanding blurred. How does the state which has already been skewed toward the propertied classes take a neutral position and maintain a balance among various classes in societies? Doesn't the state require having a labouring class skew in order to establish some forms of equality?

It is, of course, undeniable that the classes or the social categories which constitute the power have great roles in determining and shaping the nature of policies and its implementation at the grass roots. In other words, the character of the classes that are ruling and formulating the policies is significant. However, I would argue, what is more significant is the guiding ideology which would prompt the ruling classes to construct their respective policies. Not only is the ideology of the ruling classes important, but also is the ideology of the governed classes. Take the land reform acts and policies, for instance, to understand its impacts on the landless peasants of West Bengal in employment terms. During the period of colonialism, the Permanent Settlement which was marked as the beginning of colonial policy regime in regard to land was just the sheer reflection of the British capitalist interest to extract the profit from land in terms of revenues. The subsequent land policies or acts, for instance, the Bengal Tenancy Act, which have followed since, were of no exception. It may appear that those policies were having a marginal peasant category skew. But a thorough historical analysis would prove that these were aimed just at maintaining a small peasant economy which is required for continual exploitation in Bengal. All these policies, however, were doomed to failure due mainly to growing class contradiction in society, and eventually culminated in the recommendation of Floud Commission. The first part of the recommendation, i.e. the direct relation between the state and tenants, was nothing new but the imitation of indigenous tradition under which the peasants of Bengal had remained for long. The second part of the recommendation, i.e. the landlords' keeping hold of land, was drafted definitely with an aim to benefit the landlord class. But, needless to say, it was meant mainly for the enhancement of capital.

Whatever it may be, the impact of implementation of land reform acts on the peasantry varies considerably not only in terms of geography, and proximity to city, but also of its ethnographic components. For instance, take the northern part and the southern part of West Bengal for analysis. Two blocks of two districts in northern part of the state, Darjeeling and Jalpaiguri, had witnessed some kind of peasant struggle based on issues related to land reforms during the 1960s and 1970s. Hatighisa panchayat of Naxalbari block,[16] Darjeeling, is populated by the Scheduled Tribes (70 per cent) and the Scheduled caste (30 per cent), i.e. the *Rajbanshi* community, and is very close to Siliguri city. The panchayat data shows that more than around 60 per cent people of this panchayat still remain below the poverty line. The panchayat is surrounded by five tea industries. While there has been much debate in terms of a binary proposition about the relative importance of agriculture and industries in livelihood generation, this region has accommodated both agriculture and industries as employment provider since long. The *jotedar* family of the village under study unlike its counterpart in the southern part of West Bengal belongs to the SC (*Rajbanshi*) community. And the peasantry, the broad masses who once launched a big protest, belongs mainly to the STs and the Rajbanshis. The caste configuration here poses a different dynamics rendering a SC representative as the target of struggle. Notably, the peasant movement was organized in 1967 when a decade had already been passed after the enactment of land reforms. What the peasants intended to do as a form of movement was nothing but the implementation of a land reform act at the grass roots. The state had enacted the law but lacked in institutional machineries, and in local level initiatives to implement this act. However, the party of the Communists played a role in implementing the law in the ground reality of class/caste-based society. This is certainly a huge task particularly in the society wherein the interests of the classes are vastly conflicting, and the dominant class is allied and armed with the state institutions.

The landless peasants belonging to the ST community who were in the forefront of the land struggles led by the Communists could manage to get hardly any land vested and distributed by the party. Only a few among them could manage to get a meagre amount of vest land (less than a *bigha*) which was distributed by the CPI (M) party at its own discretion. There exists thus a sense of latent discontent among landless labourers as most of the land that was seized from the *jotedar* families had been distributed among the ardent followers of the top party leaders.[17] These labourers in general would labour on others' lands, and in nearby tea industries. In both workplaces, the availability of work is almost uncertain.[18] Most of the labourers from the tribal community would labour in agriculture whenever it is available on seasonal basis. They manage to obtain work from agriculture for roughly 80–90 days. Afterwards, they face a long wait for the work in tea industries. The work in tea industries is also seasonal and available sporadically, at best only for a total of 6–7 months a year. They live on a sense of insecurity in employment throughout the year. The amount of wages is, however, not up to the mark; even the rate of minimum wages as stipulated by the government has not been followed. The wages in tea industries are abysmally low, Rs. 95/day. Major portion of works in tea industries are done at piece rate basis which would definitely mount the scope of exploitation of labour manifold. Despite having various scopes of employment generation on the lands of the SC and ST families,[19] such as: flood management and river connection under the MGNREGA, the village has witnessed so far only 30 days of work for 350 job-card holders. In making the condition worse, the labourers who put their labour in the scheme under the MGNREGA three months ago are yet to receive their due payments.

On the contrary, the erstwhile *jotedars* families could retain most part of their lands, and still own around 100 *bighas* of land as informed by the present member of the panchayat. The peasant masses belonging to the *Rajbanshi* community who constitute 60 per cent of total village population are mostly marginal. Most of them are to supplement their income from agriculture, be it as cultivator or as day labourer. The villagers get some scope to involve themselves in various odd jobs owing to the village's proximity to the city. Agriculture is not considered usually gainful by most of the landowners due to the very fact that most of the lands are not multi-crop, and well-irrigated. The GRT thus seems to have not been useful in this particular area. Rather, as informed, land inside the village has often been traded with the outsiders at soaring price, thanks to the rapid urbanization. A considerable part of total land of the village has already been sold off to the investors. Moreover, when the land is mortgaged or leased in/out for the purpose of cultivation, the rate of exchange is appallingly less, e.g. Rs. 10,000/*bigha*.[20] It transpires the fact that the land is not as useful in terms of agriculture as it is in terms of trade. Therefore, despite the concentration of land in few hands, agriculture did not grow with reference to productivity of land, and the capitalist expansion in agriculture too is somewhat moderate. The surplus from land has not been accumulated in such way that the class configuration would change. The employment or livelihoods of most of the families irrespective of class and communities are not fully based on the village economy with scores of people among them increasingly fleeing the village for making both ends meet.

The plight of many families in employment terms in a village of the district Jalpaiguri seems to have been not much different. Many youths would often migrate to newer and remote places for indefinite odd jobs. A group of youths who occasionally would out-migrate for various jobs is seen to work in a scheme under MGNREGA. One among them says,

> around 20 persons have semi-permanently migrated from the village in search of jobs to Kerala, Goa and etc. They are involved in various risky kinds of jobs with no life insurance benefit. A man from this village has died recently while working in a multi-storeyed building in Kerala. His family didn't get any accident benefit or like.

The village is populated by the communities like Muslim, *Rajbanshi*, ST and Nepali. Many families, particularly from the Muslim community, do not possess any land except the homesteads. On the contrary, the ST families have benefited by way of vested lands thank to the redistributive politics initiated by the CPI (M) party. These families would possess around 2–3 *bighas* of land on an average, and have been working for a long time in the tea industries. However, their lands are being exchanged progressively with the outside investors who in most cases are exploiting the innocence of the owners in price terms.[21] Actually, this area is otherwise considered as tourist place, and some youths of this village enjoy the opportunities to work in the resorts for at least 4 months during the tourists' season. These apart, the families in general would involve themselves in work like rickshaw and van pulling, petty business and construction work. The works under MGNREGA have been available only 40–45 days on an average in the current year.[22] The families who possess some agricultural land would cultivate the same, and grow usually one crop by employing labourers or depending on self-labour. However, the lands, though not being agriculturally so productive, are extremely valuable in the land market. The village lands, as perceived by the villagers, are lucrative because of its location in the tourist map. Hence, the land is, as it were, an issue of struggle between the new entrepreneurs and the present owners. The village economy is thus characterized by unviable agriculture and fast-paced urbanization. The non-farm activities surrounding these two villages are increasing, but nevertheless are not sufficient, and several unemployed villagers would eventually survive by way of migrating in large-scale to faraway places.

The out-migration of the people from villages in the southern part of the state, however, as mentioned earlier, is no less important to understand the recent crisis in employment in rural areas. But, the issues of land and agriculture in this region seem transpire a different story. Take the two districts of Burdwan and Pashchim Medinipur, for instance, to explain this story of difference. The village under study in Burdwan district is situated just beside the Durgapur Expressway and is agriculturally immensely prosperous.[23] Most of the villagers are predominantly depended on agriculture and allied work either as cultivators or day-labourers. Several persons from the SC and ST communities commute daily, though seasonally, to work as agricultural labourer in the neighbouring district, Hooghly. The village lands have been concentrated in the hands of some Muslim families and a few Brahmin families. These families would possess maximum 10–12 *bighas* of land except one Brahmin family who owns 35 *bighas*. Around 40 per cent of total families in this village are landless. The SC and ST families constitute the category of landless. The SC and ST families who possess land have only 0.25 *bigha* of land on an average. Interestingly, as analysed separately, the SC families would hardly have any land due only to the reason that they didn't obtain almost any patta land from the then party in power. On the contrary, around 25 ST families who were passionately loyal to the erstwhile ruling party could manage to obtain 0.25 *bigha* of land each on an average. However, I try to puzzle out how the families who usually get approximately 3 months of work from agriculture manage to survive the whole year. As the SC families inform me, they would only get 2 months of work. The MGNREGA would usually supplement this main work for another 10–15 days. However, some among the ST families opt for daily commuting to other villages to work mostly as agricultural labourer in Hooghly district. This narrative transpires the fact that the village economy is characterized by farm-based work, and agriculture has been viable by way of providing employment for almost all villagers as main source of income. Non-farm work being created at the margin, even if sporadically, has also been sustained by activities associated with farming. The landowners, particularly the substantial landowners, seem to have been prospering the most by diversifying their professions into a number of other fields based mainly on sustainable agriculture thanks to the DVC canals.[24] While their counterparts in other districts of southern West Bengal are struggling to manage the cost of irrigation by STWs and DTWs that run mostly by diesel pump sets, the farmers of this district have perhaps found agriculture useful to an extent with having a privilege to use canal water at almost free cost. Besides, these farmers would also enjoy the advantage of investing incomes from other occupations, be it business and service, in farming only in order to make it more profitable. The class relations in terms of land and other occupations are sharply reflected in the village reality.

The same phenomenon is perhaps true in the social reality of the village in the district of Pashchim Medinipur. The village is characterized mainly by agricultural economy with some forms of non-farms works which provide income supplements if/once necessary. The lands are fertile and mostly bi-crop or tri-crop, provided that irrigation facilities are steady. It is perhaps unusual that the category of general castes is minority (15 per cent) though most of the village lands belong to them. Several families of the ST community (60 per cent of total population), in contrast, possess some agricultural lands, even up to 3.6 *bighas*, by virtue of the benefit of *patta* land distributed on the part of the government and the erstwhile ruling party CPI (M). Owing to this fact, like in the former village, the ST community en masse with a few exceptions are still the mass base of this party. The present ruling party, however, are trying to win over at least some of them through another kind of benefit distribution. One youth from this community, for instance, serves now the role of the supervisor of the MGNREGA programme. The people of the SC community, it seems, are still underprivileged in terms of getting the benefit from the party and panchayat. A greater proportion of people from this community has to take non-farm works as main or subsidiary occupation for livelihoods. Non-farms work constitutes sand mining, construction labour, poultry farming, etc. The work has been provided under the MGNREGA programmes so far for 30 days in this year.[25] Although agriculture has provided sufficient jobs, be it self-employment and wage labour,[26] to all sections of villagers, the overwhelming presence of the landless labouring people always create a serious level of unemployment and prompted them subsequently to take various kinds of non-farm works as livelihoods.

Interestingly, agricultural wages prevalent in both sets of villages are lower to a great extent than the wages stipulated by the government.[27] The question arises in what way the rural labourers would experience indirect outcomes from the MGNREGA when they have not even been drawing minimum wages prescribed by the government. What has been possible, as Carswell and De Neve observed (2014, 583), in Tiruppur district of Tamil Nadu, namely that the rural poor could experience some real gains of MGNREGA, is actually still a dream to the rural labourers of West Bengal. Unlike their counterparts in Tamil Nadu, the labourers in West Bengal would hardly experience 'indirect outcomes include the availability of an employment alternative, the increase in agricultural wages' and 'the improvements in labourers' bargaining power *vis-à-vis* employers' (ibid., 583). This is due not only to the fact that the programmes under the MGNREGA are not effective in terms of both creation of work and regular payment of wages, but also the very reason that the work under this act wouldn't create a pressure on the supply chain of labour-pool as mentioned earlier. Now let's examine the outcomes of implementation of the provisions meant for benefiting directly the marginal peasants i.e. the sharecroppers as well as the deprived sections like the SC and ST in terms of creating durable assets in context of caste and class. There is no doubt that the likelihood of implementation of the provisions which are thought to be skewed towards the interests of the labouring class and of the deprived social categories are often curtailed in villages wherein the dominant castes and substantial landowners are in the helm of local power. But the question is why these provisions are hardly being put in practice in villages where the SC and ST communities are numerically dominant and exclusive inhabitants. The field survey data amply show, as discussed above in this chapter, that these provisions are not at all being addressed, let alone being prioritized in the SC-ST dominated villages. Where lies the problem? In many places, belonging to the SC and ST communities, the panchayat Pradhans and the members are hardly aware of these provisions. If they are even aware of the provisions at all, the process of implementation is so bureaucratically structured that they could not succeed to put it in the ground. First of all, the panchayats in West Bengal are anything but hardly independent in terms of its functioning. These are controlled, or guided, by either the local committee if it is run by the CPI (M) party, or the core committee[28] if it is run by the ruling party TMC. These local committees and the core committees are usually led by the dominant higher caste landowning communities. As far as the prevailing caste-class dynamics in West Bengal is concerned, it seems to be not an easygoing task that the party leaders, the land owners belonging to the higher castes, would follow the order of the governments, and implement immediately. Suppose they do, and then would come the next question. The planned list of works, as a rule, has to be passed by the villagers present in the *Gram Sansad* meeting. Where there is limited resource, there is every chance of politicized distribution of benefits. Findings from the district of Uttar Dinajpur show that the expectant villagers, most of whom belonging to the ST community, are concerned about the sanction of 'land development' work on the land of a ST beneficiary. A woman who belongs to the same party with which the beneficiary has been attached candidly says, 'I am also the supporter of the CPI (M) party. However, I didn't get any benefit from the party. She does'.

The class seems also to be a factor in carrying out the provisions meant for a definite class. Would the people of the landholding class who require agricultural labourers for cultivating their lands pay attention to implement the provisions that would benefit their labourers? The instances from Darjeeling district reveal that despite the fact that the landholding class and the landless class, the would-be beneficiaries, belong to the same SC categories, these provisions have hardly been followed. The ST people in this village would barely possess land to be required to create work under the MGNREGA. In contrast, several *Rajbanshi* families possess lands in which some development works can be done. But no such works have been found. Let's turn our attention towards the south-western part of the state where the NGOs together with local administration take efforts to initiate some development work as part of these provisions under the MGN-REGA. In the districts of Purulia and Bankura, Pradan, a renowned NGO, has been devising projects of creating water harvesters on the lands of SC and ST people mainly for the purpose of irrigation. These water harvesters, locally called *Hapa*, are obviously beneficial and 'can bring substantial changes' to the livelihoods of the *hapa*-owners (Banerjee 2012, 11).[29] The acute scarcity of water for irrigation debars even the landowners to make a decent livelihood in these districts. By providing the irrigation water for agriculture, these water harvesters no doubt are changing the lives of the landowners. Various cost-benefit analyses show the way their entrepreneurship has increased, and they are cultivating various crops 'with an eye to the market'. Whether these water harvesters have changed their lives once for all, however, would remain as a question for the future. The question which probably concerns us more is about whether the lives of the landless labourers are also changing accordingly after the construction of these water harvesters? The answers are, I suppose, mostly negative. Initially, the labourers got work for some days under the scheme of 'making harvesters' as part of MGNREGA, but the creation of jobs didn't continue for long. After a while, they remain again unemployed as usual. One budding phenomenon has rather increasingly been prominent at the grass roots that the small and marginal cultivators who have in their possession the newly made water harvesters are accumulating profits accrued from the land by way of high yielding of land, multi-crop cultivation and, above all, multi-uses of water from the harvesters. They even try to make a profit by selling irrigation water to other owner cultivators, be it share-croppers or landowners. Has there been a contrast class relation emerging at the margin among the marginal peasants most of whom belong to the same community? The classes are going to be distinct, but it remains to be seen how sharp it is.

Conclusion

The issues of employment and unemployment in rural areas are thus intensely rooted in the dynamic relations of castes and classes. If we endeavour to understand the problem of unemployment in India, we must analyse the intricate relations among various castes and classes. The capitalist transformations at the rural hinterland since the early time under the British colonial rule have, of course, problematized the domain of employment in India to a great extent. The roles of the state, both the colonial and the postcolonial, in shaping the nature of issues associated with unemployment are also of immense importance. By exploring the nature of capitalist transformation in the domain of employment at the rural hinterland of West Bengal through a comparative analysis of different zones which are distinct from each other not only in terms of its proximity to city but also of its ethnographic components, this chapter reveals that the nature of employment and unemployment varies greatly on the basis of specificities of a particular social reality. The rural India has changed enormously since the liberalization of its economy began in the 1980s, and the dynamic condition of employment including its security has subsequently taken new forms all over the country. Rural West Bengal is no exception. While the 'determinant' role of capital whatsoever leads to transform the class configuration and the economy in rural areas by means of marketization of farming and other occupations, the government's attempts aimed at supporting the rural labour through particularly the MGNREGA would complicate the issue further. The question that arises is the way in which the contemporary rural is changing as a result of marketization and, similarly, in what way would the politics of rural people shape the outcomes of capitalist transformation. How do the rural people across class and caste shape the economic restructuring of global capital in their lives and livelihoods? By examining these questions critically, the chapter reveals that while the economic transformations impact differently on different classes of people in terms of employment, a specific local setting having particular forms of inequalities engender distinct capitalist dynamics.

Notes

1 *Bhadralok* means the 'gentle', the 'respectable'. The Bengali *bhadraloks* were essentially products of the property relations created by the permanent settlement. This was a class that would not labour on its land but lived off the rental income it generated. Chatterjee notes, 'the title "Babu" – a badge of bhadralok status, carried with it connotations of Hindu, frequently upper caste exclusiveness, of landed wealth, of being master, latterly in possessing the goods of education, culture and Anglicisation' (1995, 5). See more about it in Mukherjee (1993); Chatterjee (1997); and Roy (2012).

2 By quoting Gadgil (1959), Damodaran (2008) argues that the Indian society permits little mobility between one occupation and another (6).
3 See the Floud Commission (1940); Chatterjee (1984); and Mukerjee (2010).
4 The list of zamindars provided by Sarkar entails that many of them actually belong to the upper castes.
5 The sharecroppers include the *bhagchasi, bargadar* or *adhiar*.
6 In both cases, a proportion though being very small from Poundra Kshatrya and Rajbanshi has large amounts of landed property and is locally dominant. The social, political and economic dominance of this section of people are huge.
7 In this book, the word 'rich peasantry' is interchangeably used with 'the middle or dominant castes'.
8 Two other castes, namely Tili and Bhumij-Kshatriyas, had taken successfully the same way of social mobility movements.
9 Manor (2010) explains the way two *jati* clusters, Vokkaligas and Lingayats, achieved power in Karnataka by using 'the swings in the relationship between these *jati* clusters' and also from the relationship between *jatis* within the *jati*-cluster, from cooperation to rivalry and back to cooperation and by mobilizing support from groups of lesser status which comprised a sizable majority of the population.
10 It is true, as Chatterjee argues, 'whatever growth did occur was for a limited period, in specific regions and among owners of large holding' (1999, 53).
11 Downloadable at www.parliamentof india.nic.in/jpi/March2000/CHAP-5htm
12 In 1999, the NSSO report says, only 12 per cent of all pump sets used by the farmers in West Bengal are electrified.
13 The core committee of the TMC party is formed in each panchayat areas with an aim to supervise the panchayat activities.
14 This category includes the ST, the lower castes and the Muslims. As Muslims are beyond our purview of discussion, I would skip their cause.
15 When I had conducted my field work, the wage rate was around Rs.50 per day (as on 2007) in the village. But the minimum wage rate then prescribed by the central government in West Bengal for agricultural workers was Rs.74.53 (Source: www.labour.nic.in).
16 The Naxalbari movement that broke out in 1967 in Naxalbari region of the district of Darjeeling was a peasant rebellion against the zamindar-jotedar combined. This movement, which championed the issue of seizure of benami lands from local landlords and jotedars, had been initially led by the Darjeeling district committee of the CPI (M) party. But eventually a new party, the CPI (ML), was soon formed which had led the movement for a larger period. As this movement first originated in the Naxalbari block of Darjeeling district, it had been well-known as Naxalbari movement.
17 A respondent informs that the ardent followers of the top leaders of the CPI (M) party live in the neighbouring villages.
18 Agriculture as occupation did not develop much in the district of Darjeeling. The data of District Statistical Handbook (Darjeeling) show that only 44.26 per cent of total land in the district of Darjeeling has been sown during 2004–2005 economic year (GoWB 2005); 38.27 per cent of land is covered under forest. The proportion of land under *boro* paddy cultivation is also very small.
19 The MGNREGA stipulates that the work can be created on the land of SC and ST communities, and of the land reform beneficiaries.
20 The panchayat member himself has taken 4 bighas of land from a co-villager as mortgage at the rate of Rs. 10,000/bigha.
21 The respondents inform, 'there are many land brokers working in this area who misdirect the innocent ST people, and smoothly finalize the land deal. Lots of lands of these people have already changed hands, and gone to the outsiders'.
22 The labourers have not received the wages yet. The Panchayat Pradhan says, 'the new BDO has expedited the process of creating work and paying the wages to the labourers. It takes now only one month to pay the labourers whereas it used to take at least

6 months to pay the wages. The real problem in delivering the work done is actually to prepare the muster roll in a correct way. The supervisors are often unable to do it. Besides, there are also complaints of corruption. Notably, the Pradhan's brother-in-law acts as a supervisor in her own village'.
23 The village in Jougram block had been dominated by the Left Front parties for more than three decades. Though the village is dominated by the SCs and STs, the proportion of Muslims population is also high. Except 20 Brahmin families, there are no other caste Hindu families.
24 Boro paddy and potato are grown extensively by the farmers as commercial crops. The STWs and DTWs are also used for irrigation purpose, if or when necessary.
25 Some persons from the ST community complain, 'the payment for the MGNREGA work has been delayed even for 6–7 months'.
26 Several families take lease-in land from the families who have lands and cultivate it either for a season or for a year. The panchayat member informs, 'I have taken 0.75 bigha land on lease-in term at the rate of Rs. 2500/bigha/year.'
27 The man labourers earn around Rs. 150.00 with some food as breakfast in the morning as daily wages whereas the wages stipulated by the state government was Rs. 206.00 with food as daily wages during the same period.
28 The core committee is a kind of party committee of the TMC party which supervises the panchayats.
29 This is an 'Impact study of Hapa and its multiple uses in Bankura district'. The study has been conducted in Hirbandh block, Bankura, in 2012. The report of the study is downloadable at www.iwmi.cgir.org, Delhi.

References

Ambedkar, B. R. 1945. *Annihilation of Caste* (with a Reply to Mahatma Gandhi). Mumbai: Government of Maharashtra Press.
Bardhan, Pranab. 1984. *The Political Economy of Development in India*. New Delhi: Oxford University Press.
Carswell, Grace and Geert De Neve.2014. 'MGNREGA in Tamil Nadu: A Story of Success and Transformation?' *Journal of Agrarian Change* 14(4): 564–585. doi: 10.1111/joac.12054
Chatterjee, Joya. 1995. *Bengal Divided: Hindu Communalism and Partition, 1932–1947*. Cambridge: Cambridge University Press.
Chatterjee, Partha. 1984. *Bengal: 1920–1947: Land Question*. Calcutta: K P Bagchi.
Chatterjee, Partha. 1997. *The Present History of West Bengal: Essays in Political Criticism*. New Delhi: Oxford University Press.
Chatterjee, Partha. 1999. *The Partha Chatterjee Omnibus: Comprising Nationalist Thought and the Colonial World, the Nation and Its Fragments and a Possible India*. New Delhi: Oxford University Press.
Damodaran, Harish. 2008. *India's New Capitalists: Caste, Business, and Industry in Modern Nation*. Ranikhet: Permanent Black.
Dasgupta, Abhijit. 2000. 'In the Citadel of *Bhadralok* Politicians: The Scheduled Castes in West Bengal.' *Journal of Indian School of Political Economy* 12(3 & 4): 445–458.
Frankel, Francine R. and M.S.A. Rao, eds. 1990. *Dominance and State Power in Modern India: Decline of a Docial Order*, Vol. 2. New Delhi: Oxford University Press.
Gadgil, D. R. 1959. *Origins of the Modern Indian Business Class: An Interim Report*. New York: Institute of Pacific Relations.
Ghosh, Anjan. 2001. 'Cast(e) Out in West Bengal.' *Seminar* 508, December.
GoWB. 2005. District Statistical Handbook, Darjeeling. Kolkata: Bureau of Applied Economics & Statistics.

Kaviraj, Sudipta. 1989. 'A Critique of the Passive Revolution.' *Economic and Political Weekly* 23(45–47): 2429–2444.

Lama-Rewal, Stephanie Tawa. 2009. 'The Resilient Bhadralok: A Profile of the West Bengal MLAs.' In *Rise of the Plebeians? The Changing Face of Indian Legislative Assemblies*, edited by Christophe Jaffrelot and Sanjay Kumar. New Delhi: Routledge.

Manor, James. 2010. 'Prologue: Caste and Politics in Recent Times.' In *Caste in Indian Politics*, edited by Rajni Kothari and James Manor (revised). New Delhi: Orient Blackswan.

Mishra, Vandita. 2010. 'Importance of Being an Upper Caste in Bengal House.' *The Indian Express*. Downloadable at archive. Indianexpress.com/story-print/585881/

Mukerjee, Madhusree. 2010. *Churchill's Secret War: The British Empire and the Ravaging of India during World War II*. New Delhi: Tranquebar.

Mukherjee, S. N. 1993. *Calcutta: Essays in Urban History*. Calcutta: Subarnarekha.

Nielsen, Kenneth Bo and Patrik Oskarsson. 2016. 'Development Deadlocks of the New Indian State.' *Economic and Political Weekly* 51 (4): 67–69.

Roy, Dayabati. 2008. 'Whither the Subaltern Domain: An Ethnographic Enquiry.' *Economic and Political Weekly* 43(23): 31–38.

Roy, Dayabati. 2012. 'Caste and Power: An Ethnography in West Bengal, India.' *Modern Asian Studies* 46(4): 947–974.

Roy, Dayabati. 2013. *Rural Politics in India: Political Stratification and Governance in West Bengal*. New Delhi: Cambridge University Press.

Roy, Dayabati. 2017. 'Caste, Identity and Power: Making and Unmaking of Caste Mobilization in West Bengal.' In *Contested Hierarchies, Persisting Influence: Caste and Power in Twenty-First Century India*, edited by Surinder S. Jodhka and James Manor. Hyderabad: Orient BlackSwan.

Ruud, Arild E. 2014. 'Notions of Rights and State Benefits in Village West Bengal.' In *Persistence of Poverty in India*, edited by Nandini Gooptu and Jonathan Parry, 204–226. New Delhi: Social Science Press.

Sanyal, Hiteshranjan. 1981. *Social Mobility in Bengal*. Calcutta: Papyrus.

Sarkar, Benoy Kumar. 2016. *Banglar Jomidar* (In Bengali). Kolkata: Seriban.

Singh, K. S. 1993. *People of India: An Introduction*. Calcutta: Seagull.

Vanaik, Achin. 1990. *The Painful Transition: Bourgeois Democracy in India*. London: Verso.

Vasavi, A. R. 2014. 'Government Brahmin: Caste, the Educated Unemployed and the Reproduction of Inequalities.' TRG Poverty and Education, Working Paper Series, Max Weber Stiftung.

Newspapers, magazines, reports and other media

Banerjee, Partha Sarathi. 2012. 'Impact Study of Hapa and Its Multiple Uses in Bankura District.' International Water Management Institute (IWMI). Downloadable at https://agriknowledge.org/files/x633f107f

Report of the Land Revenue Commission, Bengal (Floud Commission Report). 1940. Downloadable at Archive.org

5 'Civil society', NGOs and rural employment

The idea of 'civil society' as emerged for understanding the domain outside the state in the western countries has travelled a long distance across diverse societies throughout a couple of centuries only to produce contested meanings. Despite it being a contested idea, I have no hesitation to use the term 'civil society' to categorize the *bhadralok* elites, since the latter has already been called a 'civil society' not only in media space but also widely in academic discourse. These *bhadralok* elites would dominate both the public institutions i.e. the bureaucracy and the political institutions in West Bengal, and therefore being the constitutive part of state and its institutions. Being a part and parcel of the state, while are hardly able to constitute (Chandhoke 2001, 19) 'a sphere that is oppositional to the state', these *bhadralok* elites would play roles in shaping the policies meant for the interest of broad masses, here the rural people. In place of the dichotomy between civil society and 'political society', as coined by Chatterjee (2004), if we put here another dichotomy, i.e. the elite and subaltern, and try to analyse the context, we might find a similar rendering to that of the so-called civil society and political society. This book has already explained the dynamic ways in which the upper castes as part of the political parties have been playing their roles in shaping the issues of unemployment in rural areas. Now, it is civil society's turn on behalf of which the same upper castes are performing in the domain of rural unemployment, thereby reconstructing the same through various 'civil' voluntary interventions.

Like in all modern societies, the *bhadralok* elites of West Bengal would play its roles in establishing the modern power through the passage of salvation. The modern state in all countries intends to establish, and expand its power, as Foucault (1982, 783) envisages, by means of ensuring the well-being, or the worldly 'salvation', of every individual in the whole community. As the western modern state had integrated in a new political mode an old power technique, the pastoral power, which originated in Christian institutions, the form of modern state in India and Bengal in particular, seemed to have developed likewise based partly on the compliance and charitable activities of the *bhadralok* elites. Chatterjee (2007, 2010) explains through examining critically a text the way the ancient charity or religious philanthropy evolved into the universal social work via governmental welfarism in Bengal. In our context, it might be noteworthy that the social workers, rather than the social philanthropists, who were expressively active 'in the affairs of others' with a range of salvage efforts, had significantly been reluctant in even a minimal level of reforms in rural sphere, the land reforms in particular. Take the case of Maharaja Pradyot Coomer Tagore, for instance, to explain the phenomenon that the famous personalities who were celebrated for being virtuous owing to their salvage gestures in doing goods for the broader society were seen to have been concerned about a little skew towards the interest of the *raiyats*. Maharaja Tagore was a prominent landlord, intellectual and artist, and was conferred knighthood by the British Empire (Sarkar 2016, 42) for his contribution particularly in art conservation.[1] However, when the Tenancy Act Amendment Bill was introduced in Bengal Legislative Council in the year 1928, Maharaja Tagore vehemently protested against it apprehending that it might curtail some existing rights of the *zamindars*. Maharaja Tagore as President of a Landholders' conference sent a memorandum to the concerned people like the Viceroy, the Governor of Bengal, etc. (Chatterjee 1984, 4) 'expressing its concern at the proposal to give tenants the right of transferring their holdings'. The memorandum (ibid.) mentions that

> the present occasion is most unsuitable to disturb the peace of a most influential class … any such serious change of a settled policy is likely to be followed at no distant period by general discontent among a most loyal class of His Majesty's subjects.[2]

While even the colonial government sought to make a balance between different interests like the landlords, the tenants and the *raiyats*, as it reveals, the big landholders, the *bhadralok* elites, asked instead for the maintenance of status quo.

Whatever the nature of civil society's patronage may be, the rural economy from which the *bhadralok* elites had to leave progressively during the period of late colonialism has never been of their concern during the most part of both colonial and postcolonial period. It seems that the rural has become the other and not one of the *bhadralok* elites. The other, the rural people, so to speak, belongs to the distant places, or of the distant past. The distance between these two spheres, the rural and urban, or in other words, the political society and the civil society, seems to have increased growingly in West Bengal wherein the people of the upper castes could capture most of the positions in the public sphere. As a result of this existing distance, the people of the civil society could hardly treat the rural people as equal to them, and thereby failing to act in a secular way with an aim to remove inequality whatsoever. I have argued elsewhere (2015) that the reluctance on the part of the academics in studying the rural problems empirically is perhaps partly ascribed to the upper castes' apathy towards the rural masses.

But what is equally significant as a reason behind this indifference on the part of the 'civil society' toward the rural society is certainly the hegemony of a dominant ideology over the society and the 'civil society' in particular. The people of the civil society have largely been under the sway of a dominant ideology, i.e. the liberal ideology ever since the onset of postcolonial journey of independent India. Why the liberal ideology has become a dominant ideology is simply due to the fact that it is the ruling class ideology. As Marx (1932) states, 'the ideas of the ruling class are in every epoch the ruling ideas, i.e. the class which is the ruling material force of the society, is at the same time its ruling intellectual force'.[3] It has already been argued the way the *zamindars*, mainly belonging to the upper castes, had enjoyed the privilege being collaborators of colonial agenda of revenue extraction after Permanent Settlement. This is to say, the liberal ideology has dominated the scene since. This domination grew at greater pace when this upper echelon of the society began to occupy most of the positions both in administration and legislature in context of West Bengal. The people of the 'civil society' by virtue of their capturing of most of the leading positions in administration and politics have, therefore, become the ardent intellectual force of the ruling material force. This research has already shown that the leaders of all political parties, even of the Communist parties, could hardly avoid the influence of this ideology as far as their respective programmes are concerned. Avoidance of liberal ideology seems have been more difficult for the representatives of 'civil society' given the fact that they have been one of the major constitutive parts of the government.

Whether the rural people have benefited from a trickledown effect of the economic growth is not our concern here. Whatever its positive effect may be, literally, the idea of trickledown effect is meant by the fact that 'as a result of the increasing wealth of the richest' the poorest, the lowest strata, would benefit gradually (*Oxford Dictionary*). This means, it is fully clear, even the policy makers would not expect that the poorest could directly benefit from economic reform. For instance, take a political leader's comment on land acquisition for industries to explain our purpose. When the would-be land losers were protesting against land acquisition with a plea that they would all lose their livelihoods if land is acquired, the district level leader was busy explaining the way the land losers would benefit immensely as a result of industrialization. He says (Roy and Banerjee 2006), 'I explain a woman who expressed her grief over loss of land that with industry coming up lot of people will stay here in quarters, and they will need domestic helps. You can earn more by working as maid-servants'.

The leader had, of course, no hesitation in accepting the predicament that the peasant women would take maid-servant jobs in place of cultivation which they have been pursuing on their own family land since long. Actually, this is the mindset of the people belonging to the upper strata who promote economic growth as a remedy of all economic problems. This is the way the rural, the agriculture, has been visualized by the *bhadralok* elites in West Bengal. The entire policy framework of the country at least in regard to employment seems to have been grounded on hierarchy. Why don't we consider, first of all, the rural unemployed persons as equal citizen to all of us who are thinking to solve their precarity? Here perhaps lies the problem. However, this trend of inclination, rather than prioritization, of economic growth among the urban *bhadraloks* belonging to the 'civil society', is not a new, as Chatterjee (2010) rightly argues. The 'vague but powerful feeling' that (10) 'rapid growth will solve all problems of poverty and unequal opportunities', seemed have prevailed for a long time among the urban middle class.[4] However, the level and scale of pervasiveness of this ideology has undoubtedly increased recently due to a huge augment in proportion of the middle-class people in urban areas during the last few decades, and also to the massive sway of media and information technology over the society in question.

Despite all these efforts, the issues of unemployment remain a persistent problem in the rural margins of India. The magnitude of the problem is so much so that the issues of unemployment often create a crisis in rural governance, thereby jeopardizing the processes of market. The citizens from the 'civil society' who themselves would systematically construct a grand narrative of India's development have in due course become disillusioned with the government as far as its performance in development is concerned. The growth narrative on which they had always supreme faith, however, still remains as their cherished dream. Whatever its outcomes may be, they would, it seems, refuse to consider the fact that the primacy of economic growth can be a real culprit. Instead, they seem to believe that it is the inappropriate dealing by the government with the issues of growth, and its consequences which remain a real culprit in thwarting the progress of the country. Hence, there emerges a greater initiative since 1980s to form and develop NGOs at all levels, local, national and international, under the auspices of various international associations and, most importantly, of the United Nations so as to tackle the issues concerning social and economic deficiencies within a respective country. India has thus witnessed, like its counterparts all over the world, the developing countries in particular, the burgeoning formations of NGOs in several fields. These NGOs have been seen functioning sometimes in collaboration with the government to deal with increasing deficiencies in well-being as a result of large-scale economic transformations.

However, peculiarly, West Bengal seemed have been the only state where the NGOs have rarely been able to engage in development issues during the last few decades. The NGOs were even regarded as the foreign agents trying to disrupt the normal development of the society, as a leader from the CPI (M) party comments during my field survey in 2006. It transpires the way the Communists could hinder any initiative that emerged from other than the state and state-led parties. And it is perhaps the reason behind why the East European intellectuals as well as the Chinese intellectuals, though with a 'pro-state' stance, built up a sustained challenge to the power of the Communists by invoking the concept of civil society.[5] However, a number of NGOs that had made their efforts to do something distinct through undertaking newer experiments particularly in those areas of welfare where the government has spare efforts. I try now to explain the dynamic functioning of three NGOs which have been venturing out to make their imprints in the domain of employment in rural areas of West Bengal.

While there has been a persistent attempt on the part of the academics who are concerned about the scrutiny of civil society perspective, as Hsu (2010) rightly identifies particularly in the context of the People's Republic China, to explore whether the emerging relationship between the state and NGOs is antagonistic, my work begins with a conjecture that the NGOs have basically been the part and parcel of the civil society, and its relationship with the state is, instead of being tensional and conflicting, in most cases (ibid., 260) 'one of strategic alliances and interdependence'. Moreover, I would argue that while in terms of organizational analysis, civil society's relationship with the state is 'one of strategic alliances and interdependence'; in terms of representation and ideology this relationship is simply one of organic unity. Hence, the task of my work is to demonstrate two dynamic processes. One, the NGOs in India, particularly in West Bengal, have been emerging out from among the people of the 'civil society' who mainly belonging to the upper strata of the society, and what's more, these have organically been attached with the state. Two, the workings of the NGOs are primarily based on the ideology which the state embraces as part of its avowed objectives. What the NGOs are doing is conceivably nothing but aiding the state in its all-pervasive affair of structuring the society. Furthermore, the NGOs are also aiding by way of either collaborating with the state, or supplementing the state's mission by covering the 'development' deficits whatsoever on the part of the state. In other words, the objectives of the NGOs, like most of the state, are to pursue the economic growth 'with everything included'. Why I am saying that the NGOs have also been chasing the economic growth 'with everything included' is due to the fact that they (NGOs) do also, like the state, consider the ideals of liberalism as a 'default setting', or norm. So is the economic growth, investment and the accumulation of capital. But the state, as the advocates of NGOs believe, and the state also perhaps never denies, should take care of its citizens in their distress particularly when it is caused by the very process of economic growth. In course of this process, the NGOS, instead of being 'autonomous', are strengthening the state formation, and thereby legitimizing the state to its citizenry. This is to say, the entire process that initiated on the part of both the state and the 'civil society' is actually sought finally to hegemonize the rural people.

The second section of the chapter deals with the trajectory of dynamic politicization of an NGO which has been organizing consistent agitation concerning rural employment in West Bengal, and subsequently building an apparent opposition to the state, but thereby ultimately being enabled to strengthen the state formation at the rural margin. The third section describes the fate of a 'civil society initiative' which endeavors to work hand in hand with the government to cover the development deficit through application of managerial skill. Whatever its outcome may be, the 'apolitical' combined efforts of the 'NGO and the state' partnership aiming at alleviating poverty through intensifying irrigation and agriculture, have ultimately ended up in vain except that it facilitated the state's agenda to accumulate capital. The fourth section analyses a recent phenomenon of remittance politics emerging in rural areas of West Bengal primarily based on some kind of philanthropy with and without any relationship to the state institutions. While the people belonging to a group which is an agglomeration of highly educated and most often somewhat westernized persons have been trying to take care of, albeit in a very limited capacity, a couple of issues emerging recently in rural areas, their efforts reflecting only a kind of *bhadraloks'* benevolence towards the want of so-called rustic people. The attempts of this group though apparently being of an apolitical nature are evidently emerging as a form of politics, be it conscious or unconscious, which is weakening the subaltern people's political aspiration to compel the state to look after their issues. In conclusion, this chapter elucidates that the initiatives on the part of all kinds of 'civil society' are more or less the same as far as their aims and objectives are concerned. All these 'civil societies' are, I argue, actually venturing into the lowest strata of people in order to accommodate them in this grand narrative of state formation and capitalist development. Instead of being the opposition to the state, the people of these 'societies' would act as appendages of the state and, more specifically, of institutional bureaucrats so as to aid them in their duties to govern the distressed people who are the creation of underlying processes of this unequal structure in postcolonial societies.

Civil society, political action and rural labour

At the very initial stage of my field work, when I began to give a very brief intro-duction about my purpose to interact with the person in charge of the concerned NGO, she almost immediately interrupted me and said that hers was not an NGO. It was rather a political organization, actually a trade union based in West Bengal which had been trying to organize the agricultural labourers in rural areas of West Bengal in order to 'promote the rights of agricultural workers to decent wages, work and food'. It struck me instantly. I got puzzled and then asked myself what the NGOS were above all. What is the difference between the NGOs, on the one hand, and political organization and trade union, on the other? Considering the definitions of both, I have realized, it appears that the two are more or less similar to each other, at least, as far as some of their defining characteristics are concerned. Rather, it will be fruitful in our context to explore the process through which a vol-untary organization that consists of a few concerned citizens from among the 'civil society' began to grow as political and eventually has been recognized popularly as a political organization. In fact, as the two scholars explain in context of Nepal, I demonstrate, by explaining the workings of a so-called NGO turned trade union, why an NGO needed to have been political (Shrestha and Adhikari 2011, 41) 'to become a credible actor' for not only bringing about a political change but also any kind of social change particularly in rural areas of the countries like India. As the networks of human rights NGOs in Nepal had played a central role (ibid.) 'during a crucial period of Nepal's history', this trade union/NGO under my study had equally played a substantial role in the transition of governments in West Bengal.[6] But what is significant is that although the organization in question combined with other actors in the state instigated a political change during a crucial period, it would rarely be considered as distinct from the state institutions to the extent that its agenda and ideas are concerned. To me, it is not, therefore, a dispute whether the 'civil society' or its derivative, the NGOs, is related to politics, since I have already explained that given the structure of society, the 'civil society' organiza-tions in India, particularly in West Bengal, hardly remain as non-political and even are easily going to be connected with political sphere.

Notably, the organization under my study has been founded by a few profes-sional activists who during their early days used to organize the downtrodden masses against the government certainly under political banners in both rural and urban areas. Needless to say, their activities were highly political, and their erst-while organizations used to constitute a sphere that was oppositional to the state. These activists, most of whom belong to the upper strata of the society, were likely of the opinion during that particular point of time that nothing could be achieved without a proper 'proletarian' politics and a political party. Therefore, they used to take up various pertinent issues that concerned the masses in their everyday lives and livelihoods only in order to organize them in the political party which endeavored to campaign a larger radical politics. However, the subsequent trajectory of political dynamics in West Bengal during the 1970s changed the scenario once for all.[7] These full-time activists 'who were waiting for revolution' did not so easily agree to leave the space of power they had been trying to construct. The space of power which had once been constructed by means of 'direct' political actions, has later begun to be constructed among the same downtrodden people, this is to say, the laboring people in rural areas, by way of cultural activities. But, the program of construction of power by only way of cultural activities, it seems, couldn't go far, especially, in the highly politicized society like West Bengal's. In other words, any organization which would take an apolitical stance though outwardly could hardly become a credible actor even in the space of 'civil society'. To be a credible actor among the downtrodden people, and in the activists' circle, this group had to take up issues related mainly to labour and livelihoods to mobilize the agricultural labourers towards political movements in a new distinct outfit. As a result of which, the province witnessed the birth of a new organization, i.e. the Bengal Agricultural Labourers' Association in the year 1988. This organization, be it the NGO or the trade union, whatever its identity may be, though based in Kolkata suburban areas, has been working since on issues of human rights all over West Bengal.

The name of this organization denotes that it has been primarily interested on agricultural labourers. As said by one of its leaders, the Employment Guarantee Act for agricultural labourers had been one of their main demands since the inception of this union. She said,

> since 1988, we have been campaigning for Employment Guarantee Act (EGA). We asked repeatedly if there could be an Act in Maharashtra, why West Bengal won't have one. Anyway, we started 'right to food' campaign in the whole country since 2003–2004. The issue of EGA once again came to the fore. We formed a national platform focusing the demand of EGA, and campaigned actively for it. After parliamentary elections, 2004, the UPA[8] government had included this issue in their Common Minimum Programme.

Considering the changing context of new human rights directives at the international level, this organization began to pick up various 'right' issues which were seriously undermined by the government in West Bengal. While under the sheer negligence of the government, the perpetual power in the state-like industrialists, bureaucrats and the large landowners didn't even conform to the legal provisions made recently by various international bodies to establish justice, the organization in question tried to utilize the courts of law to establish justices in the state. They had filed a couple of petitions on behalf of this organization regarding the issues like right to life, right to work, right to food, etc. until 2006.[9] But the situation began to change, so did the functioning of this organization, and starting in 2006, strong opposition against the Left Front government was slowly growing to shape.

The Agricultural Labourers' Association, which had so far been principally active in the domain of courts of law, except a few instances of joint demonstration against the prevalence of unemployment and poverty in the country, unlike most of the other NGOs, switched its focus to political agitation against the then government. While a large-scale people's movement surged all over the state following the anti-land acquisition movements in Singur and Nandigram, the broad masses from the 'civil society' came out to make a big protest against various injustices meted out to the downtrodden people as consequences of the government's policies and mal-practices. The persistent sense among civil society of Kolkata was just like that of the civil society in pre-Republic Nepal in 2006. This is to say, the political parties in the state (Shrestha and Adhikari 2011, 45) 'were ineffective' or that they were 'not doing anything' and the 'party protest' was described as 'just a ritual' 'a drama' – a 'routine but meaningless effort'.[10] As part of the 'civil society', this association couldn't remain indifferent especially when it had vowed to take care of the problems faced by agricultural labourers. One of the leaders of the association said, 'we thought that it was our duty to take part in the ongoing protest' as exactly what an activist of Network in Nepal said (ibid., 49), 'we thought, being responsible citizens and representing credible civil society groups [we have to act]'. The association began to act like a political entity and to take political efforts in collaboration with other political organizations to resist the government and its avowed programme of land acquisition for industrialization in the state. The persons belonging to the association had subsequently thrown their weights behind every protest meeting organized by any political party regarding this single issue. They were even seen to participate in resisting physically the forceful efforts on the part of the government to fence off the acquired land in Singur. When the political entrepreneurs from mainstream political parties took a moderate stance as far as its demonstrations are concerned, this association seemed to have gone often beyond its declared organizational agenda. Owing possibly to this firm stand in resistance movement, the members of this association were represented on the media, both electronic and print, on regular basis. In other words, they got a positive response also from the middle-class people in the state. Notably, a number of NGOs had opted at this juncture to participate in the ongoing anti-government movement,[11] but failed to make their presence felt. The association definitely made its mark in the field of protests that initiated on the part of the 'civil society' against the perpetual injustice in the state.

The question is: why was the association above all so vigorous in organizing the people's protest which has been considered normally the task of the political parties? The leader of this association says candidly,

we are always concerned about the predicament of agricultural labourers. They are probably the ones who have the most to lose, if agricultural land is acquired? This apart, our concern is also about the right of the general people to food. The destruction of multi-crop agricultural land, we believe, must aggravate the deficiency in food crops. We are strongly opposed to the acquisition of agricultural land.

Whatever the reasons of their action may be, these activities, the political action, did shape the mood and motive of the association to a great extent, so did the activists. Considering three components that are usually required to make a political performance successful, as suggested by Shrestha and Adhikari (2011), i.e. the script, the setting and the troupe, I would argue that all these components were fitting each other to a breakthrough in this particular case. Furthermore, the mood that the activists amassed in course of this movement seemed to have acted as motivation to pursue their agenda during the next phase of their political agitation. This is to say, the troupe have been all set to perform their part that scripted in the programme of the association. Coming in from rural areas or, most often, from the same locality, almost all the activists of this association could aptly respond to the local situational needs. Being members of the village community, the activists could well organize the labourers to perform in political agitation for want of employment.

I have mentioned earlier that the association aims mainly to base their activities on employment of agricultural labourers in West Bengal. Take the case of Purulia district, for instance, to explain the dynamic performance initiated on the part of the association. As soon as the association began to intervene in implementation of the MGNREGA in the state, its activists would confront a varied kinds of ramifications. The setting here matters a lot in how it shaped the consequence of their actions. Unlike the earlier context, the activists are now to act on a 'normal setting' in which different strata comprising the local context seem to be apparently in harmony. The agricultural labourers in Purulia, a district which is drought-prone and susceptible to unemployment, have really been in want of work for most of the year. Unavailability of work pushes the rural unemployed people either to migrate to the places of surplus of work or to starve for days. An agricultural labourer depicts the stern situation they are going to face during my field work, 'we would probably die out of starvation this year (2010) as due to drought in our district very little paddy has been produced. How can we survive if we are not able to get work?' In this context, when the actors of the association tended to play their scripted roles, the real actors of the village society, i.e. the rural classes and castes, the political parties and the local administration as well played their roles in turns, and making the situation more complicated. The leading persons of the association have given some clues the way, on the one hand, they have been playing their roles, and on the other, these local actors have been creating various impediments showing their lack of interest and initiative in implementation of the '100 days' project. One of the leaders describes, 'we had to complain even to the District Magistrate for issuing job cards for 100 persons. When the panchayat failed to provide work, and we had taken legal course so that it complied the law, the former was taking vindictive steps like sending the labourers far away, giving them harder works, imposing strict rules in measuring the work done, deferring the wages etc.'. Actually, although the government has been compelled to enact the Job Guarantee Act, it lacks the intention to provide work in the interest of a particular section of people. Another leader says,

> rather it is creating a lot of bottlenecks in every steps of its implementation. Firstly, wages are being paid belatedly. No system is created to receive the applications. Panchayat is providing work according to its whims. In several circumstances, even when we approach the panchayat for providing work, it is expressing its inability to provide work.

It clearly reveals the fact that the panchayat, being a local self-government, first, refuses to comply with legal orders, and second, remains against the agricultural labourers. The classes who have been dominating the land and labour in rural areas are here actually the panchayat. Everyone who is concerned about rural economy seems have been aware of the fact that the assurance of jobs and the payment of wages on daily basis are very important for a day-labourer. 'The convention in rural areas is that the labourers who live in a hand to mouth condition are paid within 2–3 days', a leader says, 'so that they can purchase necessary things from the weekly market. This is how they run their families. If instead they get payments after 15–20 days or after 1–2 months, how would they be able to arrange their bare needs for survival?' The crew members of the troupe, however, didn't sit idle on these problems of delayed payment. They took initiatives at local level while on the basis of their own script. The local leader who himself works as day-labourer says,

> we have raised objections at different places, but everyone associated with the project is blaming each other for the delayed payments. We have already written a complaint about it to the Assistant Labour Commissioner (ALC). The ALC says that he would pay compensation if the DM orders for the same. The DM says that he would enquire to find out who is guilty for these late payments, but nothing fruitful has happened. Until now the labourers have not received any compensation.

The chief of this association rightly detects,

> two provisions in the Act are never implemented by the state government. The first is that once you accept an application, you have to pay unemployment allowance if you cannot provide work in time. The state government doesn't even make any budgetary provision to pay unemployment allowances. We have repeatedly proved by placing evidences that despite applying for work, the people won't get work within a stipulated time of 15 days. This is the point where government has done sheer negligence. The second provision is to provide compensation if payments are delayed by more than two weeks. But here also we have experienced in course of our actions that no rules are

laid for paying this compensation: nobody knows which court to proceed to or where to approach in order to get compensation. Had these two provisions been put into practice, the Act could have been implemented in a better way.

The process of implementation, it seems, is beset by numerous problems. Does the change in regime, however, engender any change in practice as far as the implementation of the MGNREGA is concerned? One of the leaders inform, 'our experience is that the same practice continues even where the regime has changed, and a new party has come to the power'. In a block of Purulia,

> the CPI (M) people who were dominating the local panchayats had beaten the district president of our organization simply because he was committed in labourers' cause. Not only he was beaten, he was arrested in a non-bailable criminal case. Similar incident has happened with the Trinamul Congress (TMC) people. In another block, when our district president went to demand work as per the rules, he was beaten up by the TMC people. To our dismay, those who are struggling for proper implementation of the rules are being harassed and implicated in false cases, whereas those who are in power, but embezzling public fund are run free.

The chief of the association perhaps rightly assesses the power dynamics in rural areas when she says,

> The authority of the panchayat and administration would conventionally think that they are the patrons, and the poor people are their clients. They would initiate works at their will. This belief has been reversed in the MGNREGA. As it is a demand-based project, the beneficiaries are responsible for initiating the work. But they began to feel uncomfortable with this kind of method. Further, wherever the schemes under MGNREGA have been implemented at least to an extent, the wage rates are subject to an increase at the expense of landowners' interest. That is the reason behind why the landowners who are the actual power in panchayat are so adamant in resisting its implementation.

Another leader adds,

> the panchayats can't accept the power of the common people to control the things. Whoever might be in power in the panchayats, no one is in a position to accept this change, and thus creating obstacles in the way of its implementation. No difference in attitude regard to this question can be seen between the left and the right.

The troupe, the association of the activists, attempts to play roles that have been scripted by the government, of course, in collaboration with distinguished persons from among the 'civil society'. The motto of these performances is nothing but simply to establish the rule of law. The rural India, rural West Bengal in particular, is such a place where the task of even instituting a rule of law has been considered a huge task. Is it a problem that being connected only with the political society, as Chatterjee (2004) envisages? It seems not to be the fact. One of its leaders who have been working since long in rural areas says,

> our movement aims at ensuring that the rules are properly followed. Our stand is 'government follow the rules, we will be with you.' In a block of Purulia, we had filed a complaint demanding compensation. It was settled through public hearing. However, no provision was there to pay the compensation. No planning, no infrastructure was made to comply with the Act.

The narrative of the association's dynamic engagement with issues of employment elucidates one simple fact that while the actions of the activists are quite apt and political, the essence of the script they have been performing has debilitated the strength of the show. This is to say, the real culprit is a weak script. Why I am arguing in this line will be clear if we try to understand their performance from three angles, the troupe, the setting and the script. As mentioned, the members of the troupe have not only come in from rural society, but their actions are political and passionate. They can as such be considered as the 'credible actors' among the masses of the community where they perform. They could easily take up any challenge as actors within the space of their actions. Even the setting they have chosen is also perfect for this performance. Purulia seems to be the most appropriate district in West Bengal where implementation of MGNREGA could be easy-going. From the point of view of both beneficiaries as well as the administration, this must be a fact.

However, the problem is that the activists of the association didn't tend to understand the limitations of the act. If they could identify the limitations of the act itself in employment terms and also the limitations on the way of its implementation, they would have been understood what the problem is. This is the reason why their script becomes weak. The limit of the act to create employment put a limit to their performance. Are they really unaware of the limit of the act? Or, are they using this act to strengthen the larger campaign of right to work? For instance, as an activist says,

> the rural people are still unaware of their rights, the acts, and the constitutional provisions that are in their favour. We try to create awareness on these issues among the villagers. The panchayats should have created this awareness but they have never intended to do so. They seem to be reluctant because if the rural people become aware of their rights they would put pressure on the panchayats.

It is, of course, needless to say, that the awareness campaign the association is performing among rural masses is also a righteous task. However, they could have been playing a more impressing role, if they had been able to make a better script. Actually, it is not over and over again true that (Shrestha and Adhikari 2011, 41) the 'process of "de-NGOization" of everyday practices', and the doing 'as political' would enable an organization 'to become a credible actor for social change'. The content of the script also, accordingly, requires changing thoroughly so to be fitted as to obtain a fruitful result. The present script of the organization unlike the earlier has not been even pragmatic, let alone been thrilling and sensational in rural employment terms.

Civil society, managerialism, rural employment

How do we rate an organization which regards managerialism as a way of achieving success in the domain of rural employment? Does its script fit well with the troupe and setting, and combined together result in the purported goal? In a winter morning in the year 2010, when I was about to finish my extended interview with a district leader of a reputed NGO at its office in Purulia, he spoke out with somewhat a frustrated mood that, 'we have been working since long with an aim to provide employment and livelihood opportunities to the poorest section of rural areas in India but, it seems, we have failed in our attempt to secure our goal.' I was struck by this revelation especially from such a committed leader in the field of NGOs in India. This organization is undoubtedly one among those few NGOs which have made a profound impact on the development sector of India. What we do mean as a process of NGOization of development seems to be greatly reflected in the work of this organization. The organization declares as its objective that it has been working towards enabling the rural poor to enhance their livelihood capabilities. By means of providing the professional assistance for development action, the organization tries to resolve, particularly, the economic poverty of India's rural poor. But, what goes wrong in this NGO's avowed task? Is the NGO, its inherent components, itself a problem behind the failure of avowed goal? This means, the question arises about whether the process of NGOization acts as hindrance to development of livelihood capabilities as far as the rural poor are concerned. First of all, it is better to say from the very beginning that the motto of this kind of organization is broadly no different to that of the state which has been under impression that the managers (read bureaucrats) could be instrumental in reducing the rate of poverty occurrence in the countries like India. For the reason that it believes so is probably due to the dominance of a cliché idea that the unfettered growth linked with viable market could alleviate poverty. India's story of progress is, as it were, a story of economic growth, it would say. However, it has also been growingly recognized thanks to Sen and his group that the government needs also to strengthen the capabilities, especially, of the rural poor, to accrue the fruits of economic growth. This growth narrative has in fact substantial roles in shaping and transforming not only the 'civil society' but also its progeny, the NGOs. This NGO which we are talking about is here a case in point.

If we try to make a cursory exploration of the evolution of NGOs, we must find a connecting thread that the way the NGOs have come into being, and then developed in accordance with the basic economic policies that undertaken by the government. These policies, however, have evolved throughout a period of more than a half century in India. Except during the first few decades when the state had relatively been a sole player in the domain of development action, the entire period beginning particularly from the late 1980s have witnessed the spurt of NGOs which have been shouldering a range of development initiatives being either unaided or aided from whatsoever, singly or collaboratively. Back to West Bengal, the development of NGO sector, like People's Republic China especially in the period from 1949 to 1980, goes somewhat slowly as the erstwhile Left Front government used to treat the NGOs with skepticism. Actually, as Hsu (2010) argues, it seems to be correct to a great extent that the framework of civil society which is based on western political theories, and which assumes a division between state and society is not applicable in the societies of the East. However, the viewpoint of 'NGO as a organization' which Hsu proposes as a perspective to analyse the NGOs in countries of the East seems to be equally inept for understanding the emerging dynamics of our societies as far as the roles of NGOs are concerned. As organizations, it might be true that (Hsu 2010, 259) 'both NGOs and the state agencies need to ensure a constant supply of necessary resources for the firm to survive in fulfilling and discharging their own objectives and agendas'. Nevertheless, I would argue, whereas it is partially true that the NGOs require the state's assistance in question of resources, and vice versa, it is perhaps an indisputable fact that the state must mobilize the NGOs under its aegis to co-shoulder the governmental responsibilities. Which are more significant in our context are to explain, on the one hand, the dynamic reasons behind the explosion of NGOs, and on the other, the motivation of the NGOs in delivering the development deficits? The findings from both ends might facilitate the process of enquiring into why unemployment remains a perennial problem.

This apart, if we try to explain the working of NGOs in relation to the state only in terms of 'securing the flow of resources' (2010, 267), we would fail to explore not only the roles of NGOs in societal transformation, but also the dynamic reasons behind why the 'civil society' tend to get involved in development action. As I argued earlier, the economic policies are not nonpartisan in that they have evolved irrespective of any other compulsion, and of larger political economic dynamics. The Chinese NGOs have come into being, as Hsu mentions, around 1989 as consequences of market reforms, so have the NGOs of India in the 1980s. The proportion of the NGOs in India has been growing exponentially as the market reforms gathered its pace since the late 1980s in the country. With the liberalization of economy to foreign investors, the initiatives of international level agencies in realizing the development deficit have also increased the flourish of the NGO sector. The trajectory of policy intervention through 'Five-Year Plan' clearly indicates the fact that the government is asking for shouldering the responsibilities of emerging issues of development. The organization under study is perhaps a perfect example which began since its emergence to work on growth in agriculture, a catchphrase at all times of the government. The script of this NGO seems to have been as such not innovative, rather is an official agenda, which aims at increasing growth in agro-related sector by means of utilizing the resources, be it the land and the labour, available at the verge of rural societies. As we know, when the rural, or the agriculture, in India were unlocked for market reforms in the name of GRT, it would result in uneven growth in agriculture, as well as unequal consequences on the varied layers of peasantry as far as its outcomes are concerned. The development policies whatsoever undertaken by the government in order to make the labour and the land productive had largely been ineffective. In this context, the NGOs have been called on, or urged, to cooperate in.

The organization had begun to cooperate with the government, as expected, in the regions of the province where little could be done in terms of growth in agriculture. This region is commonly regarded as 'unproductive' mainly in terms of land, but also, in some instances, in terms of perhaps labour, when, particularly, the caption of the organization reads as 'enabling the rural poor to enhance their livelihood capabilities'. In other words, as conceptualized by the organization, the rural poor are needed 'professional assistance for development action'. The dynamic reason behind their economic poverty has been, as it were, the lack of the rural poor in capabilities. Simply put, the rural poor are poor since they are not capable of enhancing their livelihood as they are short of professional skills. The capability approach would often ignore a basic fact that some other factors might be liable to the predicament of the rural poor. Therefore, the professional assistance that is provided by the said NGO so as to enable the rural poor to enhance their capabilities has actually been pushing the 'target' toward the market. We describe its narrative to reveal that the script of the NGO is just a script of market reform. But, who are the managers anyway? Who has constituted the troupe? Unlike the troupe of the earlier organization, the task of the organization, i.e. managing the poverty, indicates that the troupe consists of professionals who belonging mainly to the 'civil society' or the upper strata. The organization clearly notes on its website that it requires competent and educated, at least at university level, youth who would take a challenge to work in remote villages. No matter which part of the country he/she belongs to, everyone, it believes, is suitable to work for any place. In other words, to the authority of the organization, both the group of professionals, and the rural poor are considered as a homogeneous category. On the contrary, the relation between professional 'staff' on the one hand, and the rural poor, on the other, is not only hierarchical but is also based on a difference in ideological plane. The dominant ideology that bases itself on liberalism upholds the market freedom, whereas the other is deficient in it. The way the other, the community, has been deprived by the arbitrary reign of the market with a seal of approval by the state is usually not of their interest.[12] Rather, the issue which concerns them is ostensibly in what way the people of the community can be connected with the market.

Not surprisingly, the troupe of professionals with knowledge resources has probably made no mistake, and thus chosen an appropriate region as setting in which they would get sufficient scope to apply its skills for 'enabling' the rural poor toward better livelihood solutions. Other districts of West Bengal which have already developed in terms of market reforms are obviously not of its interest. It has chosen instead the districts, the lateritic region, which suffers from uneven growth in agriculture, and requires, as the organization believes, to be connected with the market. Hence, the troupe and the settings appear as ideal as far as its script is concerned. Let's look at the dynamic trajectory of its performance and impact of the troupe on the domain of rural employment. The organization has been trying to breakthrough since its inception on employment front in the same region in which we have seen earlier in this chapter that another organization was working on but had failed to achieve any remarkable outcomes. The barriers are many standing in the way of its implementation. The political actions of the zealous members of this troupe could hardly make any difference in provision of rural employment in the said region. However, the aims of the present troupe are supposedly different when it claims to make permanent impacts on the sphere of livelihoods by implementing governmental programmes with professional skills. The inputs delivered on behalf of this organization include professional knowledge and skills, whereas the former provides political skill in the form of action as its inputs. While the political is bound to be shaped according to specificities of a local context, the managerial intervention would also see its limit in a specific situation that determines the outcome of the management whatsoever to a great extent. The question arises about what the rural poor are in need of and, similarly, what the managers have been trying to provide for the rural poor, that the government fails to do. In what way, the government lacks the needful.

This is probably a million-dollar question in our context when a leader of the organization claims that it has begun to break the chain of poverty that existed in this region since long. His words sound as if the state, the government, is absent there. As if even the rural poor are sitting idle at the mercy of these saviours. For, if this were the case, the government policies would be of no use. Furthermore, we are perhaps not unaware of the fact that the postcolonial government has been overwhelmed by a huge proportion of bureaucracies as a continuation from that of the late colonial period. This bureaucratic machinery which was 'originally built around intricate rules and procedures enshrining unfettered executive power' actually 'protects, in a well-ordered, recurrent and continuous process, those sections of the ruling classes which have interests of an all-India character'(Chatterjee 1997, 18), but it often, it seems, fails to protect the poor masses. I would attribute the retention of ICS in the bureaucracies to the reason that the government would have required the managerial or professional skills of these cadres to tackle the emerging issues of economic scarcity, owing to capitalist devastation. The managerial or professional skill, however, have hardly been of use. Had the government succeeded to protect the rural poor by means of managerial skills, these kinds of organizations would have not been come in the rural scene just in order only to enable them to enhance their capabilities.

May it be possible to think, as Nandy (2012, 40) conceptualizes, that this region has been considered as backward since it is 'culturally, ecologically and socially different'?[13] 'Irrespective of their social location and cultural features' (ibid.), a section of the people has been considered as poor, a homogenized category, simply because they are marginalized and dominated in terms of power. There is every possibility in our case to categorize the region as well as the people as backward and poor as their economy is somewhat different. It is different, I argue, more in terms of economy/ecology than of culture. While I completely agree with Nandy's influential argument, I would like to ignore the same, at least, for this moment in order only to focus on my purpose of presentation. This section of the people in that particular region is undoubtedly poor, but I wonder, whether they are poor because of the presence of the state or the market. Whether it is the case that the natural resources on which the communities, now they are called as the ST and SCs, have been dependent were seized routinely as part of the state processes. These indigenous communities who were once self-reliant ecologically are now regularly in dearth of food and other necessities since they have increasingly been alienated from the forest and community lands that they had customarily enjoyed from time immemorial. Ironically, the entire process of alienation from land, forest, knowledge and culture has been mediated with various kinds of policies, acts and legislations initiated by the state. The traditional knowledge which grew rich for centuries has begun to fade into nothing. The enormous diversity of knowledge, it seems, has become unsuitable for the new economy, and worthless to the professionals. Therefore, the people of this region become unable to enhance their livelihood opportunities and, then, require the intervention of the professionals who would help them to be enabled. For the sake of argument, I again accept this dominant argument that the skills of the professionals are needed to enable the (knowledge)-poor to find employment. Why does this professional knowledge fail to deliver then on this promise?

The organization which has bagged the Social Impact Award last year began its journey with an aim of organizing the rural women in self-help groups (SHG) on 1987 in West Bengal wherein, it is said, both government and the Left Front parties took major initiatives to intervene in the lives and livelihoods, especially, in rural areas. This is to say, it had made the SHG, an initiative of self-employment, a focus of attention initially. The prospect of this enterprise is to promote available resources in local areas, be it labour or materials, in the market, and thereby, as believed, enhancing the livelihood opportunities. The rural poor who barely have any access to market were being targeted here to mobilize toward the market-based economy. The professionals began to descend into the communities only to organize their lives and livelihoods based on the 'modern' reasoning. The role of the state and state-led parties in this effort of modernizing the rustic people was perhaps slow-going since, it appears, the culture of these people itself has acted as a hindrance to modernization process. But direct actions of the troupe of professionals seemed have made a relative impact on the rural poor, albeit on a very small section. The women are seen organized in SHGs and collaborating on behalf of these groups in various governmental policies. The organization, however, has subsequently expanded its activities to land and water resource development, as it calls it. The issue of land and water resource development has been as usual a state agenda throughout. Even the integrated watershed development project, which has become a catchphrase in recent period, came into being in 1989 under the aegis of the National Wasteland Development Board.[14] But, the motivated professionals went deep into the root even in everyday lives of the said people for transforming the land and water resources into a productive marketized commodity. As a result, it would accrue sporadic success in implementation of land and water resources development policy in the field of irrigation and agricultural production. Despite these positive results, this organization, as the district level leader informs, couldn't generate any options for the landless families. The reason behind why they barely succeeded would possibly be revealed from the narrative of construction of water harvesting structures as part of the MGNREGA in Bankura.

There are many agencies apart from the government, for example, the Ford Foundation, and Bill Gates and Melinda Gates Foundation, both at national and international level, which often grant a major support cost to fund activism of the professionals, who in due course try to stimulate the 'target' people for stepping up the course of action. Sponsored by the agencies, the professionals of this troupe try to intervene in enhancing agricultural production of the landholding people in rural areas with a presumption that the enhancement of agricultural production in a specific area would have an indirect impact on livelihood opportunities of the rural poor. A professional, trained as engineer, who was in the leadership position, informs that although this organization had begun to work on watershed development issues in collaboration with Rashtriya Sam Vikas Yojona, it has recently switched to the MGNREGA as their field of intervention. This is to say, representatives from the 'civil society' do actually intervene in mobilizing the poor, or broadly, the rustic people, toward the actualization of the state policies. Do they then facilitate to strengthen the state processes in far-flung places? In a sense, it might be true since the state would come into being by way of implementation of its policies particularly in 'different' or underdeveloped places. But their efforts to initiate state processes, rather than market processes, could barely achieve otherwise the goal of poverty alleviation by way of enhancing livelihood opportunities of the rural poor. Instead, I argue, all these processes seem have kicked off a class process at the rural fringes. Through organizing the SHGs as well as the panchayats, it is a fact that the professionals have been able to create some durable assets by way of implementing watershed development schemes under the MGNREGA on the lands of individual beneficiaries who can afterwards get a chance to enhance agricultural production. However, a few questions arise regarding the impact of the watershed construction, i.e. the *hapa* as locally called, on the communities, the poor in particular.

First of all, notably, the *hapa* is hardly a new concept, rather an age-old idea popularly held by the people of this locality. However, it has been rarely recognized as traditional knowledge by the professionals who believe that the professional knowledge is superior. What the professionals are doing is just to manage implementing the policies by way of 'reasonably' planning and designing projects. Since the procedures of its execution are now bureaucratically structured, the people of the local communities can at all comprehend the plan which often appears to them as intangible and vague. Simply put, the process of implementation has been scripted in such a way that it inevitably requires the managerial knowledge, plus the professionals, for putting it into practice. The system of policy regime helps thus to strengthen an asymmetrical structure of social relations that already exists in the country. Instead of lessening the dominance prevailing in the society, this policy regime seems to be escalating the dominance of the people of upper strata over the marginal people in rural areas.

Second, it is obvious, and a study conducted on the impact of the *hapa* construction on the local people in this region also reveals, that the *hapa* can be made on the land of those people who have at least a considerable proportion of land so that s/he can willingly spare a portion of land for its construction.[15] This means the landowner would be affected while a portion of land whatsoever is used for making a *hapa*. However, the sizeable landowners (at least one acre) who agree to spare land for the *hapa* would benefit in various ways. I would take privilege to use the study, mentioned above, done on behalf of the IWMI to supplement and clarify my arguments.[16] As the nature of the land of this region is high and lateritic, the existing Kangshabati canal system that was made as early as in 1956 has been generally of little use for agriculture. After the *hapa* construction schemes became a part of the MGNREGA, several landowners took the advantage and approached the organization for consideration.[17] As I have argued, the *hapa* owners have become well off with the increase in their annual income and also in the proportion of their landholdings.[18] Along with the increase in proportion of landholdings, the increase in use of pump machines for extracting water has been impressive. The annual income increased due to enhancement of agricultural production which is definitely the outcomes of the change in cropping pattern from mono-crop to multi-crops and also the increase in yield of crops. The study in question states that 83 per cent of the *hapa* owners now use pump machines for irrigating crops. Finally, the study states (Banerjee 2012, 7), 'the subsistence agriculture has now changed to commercial cultivation', and '93 percent of the *hapa*-owners said their social prestige had increased because of their possession of *hapa*'.

This statement elucidates the way a number of landowners of the region could possess *hapa* and then enhance the proportion of land as well as the amount of agricultural production, and thereby amassing their social prestige in the locality. This means, the formulae is, as portrayed, the *hapa* brings the social prestige by way of increasing economic prosperity. Moreover, as the data supplied by the study, the *hapas* seem to have made a rupture with the rest of the community who do not have *hapas* particularly when the sons of the *hapa*-owners, in some instances, are moving to towns for further education. In other words, the *hapa*-owners have become a new class with their connections with the market as seller, and also buyer, of produce. On the other hand, my research reveals that the people who have either no land or lesser proportion of land could hardly get employment from the *hapa*-owners once the *hapas* have been constructed. The hapa-owners usually grow vegetables on their land associated with the *hapa* since it contains a little amount of water. The cultivation of vegetables depends mainly on family labours. In course of *hapa* construction as well, the family members of the *hapa*-owners had got a considerable part of the labour-jobs as part of the MGNREGA. Except the hapa-owners, the rest of the people of the community could benefit a little from the MGNREGA, be it in durable asset terms or in employment terms.

However, the emerging class formation indicates that a section of the entrepreneur farmers are in the making at the margin with a substantial aid from the government. While there is doubt about how long these farmers would continue cultivation as prosperous farmers, as their entrepreneurship are largely based on the erratic market,[19] it has probably least doubt that a hierarchical relation among villagers comes to fore. It has also revealed that the rural poor in the underdeveloped region as well can hardly gain help for enhancing their livelihood opportunities as consequences of implementation of the MGNREGA for even the shorter term, let alone for the long term. It has perhaps been rightly said by the district leader of the organization, 'we could not do anything for the landless poor in this region'. What's wrong in the script? Is it a problem at all with the script of the organization? One problem might be palpable here in the script. The market-oriented cultivation as well as the enhancement of production is actually not the solution of the problem of unemployment, as we have already known it from the earlier chapters. Even the solvent class of farmers is not in a good position so that, it can be concluded that, at least one class would benefit in long term from the market-oriented system. The leaders of the organization perhaps miss the issues of employment of the rural poor. Had they made employment a focus of attention, they would have understood wherein the problem lies.

Civil society, remittances and 'compassion'

A new kind of voluntary effort has recently been visible in the field of 'development' at rural margin in West Bengal. This effort has primarily been based on the remittance money sent back by the diasporic community of non-resident Indians, staying particularly in the United States, at least in my case. Though this organization was established in the 1990s, it has gained its stream recently in West Bengal especially in the aftermath of anti-land acquisition movements in Singur and Nandigram whilst the people of the 'civil society' at large had registered their voice in either support of or in opposition to those movements. The members of this organization feel manifestly as Mukherjee said in 2016,[20] 'a shared sense of vulnerabilities and anxieties concerning the livelihood losses' in the place of their origin. If there is any organization which perfectly represents the people of 'civil society', and their intention of 'moral imperative' to do something for the poor and victims of their own homeland, this is this organization under our study. The association which was founded by a group of distinguished and highly established persons working aboard has declared in concrete term in its websites that the sufferings should be treated with compassion. The incidence of poverty should be eliminated with conviction and courage. However, this diasporic section of civil society, the compassionate NRIs, acts more as a funding agency than a proactive troupe of committed activists. In fact, this organization which is officially housed in the United States intends primarily to collect donations from the NRIs who in turn would like to part in the diasporic philanthropy in the field of development. The question would arise about how the organization makes its contribution in India's development. This organization, in fact, has mainly been working with the non-governmental organizations in India which are productively active in alleviating sufferings of the downtrodden people at the grass roots, as noted by one of its volunteers. As the issue of rural livelihood has also been its focus of attention, it would fund the people who are working on MGNREGA.

Undoubtedly, the issue of diasporic philanthropy in India is a burgeoning field for research due not only to the fact that 'India is the biggest receiver of remittance' in the recent period but also to an emerging phenomenon that the non-resident Indians are increasingly sending back a part of their earnings for the benefit of the people, the poor in particular, of their homeland.[21] What is the politics that emerges through these practices of remittance aiming at welfare? What motivates these non-residents for making philanthropic remittances? How do they prioritize the issues of development for their intervention? What is the impulse to this targeted remittance? The remitters belonging to this group, which is an agglomeration of highly educated and typically westernized persons, have been trying to take care of, albeit in a very limited capacity, the developmental deficits that prevail in rural areas in systematic ways. Their efforts do not seem to reflect just a spontaneous kind of *bhadraloks' dan* or gifts (donation) which have thoroughly been persisting as a customary act in Bengal since long towards the want of the poor. While the traditional kind of *dan* was 'caste-based, village-based', and somewhat spiritual, the modern manifestations of *dan* have become more complicated, extended and based on some other new features. This is to say, traditional kinds of *dan* are (Copeman 2011, 1051), 'in its contemporary Indian manifestations, mutable, and subject to a variety of complex extensions'. But, is the modern incarnation of *dan* novel? Copeman affirms us that it is hardly novel. While it is true that the contemporary extensions of *dan* differ and embody key aspects of established forms of *dan*, I attempt to extend this debate on *dan* as well as philanthropy a little further to understand theoretically the contemporary context and the politics of philanthropy in larger domain of public welfare.

The organization in question has reportedly been pursuing a combination of both traditional and modern aspects of philanthropy, and thereby forming a new kind of philanthropy. It tries to incite the conscience of the prosperous people for responding compassionately to the sufferings of the Indians in their homeland through giving *dan* or donations as well as ensuring courageously the issues towards its end. On the other hand, it tends to regulate its collection of donations so as to achieving a predetermined goal, i.e. development, India's development. In other words, it uses the impulses for collecting the *dan* and subsequently rationalizes the *dan* for purposely alleviating the sufferings of people in distress. The compassionate donation has been regulated here through a process of development action which draws its logics from disciplinary knowledge of the subject. That is, modern knowledge intervenes in shaping the reasoning behind how to tackle the sufferings of the poor in a secular way. Bornstein says (2009, 622–623), 'when the impulse of philanthropy is spontaneous and has its own beauty, giving is unregulated, it becomes deeply moving, as act of freedom'. However, she continues, the impulse 'to relieve suffering threatens rationalized charity that focuses on the long-term alleviation of need'. The question arises in our context about whether the impulse to give is tempered by its regulation, and the impulse to relieve sufferings has been threatening the rationalized philanthropy that aims at the long-term welfare of the people. First of all, I would argue that the impulse to donate in our case is not at all purely spontaneous; rather it is interested and calculated. Second, the act of regulation of this donation is similarly not based purely on social obligation. Two acts, the act of giving and the act of regulating, are being driven by some other issues which in turn engender as a result of larger political consequences.

Bornstein (ibid.) justly portrays why a gift or donation can at all be a gift or donation, in terms of both Derrida's theorization of gift giving and Hindu scriptural concepts of *dan*, if its results are intervened by the donors or givers. The organization here appeals for the donations to the would-be donors in the resident country by describing the degree of distress the poor citizens are to suffer in the country of their origin. The nature of the appeal is not spontaneous but very much calculated, and driven by a reason. The reason is that they have social obligation to liberate the fellow countrymen from abject poverty by way of development through a scientific planning. Moreover, the organization which performs its roles as a platform between the donors and the recipients is bound to inform its donors about all details regarding not only the nature of spending of these donations but also the results of these donations in development terms. This is to say, it would be obliged to let the donors know about the contribution of donations in social welfare whatsoever, or in other words, in alleviating poverty or other issues related to their anguish. On the contrary, what the donors will receive as return gifts is the tax benefit from the respective government. Gift or *dan* is here reciprocated, and it is reciprocated on behalf of the government, of course the government of the resident country. The question arises why the government attempts to intervene in operation of giving, and itself acts as a contributor as a patron of return gifts to the former donors. Whether the government's intervention can be treated as an attempt to regulate, and to provide a legal context for the donations and its results with an aim of larger interest of development? The questions are many, but the root of the questions may be easier to determine.

The organization had come into being in the United States at the very juncture when the Indian government kicked off to liberalize its economy for foreign investment, and the voluntary sector began to get a prominence in the field of development, and to be shaped increasingly by the global norms of voluntary actions. It is perhaps not unknown to us that ever since the globalization or neo-liberalization, the field of development has growingly been dominated both by the government as well as the voluntary organization or the NGOs. As Bornstein argues, it is also true that the new intelligentsia in India (ibid., 628) 'has led to an incredibly wealthy Indian diaspora, and created a new economy of Indian philanthropy'. I have already argued that this new Indian philanthropy is rational both in the efforts of fund-raising and delivering development. The fund is coming as part of social responsibility of the wealth. Whether the donors are receiving any social prestige is definitely a question here. It seems that they are supposed to gain some kind of social prestige as they don't detach their being with the donations.

Neither do they depart the space of giving after paying donations as a spontaneous response to human sufferings, nor do they lack any interest to know about the outcomes of their donations. Whatever their gains in social prestige may be, it is but clear that they are getting an economic benefit through tax-deduction. The local NGOs who are at the receiving end of these donations are, however, the direct beneficiary of these donations. Hence, there exists a number of layers of interests functional in the entire process of this philanthropy. The most significant fact regarding this Indian philanthropy is that the government, more specifically, the capitalist state, gets an add-on in its effort to alleviate abject poverty, and so gets a brief respite from social protests on the part of the distressed poor. This kind of philanthropy is highly beneficial to the capitalist system as a whole, and its caretakers, be it Indian government or the government of the United States. Bornstein might have concluded her thesis in another direction, had she tried to understand the process in terms of a larger perspective. Apparently, in a limited perspective, it might be true that the impulses urge one to give spontaneously 'in response to immediate suffering', and the regulation and social obligation reinforces 'rational accountability'. But, the efforts of both the government and NGOs in regulating the philanthropic actions, be it impulsive and rational, are supportive more to the existing system which multiplies the sufferings, than to the distressed people in the context of larger capitalist processes.

This large and multi-layered project of philanthropy that aims at alleviating sufferings can indisputably be regarded as an expression of social obligation of the wealth. However, I argue, this philanthropy has hardly been intended to address the underlying causes of sufferings of the countrymen in distress, as the organization proclaims. The trans-country network from the donor abroad to the recipient in need of a village in India has been really a complex terrain of interventions and participations of various actors. The identities and associated roles of various actors are muddled, as are the purposes. Here, donors are the individuals, whereas the NGOs being active both in the United States and India are the beneficiaries. While the NGOs of the United States have been playing a major role in determining the decision of funding, the NGOs in India as beneficiaries of the fund have been accountable to the funding NGOs for proper utilization of funds. Last but not least, the poor people who are supposedly in distress ultimately come to the scene as real beneficiaries. This is to say, three kinds of donors (e.g. the individual donors, the funding agency and the 'grass-root' NGOs) and three kinds of beneficiaries (the funding agency (United States), the local NGOS and the distressed people), would likely muddle up the sphere of development action. The efforts of regulation seem to have been operational in every step of progression only to make the situation more manageable. The question of accountability which was expected to be achieved as a consequence of regulation would actually cause to turn development action into a procedural development. Sometimes it would appear that the efforts intended for the distressed poor in a remote village are, as it were, a routine developmental ritual as part of a grand project initiated by the government. The organization which vows to seek causes of distress experienced by the poor people in India seems have engaged itself in just some palliative actions.

The troupe of performers, the new entrants in the development field, does not seem to compose a new script to narrate a novel story as far as alleviation of sufferings of the fellow countrymen is concerned. The script seems to lack the political imagination needed for producing a transformative potential for a larger change in rural grass roots. The script is apolitical, so is the troupe. Whereas the state, and the larger global perspective controlled by the global aid agencies, successfully introduces a politics of governance by involving the global 'civil society' to depoliticize the terrain of development. Actually, the roles in the script have largely corroborated with the agenda of international level aid-agencies which prompted creating these kinds of 'civil society' or NGOs as part of their own blueprint to govern the global citizenry. The organization which is concerned mainly about the sufferings and its alleviation would perhaps be unable to address the issues in terms of social inequality. The intervention in terms of funds might blur its vision to see meticulously the causes of sufferings. One of the leaders whom I interviewed, candidly informed that they, on behalf of this organization, have been working for a period of more than two decades but has yet to achieve a desired goal. In fact, the organization has made a contribution, albeit in a few pockets of West Bengal, in alternative farming with organic manures. In the Sunderban region, they have initiated organic farming primarily on lands of the marginal peasants in a few villages and have subsequently got success in production. The production apart, as a result of organic farming, the peasants got some scope for self-employment particularly when every possibility has dried out due to devastated natural calamities (e.g. Cyclone Aila). The marginal peasants who began to stop using chemical manure for cultivation and reintroduced traditional farming based on organic manure have now been benefiting from assistance provided by the local NGOs in sponsorship of the organization under our study. It is doubt, however, whether they would remain interested in future in this organic farming since it always bears some risks. The risks are basically associated with the market. There has hardly been any special provision to marketize these organic crops. The leader says, 'the decisions have to be made finally on the part of the government about how to encourage organic farming'. Hence the issues are essentially political.

The attempts of this group, though apparently being apolitical nature, are obviously the organic part of a larger politics of capitalist construction. The wealth of the wealthier section of the people is to be gathered in the name of social obligation, and is subsequently being used for the purpose of alleviation of sufferings. This is to say, the social obligations of wealth are being mobilized by the aid-agencies with an aim of responsive system of governance. Moreover, this larger domain of politics that presently pervades the entire global space has created such a situation that the 'civil society' would equally be responsible along with the state actors for managing the sufferings of people. Hence, the organization about which we are discussing has no stake in interacting with the government about its activities. It has tried to implement its own agenda by involving marginal people who are conceived as their target. I argue, this is an effort, initiated by the NGO, of de-politicization, be it conscious or unconscious, which is in subsequent periods weakening the political aspiration of subaltern people to compel the state to look after their issues whatsoever. These voluntary efforts do not provide, however, any right to the marginal peasants so that they are entitled to claim a fair livelihood. In other words, the rural people who are often organized politically against the state to structure their right-based demands related to well-being are here going to be 'unorganized' only to engage in various pro-poor schemes designed especially for them by the NGOs like this organization. These pro-poor schemes are designed in such a meticulous way that if/once the villagers would participate in it they would slowly be transformed into 'manageable unemployed' by means of some kinds of routine-based activities supervised by the volunteers. This meticulously designed routine, the daily rituals, would seem to succeed in making the sufferers oblivious to their everyday predicament of unemployment, and the subsequent demand of employment, and thereby aiding them absorbed into the mainstream.

Conclusion

As shown above, this chapter explains the way the 'civil society' and the NGOs have been intervening in domain of employment in West Bengal, and rendering this space in due course manageable from the perspective of governance. While the first organization helps strengthening the state formation through its political actions in the process of implementation of state welfare policies, the second NGO encourages the practice of managerialism as a means to enhancement of livelihood opportunities. The third one stands as a peculiar instance of the fate of Indian philanthropy which would just replicate the grand work design of the international aid-agencies in their efforts to alleviate human sufferings. These three representations of three NGOs, e.g. political action, mangerialism and philanthropy, are actually three strategies from among the myriad of strategies used by the custodians in order to govern the issues of unemployment particularly in developing countries. This chapter elucidates that the initiatives on the part of all kinds of NGOs are more or less same as far as their aims and objectives are concerned. All these NGOs are, I argue, actually venturing into the lowest strata of people in order to accommodate them in this grand narrative of capitalist state formation. Instead of being the opposition to the state, the people of the 'civil societies' through their activities within the NGOs would act as appendages of the state so as to aid in its duties to govern the distressed people who are in point of fact the creation of underlying processes of this unequal structure of postcolonial societies. More significantly, the actors of these NGOs do perform in the same fashion as the institutional bureaucrats do with purportedly an aim to manage the distressed people in various kinds of 'scientific' welfare programmes. The NGOization of development as well as of governance seems to be strengthening the domination of 'civil society' over the rural people at large by way of state-led political actions, managerialism and philanthropy. The language of development in the sphere of NGOs is not only administrational but also apolitical, and thus has become unintelligible to the average rural people. As a result of which the space of interaction between the actors of NGOs and the poor has become highly bureaucratized. Issues of rights have under these circumstances become ever more elusive. The procedural development, which sprang up as part of NGOization, would at best lessen the sufferings of the poor by means of some palliative measures, and therefore ultimately validating the system of deprivation operational in domain of employment. As the issues of economic growth get prioritized, the NGOization of development has brought into vogue. Most interestingly, the NGOs are going to be thought of as civil society in particular by the aid community, who, as Jenkins (2001, 251) argues, 'has taken the most promiscuous of ideas and fashioned it to suit its own unique culture and purposes'. Whatever the actual sense of civil society and the NGOs may be, the aid agencies have developed a culture of NGOization of development in the name of involvement of civil society only with an aim of turning the political terrain in rural areas into an apolitical terrain which promotes a culture of de-politicization and bureaucratization among the poor. These transformations which are induced by the institutional development agents have not only been thwarting the possibility of social protest, but also been averting the emerging process of right-oriented consciousness of the poor.

Notes

1 The Tagore family to which Pradyot Coomar Tagore belonged had been renowned for its consistent contribution in expansion of modern science, literature, music and medicine in undivided Bengal. This family had spent lot of money for these kinds of works throughout more than one century. See Sarkar (2016, 43).
2 Chatterjee refers for this quotation to *The Statesman*, 16 August 1928.
3 See the online version, Marx/Engels Internet Archive (Marxists.org) 2000. Downloadable at www.marxists.org/archieve/marx/works/1845/german-ideology/
4 Chatterjee believes that this trend of commitment to growth among the urban middle class is an emerging phenomenon (2010, 8–10).
5 In the People's Republic China, too, the NGOs didn't exist even as late as till 1996. The scholars reported 'that China had almost no NGOs working in the areas of social welfare, development, or environmental protection'. In last two decades, however, there has emerged an explosion of NGOs. See for details Hsu (2010, 259) and Howell (1996, 207).
6 The concerned organization had been very active in mobilizing the people of various sections particularly the agricultural labourers during the period 2006–2001 when West Bengal has witnessed large-scale demonstrations from every corner against the then government. All these demonstrations had ultimately culminated into an end of more than three decades rule by the Left Front government.
7 These activists were actually attached with the Naxalite movement that emerged in 1967 based on the peasants' issues in the northern part of the state, but soon began to shake up the youth, the educated youth of the urban areas in particular, of the entire country. After a while, this movement was severely crushed by the state police with many of the activists were tortured, murdered and put in the prison. A number of activists who could escape the police' brutality became elusive and under cover. While some activists floated NGO-like organizations to pose apolitical, some others became somewhat disillusioned with politics, and began to work as activists as part of the NGOs. The activists mentioned in our study constitute the latter.
8 The United Progressive Alliance (UPA) was an electoral alliance formed in 2004 under the leadership of the Congress party on basis of a common minimum programme.

9 On behalf of this organization, the activists filed public interest litigation (PIL) against the state government (Left Front) regarding the issues related to 'right to life' and 'right to food' in the Supreme Court. They won the case, and the judges of the Court delivered an important judgement particularly on the right to life issue.
10 See for details Thapa and Sijapati (2004).
11 The NGOs like Action Aid, DRCSC and CUTS International, and the 'civil society' organizations like Nagarik Mancha, Shramajeebi Haspatal, and NAPM were active in shaping the public opinion during that period.
12 Pradan believes, as it has written in its website, 'the poor must be enabled to break free from their past, developing an alternative vision of their future'. 'They must be equipped with the technical, organizational, negotiating and networking skill'.
13 Ashis Nandy argues that 'it became a general tendency in scholarly circles to translate geographical time into chronological space' (2012, 40).
14 See for details the website of the Department of Land Resources, Government of India–Ministry of Rural Development. www.dolr.nic.in/dolr/guidewd.asp
15 A *hapa* requires around 600–3,000 feet area though the ideal size is 5 percent of the land area where it is going to be constructed. The standard size of a *hapa*: the length 30–60 feet, the breadth 20–50 feet and the depth is 10–12 feet. See for detail Banerjee (2012).
16 The study has been conducted in the same area where I have also done my field work in the year 2010.
17 In Molian GP of Hirbandh block, the number of beneficiaries leaped to 868 in the year 2008 (Banerjee 2012, 2).
18 The proportion of landholdings has increased 0.31 acre on average. As a result of construction of hapa, the owners could convert the fallow lands into cultivable lands. (See also Banerjee 2012).
19 The extent of inputs for cultivation is now much, and the cost of the inputs is increasing. In contrast, the price of their produce is also at the mercy of the market.
20 Mukherjee, the development coordinator of the organization, informs me during an informal discussion held at Kolkata, West Bengal, in the month of January 2016. He was visiting India as part of his work and supervising the projects in rural areas which are funded by his organization.
21 See also Basu (2016), who has studied the effects and meanings that migration and collective remittances would hold for the people in places of origin, including in Gujarat.

References

Basu, Sudeep. 2016. 'Diasporas Transforming Homelands: Nuancing "Collective Remittance" Practices in Rural Gujarat.' *Economic and Political Weekly* 51 (41): 54–62.
Bornstein, Erica. 2009. 'The Impulse of Philanthropy.' *Cultural Anthropology* 24 (4): 622–651. doi: 10.1111/j.1548-1360.2009.01042.x
Chandhoke, N. 2001. 'The "Civil" and the "Political" in Civil Society.' *Democratization* 8 (2): 1–24. http://dx.doi.org/10.1080/714000194
Chatterjee, Arnab. 2007. 'Welfare, Personalism and Hegel in Colonial Night: The Forgotton Readings of Brajendranath Seal.' SARAI, CSDS Readers List.
Chatterjee, Arnab. 2010. 'Objective Helping, Hegel and Three Indian Reformers in Colonial Civil Society Prefacing the Perasonalytical History of Social Work.' *Indian Journal of Social Work* 71 (2): 145–166.
Chatterjee, Partha. 1984. *Bengal: 1920–1947: Land Question*. Calcutta: K P Bagchi.
Chatterjee, Partha. 1997. *The Present History of West Bengal: Essays in Political Criticism*. New Delhi: Oxford University Press.

Chatterjee, Partha. 2004. *The Politics of the Governed: Reflections on Popular Politics in Most of the World*. New Delhi: Permanent Black.

Copeman, Jacob. 2011. 'The Gifts and Its Forms of Life in Contemporary India.' *Modern Asian Studies* 45(5): 1051–1094. doi: 10.1017/S0026749X11000205

Foucault, Michel. 1982. 'The Subject and Power.' *Critical Inquiry* 8(4): 777–795.

Howell, J. 1996. 'NGO-State Relations in Post-Mao China.' In *NGOs, States and Donors*, edited by D. Hulme and M. Edwards, 202–215. New York: St. Martin's Press.

Hsu, Carolyn. 2010. 'Beyond Civil Society: An Organizational Perspective on State-NGO Relations in the People's Republic of China.' *Journal of Civil Society* 6 (3): 259–277. http://dx.doi.org/10.1080/17448689.2010.528949

Jenkins, Rob. 2001. 'Mistaking "Governance" for "Politics": Foreign Aid, Democracy, and the Construction of Civil Society.' In *Civil Society: History and Possibilities*, edited by Sudipta Kaviraj and Sunil Khilnani, 250–258. Cambridge: Cambridge University Press.

Marx, Karl. 1932. A Critique of the German Ideology. Online Version: Marx/Engels Internet Archive (marxists.org) 2000.

Nandy, Ashis. 2012. 'Theories of Oppression and Another Dialogue of Cultures.' *Economic and Political Weekly* 47 (30).

Sarkar, Benoy Kumar. 2016. *Banglar Jomidar* (In Bengali). Kolkata: Seriban.

Shrestha, Celayne Heaton and Ramesh Adhikari. 2011. 'NGOization and de-NGOization of Public Action in Nepal: The Role of Organizational Culture in Civil Society Politicality.' *Journal of Civil Society* 7 (1): 41–61. http://dx.doi.org/10.1080/17448689.2011.553420

Thapa, D. and B. Sijapati. 2004. *A Kingdom under Siege: Nepal's Maoist Insurgency, 1996–2004*. London: Zed.

Newspapers, magazines, reports and other media

Banerjee, Partha Sarathi. 2012. 'Impact Study of Hapa and Its Multiple Uses in Bankura District.' International Water Management Institute (IWMI). Downloadable at https://agriknowledge.org/files/x633f107f

Roy, Dayabati.2015. *Somajtottwo, Jatpat o Shreni [Sociology, Caste and Class]* (In Bengali). Kolkata: Sholoana.

Roy, Dayabati and Partha Sarathi Banerjee. 2006. Documentary Film, Abaadbhumi.

6 Women, gender and employment in rural West Bengal

Introduction

While such a precarious state of employment prevails in rural areas of West Bengal, the question is how the rural women perform on the employment front. Is their case worse than that of their male counterpart? If yes, what makes their case in employment worse? In fact, the entire field of rural employment as discussed would emerge as a different predicament, if we look at it from the standpoint of women. Thus far, we have attempted to understand the issues of employment in rural West Bengal from any perspective but the gender. Examining from the perspective of gender would disorganize and unsettle the field of rural employment in such a way that it would appear we have seemed hitherto to achieve a little as far as employment is considered. Yet, ironically, women are seen constantly busy in work whatsoever in rural areas. Let's begin to examine rural employment from the perspective of gender. That gender is a social construct, and that its social construction is configured by existing power relations, seems to be a case of belaboring the obvious, if I argue afresh. But the question that arises is whether and how gender as a social construct is being (re)constructed against the backdrop of, on the one hand, recent economic transformation, and on the other, current policy interventions in the field of work, employment and wages. This chapter seeks to explore the socio-political processes by which these gendered inequities are taking new shapes in consequences of socio-economic restructuring as well as of implementation of right-based policy in rural settings of West Bengal. It attempts to understand whether women as a gendered category would construct their individual agency in course of dealing with the right-based policy toward their own ends, and thereby levelling up underlying inequalities.

I take into account, therefore, the question of women's employment to understand, on the one hand, the prevailing gendered structure of power in the domains of work and employment, and, on the other, the impact of changing policy processes on gender and women in rural West Bengal. The right-based agenda, particularly the Employment Guarantee Act, is here case in point for explaining the way in which women are engaging with patriarchal practices to deal with their right to employment. In other words, I start by analysing the way in which women generate their agency by employing newer strategies to make use of this opportunity, albeit in a limited pace, in their own interest, and then I analyse the way the women nurture new kinds of aspirations and contestations in the course of their engagement with social policies. India has been traversing a long trajectory of transformations in gendered division of labour, particularly in women's roles, from the period of colonialism to the recent period of reform. In the period of late colonialism, the nationalist leaders of India had resolved the women's question by creating an image of 'modern (Indian) women' who were, they supposed, superior not only to the western women but also to the traditional women in general and the women belonging to lower classes or castes in particular. The nationalist argument revolved around separation of, on the one hand, the domain of culture into two spheres (the material and the spiritual), and on the other, the domain of social space into two spheres (the *ghar* (inner) and the *bahir* (outer)) (Chatterjee 1989, 1993). The inner is the domain of spiritual to which women belong, whereas the outer is the domain of material where male is represented. Chatterjee argues that this ideological underpinning, i.e. the separation of social space by the nationalists, had stipulated and shaped the gender roles in the period of colonialism, and thereby foreclosed the debate over woman issues in public space until independence. The question arises about whether this pronouncement of division of social space as well as cultural space by the nationalists would at all contribute to shape gender roles of the broad masses in India, since a considerable section of Indian people at all times live their lives beyond the control of modernization efforts of the nationalists.

It is not deniable that the *ghar* and *bahir* dichotomy has begun to decouple and take a different shape to an extent during the postcolonial period. The government has enacted various acts and legislations regarding gender-related issues and intervened in widespread discriminations against women that have been perpetuated in the *ghar*, or inner domain of the Indians. Since 1970, new waves of feminist movements have surged in India, as in many countries all over the world, and subsequently mobilized the women under their umbrellas. These efforts have also resulted in the formulation of some other policies for the benefit of women. So nothing has remained the same in sphere of gender in India. The question is about the extent to which the dichotomy of public and private as spaces are valid in rural areas of contemporary West Bengal. Finding an answer to this question is urgent since the effects of policies and enactments meant for eliminating the discrimination against women can be limited if the dichotomy of public and private still act as a barrier in garnering the actual benefit of the same. Undoubtedly, the private has now been linked with the public even in rural areas of the country, and the spiritual, the *ghar*, and the material, the *bahir*, have also been fused together more intimately in postcolonial period.[1] However, the manifestation of the linkages between the public and the private in rural areas is somewhat distinct from that of urban areas, as the rural still largely exists as a community. The private and the public as spaces here might somewhat fuse together, but the distinction between private and the public as cultural domain still matters in gender discourse. The nature and extent of gendering, however, differs also in accordance with class, caste and religion. Whatever the nature and extent of gendering may be, gendering of public and private has been ultimately a factor which determines the roles of genders in every field of social lives both in public and private spheres. Needless to say, although gendering as a process has been regulated by power at the helm of society, it is actually nurtured and shaped within the everyday lives of common masses. The outcomes of any legal intervention on the part of the state thus are mostly dependent on the notions of gender the common people cultivate among themselves.

As I mentioned, while the nationalists' resolve has mainly been confined to the urban upper strata, i.e. upper class and castes, rural societies have their own way of constructing gender through everyday social processes. The rural families belonging, particularly, to higher class and castes have in due course been absorbed into this gendered view of space and culture, and subsequently began to see the public space as assigned to men. The division and the consequential assignment of space based on gender has become a dominant *bhadralok* culture, which the rural families belonging mainly to landholding higher castes usually would aspire to emulate. Families from lower echelon of rural societies, in contrast, would merely afford to buy this gendered division of space for their lives and livelihoods. However, almost all families irrespective of caste, class and religion in rural areas of West Bengal are mostly of the belief that the domain of politics belongs to men. In order to manage the gendered bias against women, the government have made two Constitutional Amendments[2] for mandatory representation of rural women in local self-government, the Panchayati Raj Institutions (PRIs), all over India. The report of the 'Committee on Empowerment of Women' (2010) mentions that gender equity and inclusiveness will lead to better delivery of public services that would affect women's lives, and make the PRIs more accountable to the rural populace. Whether the women's empowerment, as Menon (2012, 217) argues, is 'an ally of the state project of building capitalism, essentially "empowering" women to act as agents within the overall development agenda of the state' is definitely a question at this juncture. Even if we believe, for the sake of argument, that these policies are meant for women's empowerment, do these enactments have considerable potentials to empower the rural women? Women's empowerment, as Kabeer defines (1999, 437) in a minimalistic tone, is about the process by which those who have been denied the ability to make strategic life choices acquire such ability. The ability to exercise choice, she explains (ibid.), incorporates three inter-related dimensions – resources (to include not only access but also future claims to both material, social and human resources), agency (including processes of decision making as well as less measurable manifestation such as negotiation, deception, manipulation and subversion) and achievements.

I argue that women's empowerment should be understood in terms of the perspective of gender equality without which the ability to exercise choice can't be possible. Even if one is able to acquire abilities to exercise choice, she cannot accomplish the same because of the existence of entrenched patriarchal culture. The customary law, or the family and the community, assign home, household chores or household economic practices for women, particularly those belonging to higher strata, as spaces for actions. But what do rural women themselves think about the private and public dichotomy? Do they still believe that private being an ideal space for women and public as a space suitable only for men? My earlier research reveals (2017) that the dichotomous conception of private and public is still in practice while in varied extent, and shaping significantly the women's access to power, public space and decentralized governance. The question that arises is the way in which this gendered condition would affect other issues relating to women's lives and livelihoods, and eventually determining the outcomes of implementation of the right-based agenda.

The next section explains the way in which the women's works are made invisible in rural areas, let alone transforming it as paid work. The question arises: what are the implications of these 'invisible' works on part of the women on the overall rural economy, and on the women themselves? How does the class as well as the caste impact on work practices of the women in rural West Bengal? How does the land, as ownership and devoid of ownership, act as a provider of work to women as well as a limit to work in case of the women in rural areas of West Bengal? This is to say, this section describes the dynamic processes of how gender determines the relationship of women both with land and work in rural areas. In other words, the section explains about how the gendered notions shape women's viewpoint to peasant economy, thereby creating a possibility of anti-capitalist resistance. The third section engages with the most complex phenomenon prevailing in rural West Bengal – why the works of women in most cases are not considered as work at all, let alone as employment. It examines the way in which the overwhelming participation of rural women in agriculture in turn makes it a feminized vocation; why the work executed by the women is often regarded as inferior work, and thereby often turning into a low-paid job or unpaid work. It is a truism that gender has a definite role in shaping the mode of this conceptualization. However, it requires analysing empirically the role of gender in formation of this concept. The fourth section explains the policy that having 'transformative potentials' to modify the gender roles in rural society particularly in domain of employment and wages. Although the enactment like the MGNREGA has little potential as far as employment for all is concerned as revealed in my work, this section discusses the way the rural women engage with the act and subsequently bring forward the issues of their employment on the surface. Simply put, do the women utilize the scope to demand equal wages with their male counterparts for same work as consequences of implementation of this act? The last section concludes that the private and public dichotomy still determines the women's performance in employment, and in rate of wages. The Employment Guarantee Act could have made some impact on the overall access of the women to employment, if it would have been implemented in a full-fledged way without any technical flaws. However, the act has such a little potential that the women can hardly use it for equal opportunities in employment, and for pursuing a larger political process in gender terms. As the MGNREGA becomes uncertain, the works in this programme are increasingly feminized. Thus, the greater the proportion of women in the MGNREGA doesn't necessarily ensure greater representation on the employment front. Rather, women's labour which is otherwise invisible is being used here to make land and agriculture more productive.

Women, land and work

While it is the condition that the idea of private and public space still shape women's access to power, public space and decentralized governance, it is also an emerging phenomenon that the women could discharge their duties whatsoever with utmost sincerity. In many instances, they act more efficiently 'within the overall development agenda of the state' than their male counterpart. Women are thus seen as worthwhile to pursue the state project. A block-level leader of the ruling party, for instance, says candidly,

> I had voiced my doubt about reservation of posts for the women initially. However, I realized after a short while that it was a good idea. They are more transparent; they do raise voice against corruption. Women pursue vehemently what they believe as just cause and a necessity.

Chattopadhyay and Dafflo's work (2004) on the impact of women's leadership on policy decisions also reveals that women are transparent and deliver the public goods efficiently. However, whenever I go for field work in rural areas, one thing that strikes me most is not only the women's reluctance to describe their work, but also their aversion to sit idly. When I ask about what they usually do as work, most of them would reply immediately, 'I do nothing. We do not have anything to do, anyway'. I ask the next question, why are you always busy then? They would answer, 'oh! There are no less works within a family. We are to manage our families'.[3] I would always find this contradictory answer for my two aforesaid questions. I understand that they seem to mean that their work can't be considered as work as it is unpaid. However, I realize soon that this issue is not so simple that we would easily explain it in terms of notion of wage. We need to analyse from the notions of gender.

Suppose that a woman in a marginal landholding family manages the household chores, rearing the livestock, and also sharing the farm work with her husband whenever it requires. In this ideal case, if we ask her what she does, she may reply that she does nothing. If we enquire about her husband's work, she would report without any hesitation that her husband cultivates land and thus is the principal bread earner of the family. This is to say, the question is why two persons with relatively similar characteristics hold two different identities under the same circumstances. Significantly, both of them don't earn anything as wage. What differentiates them from each other in that case as two different categories? It is perhaps nothing but their gender which turns them into two different categorical characters. The woman's works are not going to be recognized as work because she is a woman. Similarly, her husband's works are going to be recognized as work because he is a man. The difference between their works is a difference between two genders. The perception of gender does seemingly pervade the entire rural scenario of West Bengal. Even when I myself have tried to analyse the employment scenario of West Bengal, I have tried it first from the perspective of non-gender. Actually, I have done analysis from the perspective of men members of the rural families. It is undoubtedly easier to explain the domain of employment from the perspective of men as most of the policies are meant for them. However, the entire exercise of employment analysis seems to reveal a quite different predicament, if the issues of employment are to be seen from the perspective of gender. Menon (2012, 13–14) perhaps correctly, says that 'the more accurate the information the state has on the kinds of work performed by women, the more fine-tuned its policies on poverty reduction, employment generation and so on'.

While I am not sure about the postulation that the state would fine-tune its policies on employment generation if it has more accurate information on women's work, I am sure that the more accurate information on kinds of work performed by women would, at least, make women's work visible. The visibility of women's work is likely to mean a kind of recognition of their work and thereby denoting one step forward toward gender justice. But, despite the attempt by the government[4] to register the women's work in the census since 1991, the women in my survey are still likely reluctant to inform about their work. This means, the women, and the men too, in rural areas are still customarily not in a position to claim or recognize the women's works. However, the women in rural areas usually perform several kinds of tasks in an economic sphere based on their social position, as my field data transpire, apart from their stereotypical role in the reproduction of labour power in family lives. The reproduction of labour power, in other words, the field of household chores, is not only a tedious job, but a rigorous and energy-consuming affair particularly in rural areas. Why I am saying that the household chores are energy consuming and laborious is due to the fact that most of these works require heavy manual labour and venturing outside the house. Take, for instance, fetching water, collecting fuels whatever it may be, livestock rearing, etc. Women who are being confined to home for performing only household works are generally recognized as happy women in rural areas. These 'happy' women would unhesitatingly inform the data collectors that they don't do anything.

Considering the case of women in rural areas who, household chores apart, are usually engaged in several kinds of other works that are related to economic sphere, it does not seem that the rural economy is a space of men. Rather, men and women are equally but differently participating in economic activities mainly based on their class, caste and religious position, and in accordance with their views regarding public and private space. Take first, for instance, a case of a woman from a substantial landholding family in the Hooghly district. Hers is prosperous agricultural family from the *Mahishya* caste. Along with her sister-in-law, the woman does all works of the household consisting of nine members. The family possesses a couple of bullocks which are needed for cultivation on 16 bighas of land.[5] The woman members of the family have the sole responsibility to look after these animals including a number of ducks and hens the family owns. The *Mahishya* is considered as the dominant caste in this part of the district, and the *Mahishya* neighbourhood is viewed as the *bhadralok* hamlet both by themselves, and by the people belonging to SC and ST communities. There is a strong sense prevalent regarding the public and private division of space among family members including the woman. The woman as well as her sister-in-law is debarred from going to agricultural field for work or any other purposes. However, she has been engaged in agriculture-related works whatsoever within the confines of home. The works include processing of crops after harvesting, preparing the seeds for sowing, and also marketing the harvests. Most of the women from this social stratum in the village would perform the same tasks in agriculture in same way. Moreover, her mother-in-law being a veteran woman can break the social barrier between the private and public space, and would usually go to the field for various small jobs thanks to her old age. Nandy (2012, 39) nicely shows recently how the evolutionary principles had begun to be applied even to human life cycle in Europe since the eighteenth century. While he explains the way these ideas were used in early education and in childhood, we can use his ideas to explain the complexity of gender. The young wives are considered here as 'inferior, underdeveloped version of the adult' who is to be guided, 'sternly and coercively, towards productive adulthood, and "normal", "healthy" citizenship'.

Then again, we can show an instance the way caste identity stands as a marker in shaping gender roles of a woman from poor families. A *Mahishya* family in the same village does exceptionally possess no agricultural land. Her husband somehow manages the family working as an agricultural labourer. However, the woman has never worked as agricultural labourer since her family background debars her. She says, 'being a wife of a *bhadralok* family, how can I work as a day labourer on other's lands. I, therefore, try to earn some money by weaving cloths at home'. Caste here does reshape the roles of class in production of gender-based works. Let's move to another example of a woman who belongs to a SC landless family. Her family cultivates a meagre proportion of land by leasing in from a co-villager. While her husband has recently started a small business of selling vegetables, she takes the responsibility of cultivating the land in question. She is young and energetic and not debarred socially from working outside home. Like other family members, she doesn't nurture any idea of public and private space in her everyday life and enjoys working outside. She has to walk daily a distance to fetch even drinking water from a government installed tube-well. Being a leader of SHGs, and the woman's organization of the CPI (M) party, she would perform a number of roles confidently. However, when asked about the involvement of her sister-in-law who lives in the same neighbourhood, she replies, 'she doesn't come out from the house as she has recently gained her prestige. After her husband's ascendency to the post of panchayat Pradhan, she has been showing reluctance to go outside for any kind of work'. Interestingly, the Pradhan's family also depends mainly on sharecropping though a fair proportion of land (4 *bighas* of land). And, the Pradhan's wife always takes part in agricultural works that are done at home. It seems that the Pradhan's family is going to experience a budding transformation in its family character. The family has slowly adopted a *bhadralok* culture which consists in a gendered view of public and private space.

What is clearly manifested in this narrative is that the women irrespective of their social position would take part in the rural economy, while the nature and extent of their participation vary based mainly on the class position and their gendered view of space. This apart, another significant phenomenon that becomes evident is that the land stands as a pointer in determining the nature and extent of women's work in rural areas. However, notwithstanding the existence of various legislations regarding women's land rights, the women usually don't customarily enjoy the right to land. I argue that women's work in rural areas has not adequately been considered as work owing mainly to the fact that the women's legal right whatsoever are rarely put into practice. I would give ground for my argument on the basis of the evidence drawn from women's reasoning for their participation in an anti-land acquisition movement. For the first time during my decade-long field work in rural areas, I have seen the women were explicit about their own work on and achievement from land. The women of Kadampur,[6] as in other villages of West Bengal, enjoy hardly any legal right to agricultural land (Agarwal 1994) 'despite gender-progressive legislation'; however, they perceive that they would hardly survive without land. In fact, the women from different landholding sections enjoy a little of what the property inheritance laws have assigned to them, since these laws have rarely been implemented. Though 'several significant gender inequalities are embedded in the Hindu Succession Act, and their extent varying by region and community' (Agarwal 1999), the Indian Hindu women[7] are legally entitled to enjoy some inheritance rights to land and other properties. The Hindu Succession Act of 1956, by which the property rights of the Hindus are governed, and which is covering about 82 per cent of the Indian population, has been formulated in a long process of complex and contentious interaction between the state, on the one hand, and different segments of the population, on the other.[8] The agricultural land of the Hindu families in rural areas of West Bengal are usually fragmented and inherited through the lines of the male descendants. The sons are supposed to be customarily entitled to get ownership of agricultural land, and daughters are expected to be satisfied with the dowry.[9]

When asked about her land right, a woman replies,

> I don't possess any land in my own name. In rural areas, in fact, no woman inherits land. Our fathers somehow managed to get us married…. They had to spend a lot of money for paying dowry in our marriages. We are not inclined to claim a part of land from our brothers. They have also to live off depending on this ancestral land. Furthermore, if I demand a part of our ancestral land, the kinship ties would be astringent. We would not be able to visit our parental houses anymore.

This sort of reasoning seems to be common not only among the women of Kadampur, but also among the women in other areas of West Bengal. These women are hardly aware of the Hindu Succession Act, which is recognized as the chief legislation that governing the inherence of property in India. Are they entitled to, however, any right to the landed property of their in-laws' families? Another woman from a small landholding family that having one acre of agricultural land explains that 'this piece of land belongs to my father-in-law. It is the property of our family. We including all our family members do cultivate, and live off the land. Nobody can force us to part with the land'. Being completely unaware of her legal right prescribed by the Hindu Succession Act to the widows of the male successors,[10] she believes that she has a natural right to this piece of land that belongs to her husband or her in-law's family. Women belonging to the families of sharecroppers and the landless have another story which seems to have made the situation of women's land rights multifaceted. The women are generally not registered as *bargadars* or sharecroppers in West Bengal. Notwithstanding their high level of involvement in agricultural production, they are rarely recognized as *bargadars* or sharecroppers. However, a policy directive of West Bengal government in 1992 pledges that during the redistribution of land, 'to the extent possible' government-allocated land should be granted either to a woman individually or jointly to husband and wife. But the pattern of land redistribution suggests that the allocation of *pattas*[11] tends to reinforce existing gender inequalities in property right. A study shows (Development and Planning Department 2004, 36) that among the *pattas* distributed so far by the government of West Bengal, only in 9.7 per cent cases joint *pattas* have been issued in the name of both husband and wife, while only in 5.94 per cent cases, *pattas* have been issued in the name of a woman (Brown and Das Choudhury 2002). It seems that the policy has not been pursued at grass roots level, perhaps in keeping with the patriarchal tradition of the society. Even when the joint *pattas* or *pattas* are issued in the name of a woman, the women can seldom enjoy independence to use the piece of land on her own choice (Gupta 2000).

However, the women belonging to these unregistered *bargadar* families felt themselves more vulnerable, and hence vigorously participated in anti-land acquisition movement. They had perhaps anticipated that once acquisition was over, their families, since having no legal rights over the land, would rarely be entitled to any compensation or rehabilitation programme offered by the government. A woman belonging to a sharecropper family expresses a well-founded fear of loss of subsistence,

> (E)arlier we could manage food only for half the day, and had to starve for the rest. Both my husband and I have worked on other's land, sharecropped in some land and reared goats depending on the land being acquired. After years of hard labour we could have bought 5 *cottahs*[12] of land and thus at last we get into the path of a decent earning.

Thus, when the government stepped forward to acquire the land by virtue of a colonial Land Acquisition Act, 1894,[13] the peasant women, cutting across different landholding families as well as sharecropper and landless families, objected to the government move possibly by virtue of the 'subsistence ethic' (Scott 1976). In fact, the women, particularly those from the marginal peasant category, would participate in the land movement, and subsequently interact with the organized domain of politics by thoroughly pursuing their 'right to subsistence' ethic. The subsistence ethic or 'the fear of food shortages', as Scott (ibid., 2) argues, and the above-mentioned woman indicates, is 'a consequence of living so close to the margin'. In course of Singur anti-land acquisition movement, when the dominant discourse was mostly centred around a narrative of new livelihood possibilities, i.e. jobs, alternate land or compensation, whatever it may be, for either the men or, in some cases, the families as a whole, the participant women seldom bought this narrative simply due to the fear of ruin of their families. The possibility of profit maximization in a new economy as assured mainly by the government might make the women least bothered about it. What bothers the women most is the subsistence of their families.

The women did not even bother to ask about their part as women in this grand narrative advocated by the government. They rarely asked about why they were not recognized as primary stakeholders of the land that marked for acquisition, and about why they were discriminated as far as ownership of the means of livelihood is concerned. They seemed anticipated, as I have argued elsewhere (2013), that they would be the worst sufferers once the lands are acquired. Because it seemed that they were well aware of the fact that women would become the first victim once the families face a disaster. In fact, it may appear that the women of Kadampur have been much swayed by the patriarchal ideology of Hindu society in which women are treated conventionally as dependents of either their husbands or fathers or sons. Family identity can exert such a strong influence on perceptions of the Indian rural women, Sen (1990, 6–7) argues, they find the question of personal welfare unintelligible. They would interpret personal welfare in terms of their reading of the welfare of the family. The prosperity of the family seems to be recognized as the ultimate goal of the Hindu women in dominant conventional discourse. Of course, the manifestations of this convention vary according to caste, class and region, and according to some other factors, like access to modern education. In our case, the women are apparently satisfied with an arrangement in which the lands and other properties are owned or occupied by either their families or their male counterparts. And so the resistance of the women against land acquisition in the village was very much conditioned by the existing power structure, i.e. the dominant patriarchal ideology. Had it addressed the gender discrimination that persists on the issues of land right and other means of livelihood, women could have been a determining factor in the movement affecting its outcome in a more positive way. Having no gender-specific agenda, and the significant agency of its own, this resistance is, as Jeffery and Jeffery (1994, 130–131) stated, 'also limited by the extent to which the ruling ideology controls people's consciousnesses'.

While it might not be untrue that the women of Kadampur rarely bother about legal entitlement of women in landed property owing to their preoccupation with patriarchal ideology, it is also significantly true that they don't bother about legal entitlement since they are more risk-averse. I would like to extend my argument a little further in this occasion based firmly on the moral economy of the subsistence ethic. Another major reason, I argue, behind their vigorous participation in the anti-land acquisition movement since the very beginning is nothing but their 'primordial goal', i.e. a reliable subsistence (Scott 1976, 5). The fear of loss of subsistence had barred them to buy the narrative of industrialization. The subsistence security which they achieved through consistent economic efforts in everyday lives based mainly on the land, whatever their rights may be, has been of their prime importance. These practices of the 'desire of subsistence security' that grew out in the economic lives but being experienced socially 'as a pattern of moral rights', as Polanyi argues, and Scott (1976, 6) follows systematically, 'were nearly universal in traditional society and served to mark it off from the modern market economy'.[14] What I try to argue is the women in rural societies have more been likely swayed by the primordial ideal of the peasant culture. When their male counterparts have been relatively more engrossed in modern market economy and the narrative of the state, the women have been all through framing their argument based on the subsistence ethic. Not only in the said anti-land acquisition movement, but also in their normal everyday lives, they are more concerned about the subsistence security of their families.

If we consider women's activities and their frame of interpretations in the context of subsistence ethic, we may uncover different outcomes from the processes of gender in rural areas of India. We might also find a few anti-capitalist undertones if we try to understand the women' roles and arguments in terms of the subsistence ethic of peasant culture. In other words, instead of viewing women as individual achiever in gender justice term, it is better, I suggest, to analyse them from the perspective of peasant ethics for the reason that it would give us some clues to treat gender in a different way. And, this different treatment of gender would give us a scope to understand the anti-capitalist content in women's agency and in women's movements in rural areas. For instance, first take the women's perception of work for understanding gender processes in a different way. The women would rarely consider their work on individual basis particularly in rural areas. They are so organically attached with, and committed to the families, that they are even reluctant to count their work. This means, the works are organically part of the women. The family chores are, as it were, the sphere of the women. The women possess it. It is, of course, a kind of manifestation of the gendered view of home. And the mood of homemaking bestows on them the responsibilities of reproduction of labour processes as well as of protection of their families. To the extent that it is a choice, it functions as an ideological barrier against any kind of intervention from the outside, be it counter-ideological or material. But, if the aforesaid roles the women do usually play have become a compulsion, it would become an arbitrary power. In our case, the participant women in the anti-land acquisition movement endeavoured to resist the industrialization effort or, in other words, the capitalist intervention into their home and subsistence economy. The women, in fact, have been more vehement than their male counterpart who are somewhat capitalistic in their view as because of the fact that the former is relatively much engrossed in traditional peasant ethic.

Take the case of, similarly, the women's reluctance to pursue the land ownership issues in the context of legislation. It is really a fact that despite the existence of various legislations regarding women's land rights, the women rarely enjoy the right to land in practice. Why? It might be a reason that the women are hardly aware of the legislations that they could implement. But, I argue, had they been even aware of it, they would have rarely implemented the same. It is not probably, as commonly held, due to the lack of their courage to put it into practice. Instead, as they believe, these legislations are not reasonably practicable to their need.

It appears that the implementation of these legislations would incapacitate their subsistence economy whatsoever. The two instances I have mentioned earlier in this chapter have clearly revealed the apprehension of incapacitation. The former reasons why she does not want to claim her 'legal' part from her parental property. She knows that the partitioning of the landed property would certainly make her brothers' families ruin. Morally, it is perhaps not desirable in rural society. If she does parting, she would never go to the parental home as the relatives would certainly become unsociable. On the other hand, the latter does complicate the issues further when she treats the landed property of her in-laws as her own. She believes that she is the natural proprietor of this land, and she resists forcefully if anybody forces them to part with the land. All these reasons are actually lined with the subsistence ethic of peasant economy. The reasons of the peasantry seem to be different from the capitalist reasons of market economy.

Similarly, the women in land movement did throw out the capitalist narrative of prosperity, and thus didn't even engage in negotiating with the state and political parties over their predicament. They boldly resisted the acquisition of their lands, instead of even bothering a little to ask about their part as women in the proposal scripted and advocated by the government. They seemed like they didn't have any trust in governmental technology of dividing and categorizing the people who were going to lose their lands that were marked for acquisition into various stakeholders. To them, it appeared, there was a little meaning of gendered-based discrimination as far as ownership of the means of livelihood is concerned, when their entire peasant community is in serious stake. This is to mean, the patriarchal ideology is deeply rooted in women's way of life and so is the peasant ethic. As compared to the men who have long since been interacting with the market economy and outer world, the women in rural areas, though being not detached from market and capitalist production, are still culturally absorbed in peasant economy and ethics. While the peasant ethics of the women is to some extent useful so as to construct the critique of capitalist expansion, the gendered view of the women regarding work and space might hinder their access to employment in rural West Bengal.

Women, employment and wage

As I have showed in the preceding pages, the women in rural West Bengal had always been a substantial part of rural economy particularly of agriculture. But they have nowadays more growingly been participating and perhaps outnumbering their male counterparts in agriculture for some reasons. Due to the frequent crisis in agriculture, and the subsequent out-migration of male members of their families to anywhere in the world in search of jobs, the women are now involved in greater proportion in agriculture. In West Bengal, the phenomenon of out-migration is somewhat new and not so widespread like that in other states. The nature and degree of migration varies on the basis of local specificities (Roy 2013). Whatever the degree of migration may be, women in rural areas do not only labour in multifarious tasks, but also would manage the vocation of agriculture. This means the women would supervise the works of agriculture in their own capacities, and have growingly been linked with the capitalist market economy. What is the impact of their greater participation in agriculture or, broadly, in village economy on their lives and livelihoods? One impact is palpable, according to John's argument which I quote from Vasavi and Swaminathan (2010, 8), that 'the decline in rural and agrarian studies in recent decades' is related, apart from other reasons, 'to trends such as the feminization of agriculture'. While this is the case of rural and agrarian studies, the gender studies might give us some clues to understand the rural in a better way. We are now aware at the closing stage of the book of the fact that the rural economy in India, especially in West Bengal, began increasingly to languish since 1980s, and the state was required to intervene unprecedentedly in rural sphere. Why the rural economy failed to do well is not the focus of this chapter; rather I discuss here gender consequences of the failure of rural economy as far as the provision of employment is concerned. As the agriculture becomes unprofitable, many farmers chose to withdraw from agriculture. As the farmers are reluctant to continue agriculture, many marginal peasants get scope to cultivate their lands on lease, and based on sharing crops. Notably, these marginal peasants grow crops which are usually labour intensive, and which require a meagre amount of capital. They chose, therefore, vegetables, and some other crops like mustard and pulses for cultivation. However, male members of these families, like their counterpart in the families belonging to other landholding categories, tend to be involved in non-farm works since agriculture had become an insecure field for both wage earners and the cultivators. The women from all categories of families are, therefore, left to continue agriculture in the main.

As this is a budding phenomenon, its occurrence definitely varies greatly. During my field survey, I have seen women from small and marginal families busy working in agriculture either as self cultivator or agricultural labourer. For instance, take the case of a woman panchayat member belonging to ST community in the district of Bankura. She labours mainly on her own family land. Her family possesses around 2 acres of land. While she does labour only on land, her husband works as helper in masonry jobs. In all 18 villages, the same situation exists. However, the proportion of women who work as agricultural labourer is not low. In every village, a considerable proportion of women particularly who belong to the SC and ST communities, and also in some instances to the Muslim category, would earn their livelihoods working principally as agricultural labourer. Interestingly, the proportion of woman agricultural labourers varies according to the proportion of SC and ST people of a respective village betraying the phenomenon of high degree of landlessness among these two communities. The fact is that women's works in this context are not invisible unlike other forms of women's work as described earlier as a result of gendered processes, but their daily wages are gendered. Whenever and wherever during my field surveys in 18 villages I asked the rate of operational wages for both men and women, I found a gendered discrimination in wages. All the informants to whom I have enquired about wages have responded in such a way that it appeared it is quite normal to them. Both men and women respond alike as far as the discrimination in wages is concerned. The labour is gendered, so is the work. The gender imprint is so deep in the root of societies that even the political leaders belonging to all political parties, be it the left or right, don't bother about the discrimination in wages. The Equal Remuneration Act has been passed as early as in 1976, but it seems that no one has customarily been bothered about it. So is the strength of gender in rural areas.

Why don't the women themselves demand equal wages from their employers? Do they think that they are not eligible for equal wages to that of men? When asked these questions, a few of them guardedly state that the employers won't agree even if they demanded equal wages. However, most of them are typically reluctant to discuss these issues. Although they never justify gender discrimination explicitly, they appear to rationalize the system implicitly when they say that women would hardly be able to earn like men do. In other words, women consider themselves as different. Why they are different? Because what they are doing are not equal in nature with that of men? Are the works done by women really different from the works of men? If the works of two genders are different, in what way are they different? The works are, as they inform, almost the same, and related to same phase of agricultural work except the one of ploughing, which has been designated exclusively for men. For instance, take the work of plucking paddy seed plants, and the work of sowing those seed plants. In some places, the women usually do plucking, and men do sowing. Who will decide which work is heavy, or which work requires more efficiency? Actually, what Menon argues (2012, 13) is true that employers do segregate 'men and women into different parts of the labour process, and then pay less for the work that women do'. Why don't we claim that what women do actually requires more care and attention, and thus their work is more efficient? More significantly, if they are not efficient, why have they been drawn with utmost efforts into various kinds of state projects so as to alleviating poverty in rural areas?

Why I argue that women's patience and care should be more remunerative is due to the simple fact that the product of their efficient labour actually costs much. I provide you with an example to explain my argument. In many villages of West Bengal, women particularly from marginal families are engaged in craftwork on sari for a meagre amount of remuneration. The craftwork which they usually create takes long hours of tedious labour sometimes for a month to finish a sari. Suppose that one woman gives at least 6–7 hours daily for the assigned work and earns a maximum of Rs. 20.00 per day. However, a finished sari with this craftwork is generally exchanged in international market for lump sum money. The price of a sari actually varies with quality and extent of the craftwork on the respective sari. Hence, the fact is that the meticulous and sincere labour on the part of women has a value in the market. But, whenever this piece of work is going to be branded as a product of women's labour, its labour value goes down. At this juncture, what is measured is actually the type of gender. In other words, the product without a gender tag, i.e. the woman tag, costs much. The capitalist market makes profit from both ends. It profits by way of, on the one hand, exploiting the value of labour in the name of women, and on the other, selling the product in the market for huge price without naming those women who have made it with utmost care and efforts. This means, the capitalist market would exploit the gender for maximizing its profit. However, these rural women whose labour as presumed commonly as producing a little were begun to be mobilized by the government since the 1980s to play significant roles in alleviating poverty. At the very juncture when India's economy was liberalized, and when the post-liberalized consequences were mostly unpredictable, rural women were summoned to tackle the consequences whatsoever in the domain of lives and livelihoods.

It was the Self-help Groups (SHGs) by which state interventions could gain ground among rural women all over India, and thereby categorizing them with an aim of long-term management of poverty. The SHGs are now ubiquitous in all societies of rural India and of West Bengal in particular. From north to south of the state, I have noticed the vibrant presence of SHGs among women mainly from marginal families. The question that arises is notwithstanding the presence of SHGs as well as other development policies initiated principally by the panchayats for a couple of decades, why poverty, rather the problem of unemployment, has still been in full swing in rural areas of West Bengal. In all surveyed villages, the active women-centred SHGs were led either by panchayat members or by the NGOs. Through the initiatives of the panchayat or NGOs, the SHGs would act, it seems, to connect the society with market economy, as informed by Mr. Debnath in 2010, a veteran SHG 'promoter'. Being an experienced mentor and the chief functionary of an NGO, Mr. Debnath states that women are favoured more than men for the SHGs as they are less corrupt and less hankering. This means, the women as binding category play greater roles in establishing market in rural economy. Scholars have, however, doubts about the objectives, as claimed by the government, of SHGs built among women. While John (2010, 8) articulates that women of the SHGs have actually 'become the safety net for poverty alleviation and development strategies, precisely in the rural areas beset by stagnation if not crisis', Menon (2012, 216–217) believes that these are the policies of 'using women's specific skills and experience produced by their location within the patriarchal society' to make governmental agenda successful. I argue that while rural women are targeted for preparing their families towards major social and cultural transformations in near future, their gendered skills and experiences are meaningfully used as the safety net for managing poverty in rural areas by means of the SHGs and other programmes, Moreover, their skills, money and resources, whatever they may be, are going to be tapped for larger business in market economy.

As discussed in the preceding chapter, an NGO which began its work during the late 1980s in the district of Purulia endeavoured first to form SHGs among women from marginal families with a single aim to curb abject poverty. The question that arises is why the women are its preferred target. Notably, when it would embark on this project of SHGs, the government too had already considered SHGs as an anti-poverty measure. Because, the leader of the said NGO replied,

> the women can play greater roles in managing the menace of poverty. Through their small savings, they can do lot of things. They can start small business,

trade and even horticulture with the capital they can get on credit. We have got effective results from the activities of women's SHGs in this regard.

I agree, for the sake of the argument, that woman members of the SHGs would achieve a favourable condition to start a business, trade or horticulture in villages. No matter what the infrastructural hindrances are. Would they however be able to perform successfully the trade they have attempted to pursue in current climate of neoliberalism? During my previous field work conducted in two villages of Hooghly district in 2006, I found the way the women who had made their living through preparing and exchanging parched rice commercially were doomed to be impoverished when a couple of high-tech machines being installed for doing the same perched rice business in the locality. In other words, it is perhaps certain that there is hardly any safe space or a well-demarcated 'non-corporate zone', as Chatterjee argues (2004), where the peasantry or marginal people in rural areas can do their business without experiencing any coercion from the big or corporate capital. In face of the competition with corporate capital, these micro-credit businesses tend normally to decline. Wherever and whenever these micro-credit businesses are helpfully managed by way of some encouraging interventions, rather supports, on the part of the government, the NGOs or the political parties, women in SHGs ably keep hold of the business though only at a subsistence level. In fact, the enterprising women can only manage to get just a cost of their labour, albeit at a very irrational rate, in the exchange processes. This means the domain of women's small enterprises becomes a field of exploitation by big capital. One can gauge a palpable discrimination in prices of the products made by the women's SHGs especially in big corporate showrooms. While women earn a meagre amount of money in lieu of their labour, and even of their savings or capital whatsoever, the big businesses can accumulate the whole profits.

The same scenario seems to persist all over rural West Bengal. Along with local material resources and skilled labour, patience and transparency of rural women have directly been tapped through the capitalist market processes. And there is as such no Chinese wall between the 'corporate capital' and 'non-corporate capital' so that women's efforts in business sector can be protected from the wrath of big capital. Whatever the extent and nature of exploitation may be, the linkages of both women's labour and local resources with the larger market are having long-term impact on rural economy. Moreover, I could find two more interesting phenomena that are budding at rural grass roots. First, while the women's way of life is utilized for poverty management, and for tapping the local resources including labour for the purpose of capitalist expansion, their lives are also being intended for a change towards a capitalist mode of life. Two, they have eventually become the drivers of putting various policies or agenda of the government in practice. Many NGOs are working at the grass roots so as to 'educate' the women through the platform of the SHGs. For instance, take the NGO I have already mentioned to explain the way the NGOs have been grooming the women. The women are not only taught by the NGO leaders who have the responsibilities to manage the SHGs, but also are trained about how to deal with everyday lives. I have taken a look at the entire process through which the savings and credits are being managed by the women. It is really not just an account-keeping job in which the leaders of the NGOs would intervene and manage; it is also a question of leadership which rural women would automatically possess as part of their daily lives. The rural women seem have been chosen for these 'group-based activities' owing to their organic relationship among themselves, and to their emotional commitment to the distress of other women. The gendered attributes of the women are harnessed here for the purpose of development whatsoever.

Many attempts have thus been taken to inculcate the ways of modern living. The leaders of the NGOs would train and educate the women in SHGs on daily basis as part of their programmes. Paying a surprise visit to a block-level office of this NGO, I realized that they have several tasks to do except the micro-credit things. Interestingly, a couple of staff members of the office are designated as community leaders who have the tasks of making the women in particular aware of 'socially unjust issues', and motivating them to be proactive to do away with the same through rigorous campaigns. The rural women are, therefore, not only familiar with development terminologies like beneficiary, scheme, action plan, sub-plan, implementation, community, awareness campaign, group, and many social policies implemented by the panchayat, but are also to be habituated to consume various items which have been introduced recently as consequences of their 'group' activities and campaigns.[15] Debnath, the veteran NGO leader, perhaps rightly interprets that 'the corporate groups are interested to form and expand the network of SHGs with a single aim to promote their products '. Women are the appropriate category for motivating towards new consumer goods as they would usually decide about what to buy for family consumption. Moreover, the networks of the SHGs have been a good platform to mobilize the votes among them for or against the respective political parties. As the women who have been active in SHGs are also often involved either with parties or the panchayats in rural areas, it is easygoing task for the political leaders to propagate their electoral politics among women through the SHGs. A woman panchayat pradhan, North 24 Parganas district, who happens to be a leader of SHGs candidly says, 'I do supervise these SHGs since long. I was first active in SHGs, and have gradually become interested in politics, and subsequently become the panchayat pradhan'. This is to mean, two types of activities here complement each other. And, more significantly, being a leader of the panchayat and the party as well as the SHGs, she has been enjoying a privilege to utilize the platform of SHGs for influencing the half the sky of rural society on her party's behalf. Hence, the SHGs which are usually thought as part of 'civil society' or 'civil society space' in the NGO's vocabulary are actually very much politicized, and most often act upon the appendage of political parties.

In course of my discussion with leaders of two NGOs, I realize that the SHGs are favoured by the NGOs in their several collaborative efforts with the government to implement various policies. The involvements of women from the SHGs are actually here factor functional to structure and implement various policies and acts like the MGNREGA and SGSY. In its bid to construct watershed projects as part of the MGNREGA, the NGO working in Purulia has used energetic efforts of the women who are active in SHGs not only for making a consensus among the community members in favour of the scheme, but also for supervising the process of implementation effectively. The gendered virtues of the women are therefore here cases in point. Women's unity actually matters much in pursuing policies towards its implementation. It reveals that women would quickly reach a unity. Around nine woman panchayat members of a GP in the district of Murshidabad inform in unison that they reach a unity instantaneously among themselves, no matter what their party affiliations are, on various issues. This means, the issues are more important to them than the party identities. Likewise, when the NGO faced a problem of disunity among the villagers regarding a watershed development, it called for the support of the women from SHGs to clinch the matter. Some of the villagers had actually expressed, on the one hand, their doubt about the extent of benefit from the scheme, and on the other, their fear of the loss of land that was needed for making a watershed. The women took a role to convince their counterparts that the watershed might be of their benefit, and eventually became a stakeholder to supervise the schemes. The women who are, inherently, as I argue, part of the moral economy, and effectively away from the narrative of mainstream development have actually growingly become a driving force of market economy and the state projects. Their gendered roles and views are being used here to accomplish the larger mission of the state. While the women have been a budding but influential category to make the state deeper, they have hardly been benefiting from the legislations like the Equal Remuneration Act enacted in 1976 that aimed at establishing gender justice at least to an extent.

Policies, gender and social transformation

The social policies that are meant for social transformation, be it direct or knock-on, have actually been becoming spaces of domestication of gender in rural areas. And, the labour markets, as we know and Elson has rightly reconceptualised (1999), are gendered institutions. It is also not unknown to us, as Razavi rightly reasserts (2012), that gender justice will not occur automatically until and unless interventions are made by way of social mechanism to curb the power that shapes the gender inequalities in a particular society. The labour markets in agriculture and off-farm work, as Carswell and De Neve (2013b, 82) argue, 'remain highly segregated, wage gaps continue to be substantial', 'and women's mobility and access to rural and urban employment severely constrained'. In our case, I find that the wage gaps between men and women remains around at least Rs.20–Rs.30 in all villages I have conducted field work in West Bengal. This wage gap persists in all cases due mainly to the segregation of work based on gender norms and power inequalities. Razavi (2012, 249) finds a solution 'in the creation of social mechanisms that reduce wage gaps through effective institutions', but Carswell and De Neve (ibid.) are correct when they ask what such social mechanisms might consist of. Critiquing the World Development Report (WDR 2011) which emphasizes 'the importance of reshaping markets and institutions to reduce the gender gaps', the scholars consider 'the recent rise of social protection policies' as well as the MGNREGA

(Carswell and De Neve 2013b, 82) 'that have begun to make significant impacts on men and women alike'. I would, however, question the scholars' conviction that the MGNREGA's gender-friendly design (82–92) 'significantly shaped how it is implemented, who benefits from it, and what its gender-related impacts are' and thereby playing 'as important a role in shaping gender relations as policies and development interventions that are explicitly designed to address gender inequity'. The question that arises here: when even the acts like the Equal Remuneration Act has hardly been implemented in rural areas, how does the Employment Guarantee Act, which didn't take gender equality as its primary objective, play a role in delivering gender justice?

First of all, it is always to be kept in mind that labour markets are not only gendered institutions, but also are class-based institution. And, thus capital plays an important role in determining the dynamics of labour markets in the capitalist regime. If we try to understand the gender component of a particular policy in terms of class processes and mode of production, we would definitely locate a varied and complex understanding of its outcome. An incisive reading of the regulatory framework of the MGNREGA in context of both class and capital can thus give us a different rendering of the act. Had they read it with a lens of class or capital, they would have understood that this act can hardly address gender inequity prevalent in wider rural society. I have argued in detail in the earlier chapters about why the act has very limited scope to provide employment for the rural unemployed people in the long term, and why it is ultimately going to benefit the rural propertied classes. The WDR has actually done justice to the MGNREGA when it is 'silent on … the employment guarantee schemes' that have, as Carswell and De Neve (ibid., 82) expect, 'begun to make significant impacts on men and women alike'. Given the overall limitations, the act has hardly benefited rural women in terms of gender. Instead, as agriculture is increasingly feminized, the MGNREGA follows suit. The question that arises: why is it so? It might appear that women would fare well as far as the extent of their participation in the programme is concerned. But, this phenomenon is nothing but the domestication of gender in a state-initiated project, if we analyse it in terms of gender. Although the women's greater participation in the schemes under the MGNEGA ensures at least to an extent some wage-based work for them, (WDR 2011, 16) 'this increased participation has not translated into equal employment opportunities or equal earnings for men and women'. The WDR has rightly conceptualized, and Carswell and De Neve who quote these words seem also agree with this point, that the increased participation of women in labour market would not automatically translate into gender-just employment and earnings. Had it been translated into gender-just earnings, the women who now dominate agriculture numerically would have earned equal wages with men.

In their own research, the data indicate that the majority of workers in the MGNREGA are dalits and the women. This piece of information is true in both cases – the state level data for Tamil Nadu, and the village level data in their study villages.[16] Of the total sample, it states, 88 per cent of MGNREGA workers are women, and, it might not be out of our context, 47 per cent of the workers have no education at all. The case of West Bengal seems have been somewhat different from that of Tamil Nadu. The state level data indicate that the number of women in the said work is marginally higher than the number of man workers in West Bengal. However, my field survey in West Bengal reveals that the women as compared to men have been taking much interest in the MGNREGA work. The question arises: what does this phenomenon of feminization indicate in our context? I take a clue from the research by the same scholars (Carswell and De Neve 2013b, 86) that 'MGNREGA attracts workers from whom it is increasingly difficult to do other work'. This means, a substantial proportion of women, along with the *Dalits* (76 per cent), in rural Tamil Nadu, as they argue, are barred from mainstream labour markets. The labour markets there, in other words, are so masculinised and dominated by upper castes, that the women, and the *Dalits*, rarely get opportunities to enter. However, the works in the MGNREGA are 'less popular among male workers due to the higher wages they can earn elsewhere', and being subsequently popular among the women, and thereby making the MGNREGA 'successful'. Surprisingly, despite having these clear evidence-based indications in their research, the scholars have failed to interpret that the greater participation of women in MGNREGA has nothing but a manifestation of stereotype gender roles in the labour markets of Tamil Nadu. As the men have left space generated by the MGNREGA, the women got the opportunity to work in large scale with lesser wages from the market rate. Whatever successes the implementations of the MGNREGA have obtained in Tamil Nadu are at best the fulfilment of its target to employ the unemployed poor in rural areas. Whether the implementation of MGNREGA has made any gendered impacts in rural society is to be understood in terms of analysing some other social dynamics. If the wage gap between men and women is one such issue, another is knock-on effect of women's participation on the stereotype gender roles.

Both researches done by Carswell and De Neve (2013b) and Chopra (2015) have tried to show that the MGNREGA includes some 'women-friendly provisions' which would address gender-based inequalities in the labour market, despite its intended goal is not the transformation of gender inequalities. What are those provisions, anyway? First of all, the Schedule II (6) which has given priorities to women for work specifies that the one-third of workers at the worksites must be women (Ministry of Law and Justice, 2005). The question arises about why the act ensures only the one third, a disproportionate representation, of women in the workforce, when it is prioritizing the women for work. It should have guaranteed the proportion of women's participation at least to 50 per cent of workers. The act has thus tried to ensure women's participation in work but with a gender bias. The Schedule II (ibid., 34) which prohibits gender discrimination of wages seems to be nothing new as an earlier act, i.e. the Equal Remuneration Act, 1976, already legally bans gender discrimination in wages for the same work. But the gender discrimination in wages would largely persist in the name of gender-based segregation of works. Here lies the scope of gender discrimination in wages for work under the MGNREGA. The MGNREGA too has retained this loophole for gender discrimination when it categorically mentions that it ensures 'the same wages for the same work'. Actually, we might drop the gender perspective midway if we prioritize women's participation in various so-called development agenda. For instance, I would mention here the version of development ideologues who would address the gender equality in terms of development. The aim of greater gender equality, to them, is to (WDR 2011, xx) 'enhance productivity, improve development outcomes', 'and make institutions more representative'.

Hence, the extent of participation of women in the MGNREGA does not alone seem to make any difference about whether the act would enhance or reduce gender inequalities in rural India. The question is, instead, whether the participation of women in works under the MGNREGA has made any positive impact to decrease the wage gap between men and women both in the said public work, and in larger labour markets. It is also important to enquire about whether the gap in wage between the labour markets and the MGNREGA work has decreased at all owing to the introduction of the MGNREGA in respective areas. Why I am considering it as significant is due to the sheer fact that the wage gap between the labour market and the MGNREGA is a factor that can influence effectively the extent of women's participation. If wages in the labour market are greater than that of the MGNREGA, there is a possibility that the women would participate more in the MGNREGA since men would obviously favour the labour markets for earning a greater wages. Similarly, if the MGNREGA offers greater wages than the operational wages in the labour markets, men would chose to work in the MGNREGA by reducing the possibilities of women's participation. In my own research, like mostly the aforesaid research in Tamil Nadu, it reveals that the gender-based discrimination persists vastly in agricultural labour markets even for the same works as well as in the name of different works.

On the other hand, while the agricultural labourers irrespective of gender have rarely been getting minimum wages in villages of West Bengal, the wages for agricultural labourers would vary a great extent from region to region, even from one panchayat area to another. In several cases, wages in the labour market are much lesser than that of the MGNREGA particularly in the villages I have conducted my field survey. The wages for agricultural labourers vary ranging from Rs. 110.00 to Rs. 190.00 in West Bengal. The wages for the same work for different genders seem to vary not only greatly but also complexly. It is thus expected that man job-seekers in the low-wage areas would opt for the work under the MGNREGA if it is available. And, as soon as men would choose to go for the works in the MGNREGA, the chances for the women to work in the MGNREGA would be little. It is perhaps one of the main reasons why the proportion of women's participation in the MGNREGA in West Bengal is not as much higher as compared to the proportion of woman participants in Tamil Nadu. The proportion of women in MGNREGA of West Bengal has not been so far more than 57 per cent of total workforce.[17] However, the proportion of woman participants in the MGNREGA has growingly been increasing over the years, and the works become feminized by way of representing the women disproportionately in the said act. The extent of feminization has been still somewhat moderate as man workers in the state often find the MGNREGA more gainful as the agricultural wages in the labour markets are lower in comparison with the wages under MGNREGA work. The women are, however, lately getting significant scope to work in the MGNREGA since their men counterpart have been forced to leave the countryside for better earnings. The case in West Bengal is not so different from its counterparts since in the state as well the women who have prior experience of working either as agricultural labourer or marginal cultivator are to join in the work under MGNREGA.

In other words, more and more women belonging to landless and marginal landholding categories are seen working in the MGNREGA schemes in the state. Needless to say, they belong mostly to the SC and ST categories as caste and landholding class are overlapping categories in West Bengal. This means, whatever the nature of discussion may be, we are discussing mainly about the SC and ST women who mostly toil on lands. Notwithstanding the greater wages in the MGNREGA, many man workers in rural West Bengal do not at all rely on works under the act due to its uncertain nature of implementation. If some rules of the regulatory framework of the act had been improvised based on local specificities of the state as being done in Tamil Nadu, albeit in a limited degree, men would have been more interested to work in the schemes under the act. I have argued in detail in the earlier chapters about why implementations of the MGNREGA in West Bengal would hardly attract the rural unemployed men for wage-work, and subsequently limiting further the limit inherent in the design of the act. The works under the act are dependable neither in terms of timely creation of work nor in terms of timely wages. The works as well as its wages have become just an occasional stroke of luck to the expectant rural unemployed in West Bengal. The works under this act do not emerge as a 'last resort' for the rural poor, let alone any positive impact on the gendered discrimination at least in agricultural wages. My work doesn't find any concrete evidence that wages in the labour market have increased, and wage-gap between men and women has reduced as a result of the implementation of the MGNREGA.

The aggregated wages for around a fortnight or so are undoubtedly assets particularly for the rural poor who have always been deficient in means for living. How do the rural poor, however, interpret these earnings? The man informants with whom I have talked have not at all considered these earnings as source of income mainly because of its nature of uncertainty. To them, it is, as it were, an ad-hocism. The women, on the other hand, who have already worked under the act are relatively, as it seems, concerned about the MGNREGA works. They have several criticisms about the foundations of the act and its implementations. Despite the fact that they have expectations, the women scarcely believe that the works under the MGNREGA are an important source of income. This is to mean, the act as it stands now is in no case of the women's interest for a reliable source of income, be it primary or secondary. The women's own words here can give us a clue about what they think about the act. About the limit of work only to 100 days for a family, women have several grievances. A woman participant in the district of Purulia states, 'one job card has been issued for my family having 5–7 members. Hence a few days work for each member of the family is fulfilling the hundred days' quota. We have been denied any more jobs' (Roy 2011). However, they are seemingly more concerned about the non-implementation of the act. Another woman from the same village says (ibid.), 'if we get 100 days' work that would definitely benefit us. But how can it be beneficial if we get only 30–40 days work?'

From north to south or from east to west we might hear the same grievances from the women who have a little interest about the work. A woman from Bankura has the same observation when she candidly informs,

> though 100 days work should be given, we don't hope to get it ever. We last worked in this project three months ago. Now we get this work order for 6 days. We have no power, and cannot even guess when we will get work next time. We depend mainly on raising our livestock. We have to wait indefinitely after putting in our application for work.

The woman from North 24 Parganas may have a different opinion. She says,

> they have arranged this work for now. Then there will be no work, say, for one and half months. Moreover, we have to wait at least for two months to get our wages. We are working dawn to dusk with an empty stomach in this project, but one might even die before he/she gets the payments.

It seems that women in rural areas who have been working under this act are more concerned about the delay of payment for their work. Surprisingly, the act stipulates categorically that the wages under the MGNREGA have to be given within a fortnight. Almost nowhere in West Bengal did I find that the wages were given properly. The same grievances were expressed everywhere. Hence, most of the men folk are beginning to migrate, while women are compellingly joining in the works under MGNREGA in greater number.

This is to mean, the women though having some expectations about the act don't depend on it, at least as it stands now, for their livelihood. They don't even seem consider it as secondary source of income. During the recent past, however, after the change in regime in the year 2011, the state has witnessed a kind of urgency for implementing the MGNREGA on the part mainly of the bureaucracies. After the end of all-pervasive party system maintained by the Left Front government which had been prevailing for more than three decades throughout West Bengal (Roy 2013), the people who were concerned about the issues of unemployment in the state expected to an extent that at least a change would occur in style of implementation of the policies and acts, notwithstanding the fact that many didn't know which way the things were turning. Despite a consistent pressure from the command of the top echelon to arbitrarily implement the MGNREGA, and a direct intervention on the part of the BDOs in village level activities, the act seems to be hardly of relevance to the rural people in West Bengal as far as generation of employments are concerned. By replacing the earlier party system, a different kind of party system have emerged in the state in which a number of power blocks would operate even in a small region, and thereby counteracting each other only to disrupt the policy implementation. This apart, the procedural bureaucracy as well as the existing loopholes in regulatory framework turn the process of implementation into a tiresome task. In several villages, the issues of corruption and the paucity of infrastructure are cited as the main culprits for the poor performance of the act. The increased participation of women in labour market would not, therefore, automatically translate into gender-just employment and earnings.

The *nirmansahayak* (construction assistant) of a GP in the Cooch Behar district perhaps rightly interprets the act when he says that they lack the minimum infrastructure that are required to run the act smoothly. He said (2015),

> we can't implement the programme without an internet connection as official works have to be carried out through online. We don't have any net connection in this entire panchayat area. We are to use the net connections that available in neighbouring panchayat area for accomplishing our tasks. There too, the server remains down in most part of the day.

However, the question is at this point: what the state would have experienced in terms of gender, had the new government improvised the act for better implementation as the government in Tamil Nadu has done. In Tamil Nadu, the AIDMK government had made two important revisions in the regulatory framework, i.e. the issuance of job cards in the name of both men and women of a particular family, and the cash payment of wages on weekly basis. The first revision has recognized the existence of woman in a family officially through mentioning their names as job-seekers. The second one would, on the one hand, fulfil the aims of the act by giving wages in time and need, and on the other, encourage the day-labourers in rural areas in participating in works under the MGNREGA by way of daily wages.[18]

Whether the MGNREGA has a positive impact on the labour market as well as on the wage gap between men and women is actually not at all a question in our context since, I have argued elaborately, the MGNREGA has not been fared well in West Bengal as far as its over-all implementation is concerned. Though the workers would earn wages sooner or later if they get a chance to work under the MGNREGA, the act, in case of West Bengal, does have limited potential to influence the increase in wage in labour markets what has been observed, arguably, in other states (Berg et al. 2012; Dutta et al. 2012; Jeyaranjan 2011). However, agricultural wages have increased, albeit a little, during the last decade everywhere in West Bengal while variably based on the local specificities. As I am not sure about whether the increase is due to the impact of the MGNREGA, the question remains to be answered later. What is interesting in our case is that the MGNREGA has become so uncertain that it gets feminized. In other words, gendered roles are domesticated here too. Women's labour is being used to make the land and labour productive in rural areas. It is needless to say that women would enjoy greater dignity in the government work as compared to the work offered by the local landholding families. And, women, including their male counterparts, indulge and enjoy some liberties to work arbitrarily in these kinds of government work.

Conclusion

The aim of this chapter, as I set to explore, is to take stock of gender in work and employment as well as in policies and acts in rural areas of West Bengal. It reveals that the gender stereotype does not only shape roles of the women in work and employment, but also does influence the policies and acts that are meant for 'development' in general, and gender justice in particular. The existing gender stereotype has most often been domesticated in the institutions set up at rural grass roots under the aegis of the state, and thereby recreates inequalities that are undoubtedly durable (Tilly 1999). Although the patterns of works of both genders are changing, gender remains either to shape the new forms of works or to creep in new works and policies in considerable ways. The views regarding the public and private space would change over time among both men and women but still matter substantially to determine the women's work and employment, and also their wages in rural areas. The gendered outlook that the women are weak and inexpert in the works in particular outside their home is largely in vogue. It seems to be thus no respite from gendered discrimination in work and employment in rural West Bengal. The policies and the acts whatsoever meant for establishing gender justice have hardly been in use in rural West Bengal. The MGNREGA, which is considered by the scholars as part of the 'New Rights Agenda', does make any difference as far as women's right to work is concerned. The rural women who belong to marginal peasant families in general and to the SC and ST categories in particular are increasingly participating in agriculture, and the public works that emerged sporadically through implementation of the MGNREGA are hardly experiencing any transformation, as Roy (2014) has argued. While it is true, as Roy (2014) analyses, that rural women's participation in MGNREGA represent no 'rational coping' strategies and tactics of 'everyday resistance', it is also not true as revealed from my analysis, that their actions are 'a series of encroachments into the extant social customs, norms and habits in India', as Roy hypothesizes (22). The increased participation of women in labour market, however, I propose, would not automatically translate into gender-just employment and earnings until and unless some social mechanisms are created to transform the gender-based views.

Notes

1 Owing to the rapid expansion of market economy in the country, the *ghar*, or the private space, has been greatly influenced by the same. The rural societies are of no exception. The family, its consumption pattern and religiosity are closely linked with market and capitalist way of living.

2 The 73rd Constitutional Amendment has made a mandatory provision that no less than the 33 per cent of total seats of the panchayat at all levels, and also of no less than 33 per cent of the total number of offices of the chairpersons in the panchayat at all level would be reserved for the women. Another Constitutional Amendment, which is called the 110th Constitutional Amendment Bill, was passed in 2009 for further enhancement of reservation for the women in all tiers of the panchayat. In 2010, following this latest enactment, the West Bengal government has enhanced reservations for women 33–50 per cent in all panchayat seats, in offices of the chairpersons and also in seats

and offices of the chairpersons reserved for scheduled caste and scheduled tribe in all tiers of Panchayati Raj system.

3 *Sonshare tow awnek kaaj!* (In Bengali).
4 Due to the consistent pressure by the feminists, the government has agreed to collect detailed data about the women since 1991.
5 The lands are very fertile with a multi-cropping character. The family grows potato and boro in those lands as commercial crops.
6 Kadampur is a fictitious name of a village I had studied as part of my doctoral thesis. The village is situated in Singur block, Hooghly.
7 I am referring here only the Hindu women and Hindu Succession Act as most of the people of Kadampur belong to Hindu religion. The women belonging to other religions in India are also more or less legally entitled to enjoy some inheritance rights to land.
8 Agarwal mentions three kinds of inequalities in relation to succession.

> First, among several religious groups, women are entitled to smaller shares than men's. Second, there are specific gender biases pertaining to the devolution of agricultural land.... Third, tribal communities of the north-eastern states continue to be governed by un-codified customary law under which, among patri-lineal tribes, women's rights in land are severely circumscribed and typically limited to usufruct.

9 The system of dowry is still prevalent in India despite the Dowry Prohibition Act passed as long as in 1961. Dowry can be defined as the amount of assets, marriage gifts and cash payments given by the bride's family to the bridegroom's family. Sharma observed that there has been a total shift from bride price to dowry amongst all but the lower castes, and not only among those where women have withdrawn from outdoor labour. Also, the amounts paid in dowry, even among agricultural labourers, are noted to have increased several folds in this state (Randeria and Visaria 1984). The state of West Bengal has seemingly been witnessing the same trend of dowry practice these days.
10 Under the act, in case of a Hindu male dying intestate, all his separate or self-acquired property, in the first instance, devolves equally upon his sons, daughters, widow, and mother.... In Dayabhaga rules of inheritance, women inherited an interest in all property, irrespective of whether it was ancestral or separate. In West Bengal the traditional rule of inheritance follows the Dayabhaga code. But these religious codes are seldom implemented in reality.
11 *Patta* is a piece of paper recognizing the ownership right of the beneficiary to a plot of land distributed by the government under the Land Reforms Act.
12 1 *Cottah* = .05 *bigha*.
13 According to this law, land can be acquired only for the purpose of 'public interest' and in that case no sanction of the landowners was required for acquiring the land. Interestingly, the Left Front government had been projecting this land acquisition for the Tata Motors' car plant as the purpose of 'public interest'.
14 See for details Polanyi (1957).
15 In a tribal village in the district of Bankura, I have seen that the families of the SHG members began to use toothpaste, soap, phenyl, bleaching powder and etc. in their everyday lives.
16 Women's participation in the works under the MGNREGA has been consistently high in Tamil Nadu ever since its inception. In two consecutive years, 2006–2007 and 2007–2008, the data shows that Tamil Nadu stands first in the country as far as the proportion of women are concerned. See also Carswell (2013).
17 See for details the website of West Bengal Government, Downloadable at www.wbprd. gov.in/HtmlPage/NREGA.
18 Except in Tamil Nadu, the rule is to pay wages to the workers through bank account. The surveys conducted throughout India show that the respondents prefer payments through banks to the cash payments. See for details, Khera and Nayak (2009); Adhikari and Bhatia (2010); and Carswell (2013).

References

Adhikari, A. and K. Bhatia. 2010. 'NREGA Wage Payments: Can We Bank on the Banks?' *Economic and Political Weekly* 45 (1): 30–37.

Agarwal, Bina. 1994. *A Field of One's Own*. Cambridge, UK and New Delhi: Cambridge University Press.

Agarwal, Bina. 1999. *Gender and Legal Rights in Landed Property in India*. New Delhi: Kali for Women.

Carswell, Grace. 2013. 'Dalits and Local Labour Markets in Rural India: Experiences from the Tiruppur Textile Region in Tamil Nadu.' *Transactions of Institute of British Geographers* 38 (2): 325–338.

Carswell, Grace and Geert De Neve. 2013b. 'Women at the Crossroads: A Study of MGNREGA Implementation in Rural Tamil Nadu.' *Economic and Political Weekly* 48 (52): 82–93.

Chatterjee, Partha. 1989. 'Colonialism, Nationalism, and Colonialized Women: The Contest in India.' *American Ethnologist* 16 (4): 622–633.

Chatterjee, Partha. 1993. *The Nation and Its Fragments: Colonial and Postcolonial Histories*. Princeton: Princeton University Press.

Chatterjee, Partha. 2004. *The Politics of the Governed: Reflections on Popular Politics in Most of the World*. New Delhi: Permanent Black.

Chattopadhyay, Raghabendra and Esther Duflo. 2004. 'Women as Policy Makers: Evidence from a Randomized Policy Experiment in India.' *Ecomometrica* 72 (5): 1409–1443.

Dutta, P. et al. 2012. 'Does India's Employment Guarantee Scheme Guarantee Employment?' *Economic and Political Weekly* 47 (16): 55–64.

Elson, Diane. 1999. 'Labor Markets as Gendered Institutions: Equality, Efficiency and Empowerment Issues.' *World Development* 27 (3): 611–627.

Jeffery, Patricia and Roger Jeffery. 1994. 'Killing My Heart's Desire: Education and Female Autonomy in Rural North India.' In *Women as Subjects: South Asian Histories*, edited by Nita Kumar, 125–171. Charlottesville: University of Virginia Press.

Jeyaranjan, J. 2011. 'Women and Pro-Poor Policies in Rural Tamil Nadu: An Examination of Practices and Responses.' *Economic and Political Weekly* 46 (43): 64–74.

Kabeer, Naila. 1999. 'Resources, Agency and Achievement: Reflections on the Measurement of Women's Empowerment.' *Development and Change* 30 (3): 435–464.

Khera, Ritika and Nandini Nayak. 2009. 'Women Workers and Perceptions of the National Rural Employment Guarantee Act.' *Economic and Political Weekly* 44 (43): 49–57.

Menon, Nivedita. 2012. *Seeing Like a Feminist*. New Delhi: Penguin Books.

Nandy, Ashis. 2012. 'Theories of Oppression and Another Dialogue of Cultures.' *Economic and Political Weekly* 47 (30): 39–44.

Polanyi, Karl. 1957. *The Great Transformation: The Political and Economic Origins of our Time*. Boston: Beacon Press.

Randeria, Shalini and Leela Visaria. 1984. 'Sociology of Bride-Price and Dowry.' *Economic and Political Weekly* 19 (15).

Razavi, Shahra. 2012. 'World Development Report 2012: Gender Equality and Development: A Commentary.' *Development and Change* 43 (1): 423–437. doi:10.1111/j.1467-7660.2012.01743.x

Roy, Dayabati. 2013. *Rural Politics in India: Political Stratification and Governance in West Bengal*. New Delhi: Cambridge University Press.

Roy, Dayabati. 2017. 'Women in Panchayat of West Bengal: Access, Attainment or Empowerment?' In *In Pursuit of Inclusive Development: Essays for Manabi Majumdar*, edited by Dayabati Roy and Sreemoyee Ghosh. Kolkata: Purbalok Publication.

Roy, Indrajit. 2014. 'Reserve Labor, Unreserved Politics: Dignified Encroachments under India's National Rural Employment Guarantee Act.' *The Journal of Peasant Studies* 41 (4). doi: 10.1080/03066150.2014.922551

Scott, James C. 1976. *The Moral Economy of the Peasants: Rebellion and Subsistence in Southeast Asia*. London: Yale University Press.

Sen, Amartya K. 1990. 'Gender and Cooperative Conflicts.' In *Persistent Inequalities: Women and World Development*, edited by Irene Tinker, 123–149. New York: Oxford University Press.

Tilly, Charles. 1999. *Durable Inequality*. Berkeley: University of California Press.

Newspapers, magazines, reports and other media

Berg, Erlend, Sambit Bhattacharyya, Rajasekhar Durgam and Manjula Ramachandra. 2012. 'Can Rural Public Works Affect Agricultural Wages? Evidence from India.' CSAE Working Paper, WPS/2012-05, University of Oxford, Oxford.

Brown, Jennifer and Sujata Das Choudhury. 2002. *Women's Land Rights in West Bengal: A Field Study*. Seattle, USA: RDI.

Chopra, Deepta. 2015. 'Political Commitment in India's Social Policy Implementation: Shaping the Performance of MGNREGA.' ESID Working Paper No 50. Manchester, UK: University of Manchester. Downloadable at www.effective-states.org

Development and Planning Department. 2004. *West Bengal Human Development Report 2004*. Kolkata: Government of West Bengal.

Gupta, Jayoti. 2000. 'Women, Land and Law: Dispute Resolution at the Village Level.' Occasional Paper No 3. Calcutta: Sachetana Information Centre.

John, Mary. 2010. 'Agrarian and Rural Studies: Trends, Texts and Pedagogies.' In *Consultation with Participants in Conference–Cum–Consultation*. Bangalore: National Institute of Advanced Studies.

Ministry of Law and Justice. 2005. *The National Rural Employment Guarantee Act, 2005*. New Delhi: Government of India.

Roy, Dayabati, dir. 2011. Hundred Days, Documentary Film.

Vasavi, Aninhalli R. and Padmini Swaminathan. 2010. 'Agrarian and Rural Studies: Trends, Texts and Pedagogies.' In *Report of the Conference–Cum–Consultation*. Bangalore: National Institute of Advanced Studies.

World Development Report 2012. 2011. *Gender Equality and Development*. Washington, DC: The World Bank.

7 Conclusion

Employment, capital and the state in rural India

Why has the level of poverty not been curbed in rural areas of India? How does the rate of poverty rise over the years in rural areas despite even the soaring growth in agriculture? Why did the economic and welfare policies that aimed at curbing poverty almost fail to reduce the level of poverty in rural West Bengal? Keeping these questions in mind, I had embarked on my research since a couple of years ago. Again and again, particularly when I did visit the rural areas of West Bengal, these questions kept haunt me to uncover a fundamental reason for the persistence of poverty in rural areas. While the years passed, I figured out that the poverty was a discursive concept created by the government or, in other words, by the state that required managing or, in other words, ruling its subjects. Actually, the poor are poor as they are unemployed or underemployed. I quickly realized that we had to understand the causes of unemployment if we were really desirous of finding some measures to get rid of poverty in rural areas. I began to alter the entire perspective of my research and framed the aforesaid questions in a different manner. Why are the rural poor unemployed? Why did the economic transformations whatsoever fail to settle the problem of rural unemployment? Despite all the efforts on the part of the government, the Central and the state, why does the rate of unemployment rise in rural India and in West Bengal in particular? These inquiries brought me into a new hypothesis. I have revealed that unemployment, be it the rural or the urban, is a political process, and thus the eradication of unemployment must have its roots in politics of the victims of unemployment. The confluence of three stakeholders, i.e. the capital, the state, and the people, who being classified or stratified, as I argue, does create and recreate the dynamic occurrence of unemployment. This research thus reveals three key facts. First, the problem of poverty or well-being has to be understood mainly in terms of unemployment and underemployment. Second, the unemployment as a political process has to be studied from the perspective of emerging politics among different constituent groups of the said process. Third, the problem of unemployment and its solutions are actually a part of an interdisciplinary research agenda.

Why I am saying that the poverty is a discursive concept created and nurtured by the government, and that we must have to understand the dynamic nature of unemployment if we are really in want of eradicating poverty is due not to the fact only that poverty is a conceptual category to see people from the perspective of government, and that unemployment is an empirical problem, particularly if seen, from the perspective of the governed. But, it is due also to the fact that poverty is a governmental technology purposefully created for managing the lack of employment, while unemployment as experienced by the rural people has constantly been created as well as recreated as a consequence of both the capitalist and state intervention in the domain of rural economy. If unemployment is the outcome of capitalist and state intervention in economy, poverty, whatever its level may be, is the manifestation of the phenomenon of unemployment. Thus, the interventions on the part of the government into the alleviation of poverty are nothing but a palliative attempt to lessen the agony of unemployment. It is not only an effort to lessen the pain of unemployment but also an attempt to cover a burning social phenomenon like unemployment. The governmental discourse is so influenceable that a majority of scholarships easily often take poverty into consideration to gauge the level of well-being of the people in a particular society. Upon considering the poverty, these scholarships have not only made poverty as a perennial problem, but have made unemployment as a default phenomenon too. Ignoring the issues of unemployment, they, in fact, turn unconcerned about the contribution of the capitalist expansion, and the subsequent state intervention in creating and shaping the phenomenon of unemployment. Here lies the problem. I argue that the perspective of unemployment would not only help us to understand the causes of both unemployment and poverty, but would also offer us some possibilities to cope with these causes by way of questioning the role of capitalist expansion in creation of unemployment. To the extent that we intend to understand the role of capitalist and state expansion in shaping unemployment, we would be able to find the remedy of unemployment as well as poverty.

I have tried to discuss in detail in the preceding chapters about the issues of capitalist expansion in societies, and about the subsequent role of the state in it. I have described the way the state emerges and develops based mainly on the dynamics of capitalist expansion particularly in the rural areas of India. The way the state does mediate between the capital, rather the capitalist class, on the one hand, and the labour, the broad masses, on the other, is my focus. In its bid to do this, the state is to regulate the level of expansion of capital in order to provide a minimum well-being for the people whom it has the responsibility to govern. The state's regulation in matter of capitalist expansion as well as in provision of well-being to the masses is deemed necessary due actually to the reasons that the capitalist accumulation germinates unemployment, and that the unemployment causes poverty. What is the nature of the state does vary, therefore, depending on the way the state intervenes in the capitalist expansion and in public welfare within a respective country. Whatever the nature of the state may be, it is evident that almost all the state's guiding ideology is essentially liberalism. I attempt to unsettle the quintessence of this dominant discourse for imagining a possible critique to the evolving promises of liberalism, and thereby essaying a possibility of alternative politics to resist against the ongoing sufferings of abject poverty and unemployment in postcolonial countries like India. When there is remotely a scope to go beyond the liberal framework, the alternative politics does at least offer a strategy for effectively regulating the capitalist expansion with a skew to employment, and for nurturing a real public welfare based on the issues of employment. In other words, the aim of alternative politics is to maintain a balance between the two processes with a primary emphasis on employment. In fact, the normative liberal agenda, I have argued, advocates two simultaneous processes, if one is the advancement of economic growth, another is the management of issues like poverty, in other words, unemployment. Two processes are actually counter to each other. The economic precarity of Indian rural people seems to be a direct fall out of the practice of this politics. An incisive survey has vividly reflected the way in which the postcolonial state in India has intervened, however futilely, in the rural economy with an aim to make it prosperous based mainly on the vision of capitalist expansion, i.e. economic growth.

India is often presumed to signify abject poverty, unemployment and 'underdevelopment'. Hundreds of millions of poverty-stricken people have been, as it were, just striving hard to make ends meet in India, particularly in rural part of India since time immemorial. Of late, in view of the fact that two faces of India, if one is shining while another being the other of it,[1] often being juxtaposed as starkly different in many ways mainly in terms of inequality, the above saying is perhaps gaining ground. Even the ideas that economic 'precarity', as Gupta denotes (2016), had been one of the inherent features of India, and that the British colonialists appreciatively began to cause the progress of that economy by means of initiating capitalist development as well as expansion of market are also not rare both in popular and academic discourse. I have argued in this book that Bengal, 'which is in miniature the history of India itself', though 'long been synonymous with hunger' (Mukerjee 2010, xiv), had never been a poor state, and that the moment when modernization began its journey is actually the juncture at which India was intervened devastating to its doom. The trajectories of transformation in the domain of employment have thus to be mapped ever since the period when India was intervened by the colonial power. Although India and its rural spaces have their own intrinsic complexities and problems, it had been anything but impoverished before the British colonialists came. Take Bengal, the present West Bengal, for instance. As I have argued, several historical accounts show that its economy was 'the finest and most fruitful country' as early as around in 1665 when, as Bernier describes (1891, 437–438), 'the rich exuberance of the country … has given rise to a proverb in common use among the Portuguese, English and Dutch, that the Kingdom of Bengale has hundred gates open for entrance, but not one for departure'.

I would like to mention here an old debate to draw the readers' attention to a significant line of thinking in the past and its present incarnations, since it might still provide us some theoretical underpinnings which are relevant in our context. Rammohan Roy (1722–1833) used to proactively promote an idea that the free trade would strengthen the expansion of industries, thereby making the Indian economy flourish by way of generating employment at large scale. Interestingly, he was trying to promote this idea at the very juncture when British imperialists had been destroying the indigenous industries as well as the Indian small peasant economy in order to monopolize its own trade and commerce.[2] Whether he will be called the father of our modernity/nationalism has still, after around one and half centuries, been a point of debate particularly since Roy is identified (Sen 1975) 'as a collaborator in British imperialist's efforts to plunder the economy in the name of free trade'. However, whether he was a nationalist or a liberal is actually not my point of concern since nationalism as an idea was actually impossible to be present during his time.[3] What I focus here is rather on the way the idea of liberalism that was originated in the early period of colonial modernity has still been regarded as supreme among the policy makers, social thinkers and even academics. If Roy is branded as anti-national and as a collaborator in British imperialists' efforts to plunder the Indian economy, how should we position the contemporary liberals who believe that free trade would make the Indian economy flourish.

In this book, I explore the way the issues of unemployment have been created and shaped through a complex process of capitalist transformations and the subsequent state intervention in the domain of rural economy. This means, the book analyses the nature of capitalist transformation in the domain of employment at the rural hinterland of West Bengal, an Indian state, through a comparative study of some villages which are distinct from each other not only in terms of their ecological specificities and of their proximity to city, but also of their ethnographic components. Set in a historical perspective, the book understands the dynamic changes in condition of employment in rural areas during three broad phases of political and economic transformations. These three broad phases include the British colonial period, the first four decades of the postcolonial period and the so-called neoliberal or hyper-liberal period. While the determinant role of capital whatsoever leads to transform the class configuration and the economy in rural areas by means of marketization of farming and other occupations, the government's attempts aimed at supporting the rural labour through various kinds of policies complicate the issue further. The question is about the way in which the rural has been changing as a result of marketization and, similarly, in what way has the politics of rural people been shaping the outcomes of capitalist transformation. How do the rural people across class, caste, religion and gender shape the economic restructuring of global capital in their lives? By examining these questions critically, the book reveals that not only do the economic transformations impact differently on different classes of people, but also does a specific local setting having particular inequalities engender specific capitalist dynamics. Moreover, which is seemingly more significant in our context, is to look at the change in pattern of governance in rural areas over the years based on the want of a particular emerging system primarily with an aim of managing the population towards a definite economic goal.

Rural unemployment

Why I am saying that the advent of British colonialism is marked as a beginning of an era is due to the fact that it introduces two simultaneous processes, as I have mentioned, that is, the capitalist transformation in rural economy, and the management of rural population through the intervention of the modern state. Two processes are, however, unsurprisingly, not at all in proportion to each other.

While the extent of capitalist accumulation was aggressively overwhelming, the budding state was just setting its foot on the ground. The Permanent Settlement was a major intervention on the part of the British Colonialists in the domain of land relations which had transformed overwhelmingly the rural economy once for all. And the small-scale industries that began to grow sustainably in rural areas were routinely bankrupt by the violent penetration of British trade and business. Ever since the introduction of the Permanent Settlement, the condition of rural Bengal began to deteriorate in such a manner that it couldn't recuperate any more. Worst affected of all was the domain on employment in rural areas. The change in land rights, both proprietary and occupancy, pushed the small peasantry as well as even the rentier class while in late colonial period into an economic crisis mainly in the question of livelihoods. As the level of capitalist expansion in agriculture mounted, the small peasant economy grew worse, even notwithstanding the British colonialists were always in favour of the continuance of the small peasant economy in Bengal. Becoming landless was a routine process for the small peasants as consequence of extraction of exorbitant revenue and of impoverishment of farming due to several reasons.[4] Most of the peasants who were once labouring on their own lands had afterwards become landless labourers, and began to labour on their erstwhile lands. This means, which is significant is that the rural economy got devastated.

The British officials were not uninformed of this agricultural crisis, and actually they were concerned about the subsequent landlessness and unemployment in the rural field. To them, it was an urgent requirement to sustain the small peasant economy only for the purpose of unhindered revenue collections. They had thus tried to regulate the rural economy, the land revenue structure, and the system of land proprietorship as well as land occupation, by introducing a number of acts and policies on regular basis since 1859. These acts had some safeguards to protect the tenants (though being as such not pro-tenant); they were, however, amended several times under the pressure of the vested interests on lands. There were possibilities that these acts and policies were not put in practice. Hence, which was in advance anticipated that the rural economy might be headed to its doom became at last true in the first half of twentieth century. This was not only due to the failure of the legal endeavour on the part of the colonial government, but also due mainly to the fact that both colonial power and the rentier class squeezed the rural economy for maximizing their own profit. On the other hand, as a result of various legal interventions, and the simultaneous persistence of customary practices, the peasantry were sectioned both horizontally and vertically to a variety of categories, for which they themselves were confused. If the layers of landowners, rentier classes, the revenue payers, the sharecroppers and landless peasants are the example of vertical sections, the horizontal sections at the bottom of the rural society include the sharecroppers, tenants, *raiyats*, under *raiyats*, *aadhiar* and etc. As these lower sections of the rural classes had increasingly been turned into landless and poor peasants, they began to get politicized, and subsequently organized in 'no rent' movement. The rentier class was thus no exception to the general trend of rural impoverishment. The rural economy of Bengal culminated in a huge disaster in terms of employment just before the end of colonial power simply as part of the intervening role of capital and state in it.

The roles of capital and state in postcolonial period though being essentially nothing new but the same as earlier have more and more been shaped and influenced intricately by a myriad of party-politics in the country. What the government was due to plan concretely is nothing but major agrarian reforms at rural grass roots. The central government kicked off its journey by stepping in the tasks of land reforms in particular. However, the way the government tended to step in land reforms was even short of provisions that the colonial administrators already recommended. Although it is most often said though in popular discourse that the policies of land reform have been the outcomes of the people's consistent movement led by particularly the Communist left of all hues in case of West Bengal, it has actually been just a repetition of an erstwhile policy grew out in the late colonial period by the then British empire. The Floud Commission's recommendations are here cases in point. The commission did recommend not only to acquire superior interests in agricultural land, but also to assume a direct relationship between the actual cultivators and the government in view of, on the one hand, the uncertain tax collection, and on the other, the growing landlessness, poverty and unemployment, and the subsequent peasant protests at the rural fringes. In fact, the commission was of opinion (Report of Floud Commission 1940, sec 10) 'to abolish the *zamindari* system in its entirety'. I have mentioned in the earlier chapters that the Floud Commission was even in favour of granting the legal entitlement to the landless but the actual cultivators, i.e. the *bargadars* and sharecroppers, and of stipulating a proportion of share, which would be legally recoverable, of the produced crops for them. (Floud Commission: Para, 146).[5]

The question that arises is about how we would interpret Floud Commission's recommendations for our purpose to explain the roles of capital and the state in shaping the domain of employment. The Floud's recommendations are nothing but an attempt of maintaining a balance between two simultaneous efforts on the part of the state. By recommending for a major agrarian restructuration, the Floud Commission aims at achieving, on the one hand, the goal of capitalist expansion in agriculture, and on the other, the goal of public welfare through granting the cultivators some legal rights to land. The commission realized that the capitalist expansion in agriculture would not be possible unless the cultivators could enjoy a freedom to cultivate their own lands. Upon considering this angle, the commission's recommendations can be called at best as a part of capitalist agenda. In other words, the commission, being a part of the colonial state, attempted to regulate the functions of capital by way of facilitating capitalist growth, and of widening the scope of public welfare by means of recognizing the part of actual cultivators in development of agriculture. But we didn't get scope to know about the nature and extent of the impacts of the Floud Commission's recommendations on capitalist development in agriculture as well as on the peasantry as a whole during the colonial period since the said report could never manage to get the colonial government's seal on it. The postcolonial rural Bengal thus began its journey carrying a strong existence of landlessness, indebtedness and unemployment in the rural landscape as well as a strong sense of expectations for agrarian prosperity that grew out of India's independence. In order to bring the agrarian prosperity, the postcolonial state made use of the Floud Commission's recommendations to formulate various land-related acts and policies. We might get an idea on whether the Floud Commission's recommendation are effective as far as its avowed objectives are concerned, if we analyse the dynamic impacts of various land reform policies that were undertaken in the postcolonial period.

It is undeniable that agriculture and its growth have expanded and improved all over India due to the implementations of land reform policies in general, and the Estate Abolition Act in particular which were formulated in early postcolonial period mainly in conceptual line of Floud Commission. But what is truer is that the expansion of market as well as of capital has enormously grown as expected owing to the implementations of land reforms during the same period. Floud thus seemed right in his position, if we judge the potential of his recommendations from the perspective of capital. However, in our context, interestingly, despite the relative success of land reforms, not only does agriculture become unprofitable, but also the small peasantry growingly become vulnerable for the very purpose of capital. Actually, capital as well as market gets increasingly thriving ever since the moment of land reforms at the cost of agriculture, and of the lives and livelihoods of small peasantry. Through exploiting the input provision and the harvest procurement in agricultural sector, market has become strengthened, and capital thereafter gets accumulated at a higher level at the rural grass roots. The application of GRT which is deemed as a dream project by the policy makers has not only prompted to increase the application of inputs in cultivation but also to reduce the fertility of the soil, and subsequent slump in production which anyone can assume once s/he sets foot in the village. In course of all these major steps on the part of the government in regard to land reform and expansion of agriculture, capital only gains its strength through utilizing the thriving sphere of peasant economy.

The implementations and improvization of land reform acts in the case of West Bengal have always been the concern for good reasons of the academics, let alone the popular section. I have showed in detail in the earlier chapters of this book and also elsewhere (Roy 2013) the limit of land reforms in rural West Bengal both in terms of their implementations and consequences. While whether the phenomenon of landlessness and unemployment are going to be increased is my focus, Bardhan et al. (2011, 3) recently explains the roles of land reforms and demographic alteration in changes in land distribution in West Bengal in the period of 1967–2004 using a large-scale data from 89 villages of the state.[6] They find that the pattern of land distribution has changed, so has the extent of land inequality. But (ibid.) 'the land reforms involved a relatively small fraction of agricultural land', and have hardly any effective role in 'lowering land inequality'. In fact, 'high rates of household division, immigration, and land market transactions' have roles in growing reductions in per capita and per household landownership. While I do agree with Bardhan et al. that the role of the land reforms is insignificant in changes of land distribution as well as in lowering land inequality, and that high rates of household division and market transactions play roles to change land distribution, I would strongly contend that the expansion of capitalist market is one of the main culprits for the rise of land inequality. And the level of unemployment must increase, given the condition that land is (ibid., 1) 'the primary determinant of livelihoods of the poor' in rural areas. In other words, the extent of landlessness, i.e. nearly a half of village population, signifies that unemployment is a dominant phenomenon in rural West Bengal.

But, interestingly, the capitalist expansion in rural areas in general and in agriculture in particular was once thought to be a solution to the mounting food crisis and poverty that the country faced during the late 1960s. The central government launched GRT to curb the food crisis all over India, which in turn did easily facilitate the capitalist expansion in rural areas, particularly, in agriculture. The capitalist expansion in agriculture in the name of GRT was clearly an intervention on the part of the state, but it has been considered by the social analysts as a respite not only from food crisis but also from rural unemployment. The capitalist expansion has always been made indispensible by the respective state in the aforesaid fashion. The narrative of the modern state is, as I argue, the narrative of capital. Whenever the state faces a major crisis, particularly, in regard to employment and food, it opts for further capitalist expansion. It promotes the expansion of capital in such a manner as if there is no other way to come out from the crisis. For, instance, take land acquisition in Singur and Nadigram, the then government even demonstrated its land acquisition move for industrialization as public interest as, it argues, the latter would create more employments. Whether the proposed industrialization would be more of a loss of employment than it helps to create employment has still been a question of contention. But, which is more perplexing is the Communists' exhortation of the rhetoric which has been usually nurtured by the liberal capitalists. Both the Communists and the liberals are here exhorting the same rhetoric that the increase in investment means increase in employment, and that the land has to be acquired by any means, whatever action is needed. I would remind the readers once again at this juncture that Marx (1853), like the Bengal's Communists, had justified the British colonial exploitation in India on the ground that England was 'causing a social revolution in Hindostan' without which, he thought; mankind could hardly 'fulfil its destiny'. Although late Marx had begun to rethink his early writings about 'the British rule in India' as Chatterjee (2000) argues, it carries little importance to us at this moment since contemporary Communists, at least in India, do still reiterate the proposition of early Marx. The Marxists and the liberals including even the colonialists do converge here on a major point. The converging point of these two distinct camps is, as it seems, the indispensability of the capitalist expansion in economy. The capitalist expansion, these camps believe, must have the potential to push the economy, whatever it may be, towards its higher stage. This stage theory binds into one thread these two camps though each of them appears as relatively different from each other.

It is surprising that the academics in general are also often seen to opine that capitalist accumulation and market are prefixed, and that the governmental state should facilitate the free market and capitalist expansion so that, as they imagine, a particular economy would create more employment opportunities. Thus, turning a blind eye to capitalist fall out, some scholars don't even bother a little even to argue that the poor are poor as they lack in capabilities. As the capability approach has gained ground, so has the capitalist expansion. In our context, it reveals that the application of the GRT in agriculture gave some respite to the peasants at least for a while as far as production and employment are concerned. It is also true that the application of the GRT in the state didn't take a uniform pathway since a number of components that are specific to each particular regions have been functional to determine the nature of application of this technology. As a matter of this fact, the state has witnessed an uneven development in agriculture. The question arises about why the success of the GRT evaporated so quickly. I argue that the GRT has its own limitation to sustain agriculture for a longer period and, therefore, after a while the growth in agriculture begins to shrink. However, the problem is not so simple in our case that we would settle the issues effortlessly. The intervention of the state has made the situation worse by liberalizing the country's economy for market forces, whatever its nature may be, since late 1980s. The withdrawal of subsidies from agriculture, and the capitalist manipulation in input provision, as well as in harvest procurement, put the final nail in the coffin of the rural economy.[7] The capitalist expansion which was required once to create employment opportunities has actually become eventually a major dynamic for causing unemployment and poverty at the rural fringes. However, this situation again calls for reiteration of the same cycle of capitalist expansion only to bring in another crisis.

While the state has been in action to encourage the capital for forceful expansion through liberalizing India's economy since the late 1980s, it cannot afford to overlook dealing with the negative consequences of this new sort of capitalist expansion. The central government has perhaps for the first time in its half-century-or-so-long journey declared officially that 'the international political and economic order is being restructured everyday', and thus 'in many areas of activity, development can best be ensured by freeing them of unnecessary controls and regulations and withdrawing state intervention' (8th Five-Year Plan, Foreword). The 8th Five-Year Plan was thus meant for (Preface) 'managing the transition from centrally planned economy to market-led economy' when, as the policy makers recognized in the same document, a third of the country's population lived in abject poverty and unemployment. There was in point of fact no end, as many had assumed that the neoliberal period meant the withdrawal of the state in every respect of the welfare policies on the part of the government. While the earlier policy interventions were such welfare programmes that provided 'tangible services and assets', as Sharma and Gupta (2006) envisage, the contemporary policy regime (like the MGNREGA) as an empowerment programme aims at helping the rural to become autonomous rather than dependent clients who are waiting for the redistribution of resources. I have explained in the pages of the book that the policies, far from concerned with empowerment and self-help characteristics of 'neoliberal governmentality', have still been rendering the individuals 'dependent clients of the state'. It is thus not the end of welfare and its replacement with workfare, as the scholars (ibid.) propose, but the simultaneous expansion of both kinds of programmes.

Neoliberal forms of government feature not only direct intervention by means of empowered and specialized state apparatuses, but also characteristically develop indirect techniques for leading and controlling individuals. The strategy of rendering individual subjects "responsible" entails shifting the responsibility for social risks such as illness, unemployment, poverty, etc. and for life in society to a domain wherein the individual is responsible, and transforming it into a problem of "self-care" (ibid., 12; Rose and Miller 1992, 34). In the Mandate and Objectives section of the Ministry of Law and Justice (2005), it has been mentioned that 'MGNREGA marks a paradigm shift from the previous one because its design is bottom-up, people-centred, demand-driven (where provision of work triggered by the demand for work by wage seekers), self-selecting and right-based'. Also, 'it has an integrated natural resource management and livelihood generation perspective.' These words clearly reveal that this act as a governmental technology encourages entrepreneurship which means, in normative sense, any adult individual in rural India 'make[s] their decisions, pursue[s] their preferences, and seek[s] to maximize the quality of their lives by demanding employment'. But, while the MGNREGA encourages entrepreneurship, it limits the sphere of entrepreneurship. The contradiction, in fact, lies in the conceptualization of the act. While it declares legal guarantee of wage employment on demand, and recognizes it, to some extent, as a 'right to work', it restricts at the same time the guarantee of employment to only a limited days – 100 days. Whatever the case may be, one point is clear: the policies of employment generation have been interpreted and delivered in a different way, thereby creating a new kind of management of unemployment. However, what is not new is the way the 'idle labour' in rural areas is being used for making both the land and capital productive in the name of employment generation. The question is the way the political parties have been intervening in employment concerns.

The political parties

The political parties of all hues, as I have argued, are not different from each other as well as from the state as far as the politics of employment are concerned. The politics of the political parties is more or less the same as the state's for the reason that they both construct their politics based on the grand narrative of state which emphasizes capital which, as believed, has potential to create employment. This narrative, as I have shown, is actually a contradictory narration of two processes, i.e. the capitalist accumulation and the employment generation. That the expansion of capital though requires labour as an indispensable component does inevitably, in turn, counteract the possibility of employment generation has often been overlooked consciously or unconsciously in this grand narrative. The political parties, it seems, don't bother to see anything beyond this narrative. Unemployment and underemployment in the rural economy is, supposedly, being considered by the advocates of various political parties as a normal phenomenon which, as they believe, would be ameliorated in course of capitalist development. Even the Communist lefts who do at least recognize the capital as a cause of inequality and unemployment have been reiterating the same practices. Left politics does not manifest any sign of alternate thinking regarding the issues of unemployment. The question that arises is whether the Communist narrative in India is at all different from the dominant narrative.

There is no question that the political parties that emerge out from the encounter between the state and the people do play roles in mediating between the state and the people in order not only to resolve the issues related to the people's lives and livelihoods but also to regulate the expansion of capital. Despite the appearance that members of the political parties are the people's representatives, they are actually more the representatives of the state than of the people. What I am saying is due to the fact that all the parliamentary parties are the driving force of the state project of capitalist management. However, the representatives of political parties also would raise the perspective of the people, in more concrete terms, the perspective of different sections of the people depending on principles of a respective party before the state. Immediately after a political party sets foot in the parliamentary politics, it enters the domain of capitalist or liberal discourse. I have discussed in an earlier chapter about the way the political parties would make the state and its project of capitalist development grounded among the masses of West Bengal at the grass roots. I emphasize here, first of all, the point is that the major political parties hardly bother about employments of the rural poor since most of the leaders of these parties belonging to the upper class and upper castes.

The leaders of these parties don't consider unemployment as a problem owing probably to the fact that they regard the phenomenon of unemployment prevalent in rural areas as normal or, at best, the new normal. Leaders do not consider unemployment as a serious problem since, as I argue, they usually belong to the upper class and upper caste groups, and the people who experience rural unemployment mostly belong to the disadvantaged social groups, i.e. the so-called lower class, lower caste and tribal groups. The disadvantaged masses who constitute the unemployed troops in rural areas are none but the vast workforce and service providers engaged by the landholding classes at least for occasional periods and purposes. Even the elite class as well as the middle class in cities and urban areas also enjoy considerably the services of cheap labour of the people from these rural disadvantaged groups. Who do want to lose the privilege of parasitic living feeding off of others' labour? Why do the so-called social proprietors bother to recognize the predicament of unemployment that has been experienced by the mass of laboring people who are considered in particular as the subaltern groups in rural parlance? When many from these so-called subaltern groups are unemployed or underemployed for most part of the year, the people of the landholding class in general, as I have observed during my field work, look somewhat dispirited, and say that the laboring people have performed such a level economically during the recent period that it is difficult to identify them as belonging to laboring class. That the laboring people can avail the scope whatsoever beyond farm and non-farm work in rural areas seems has been the concern of the rural elites. In other words, the solvent section of rural people seem to consider it as normal that the laboring masses would live in midst of unemployment and the subsequent economic poverty. Hence, the leaders of the political parties who do not even believe that unemployment is a serious and common problem in rural areas are barely expected to consider unemployment as central to their politics.

Second, the leaders of the political parties hardly consider 'full employment' as one of their main political goals to achieve due also to the fact that their politics as essentially being shaped by the ideals of liberalism which presumes that economic growth would eliminate unemployment automatically. Liberalism as a political viewpoint set the perspective of capital which endorses the belief that free market and investment would liberate the people from unemployment and poverty. I argue that the leaders of political parties are blind at least to an extent to the economic realities of unemployment since their politics does not go beyond the purview of liberal politics. Whether there is any scope to go beyond the purview of liberal politics while or once a party participates in parliamentary politics is not our concern here. I have only argued that all the political parties that do a matter in the politics of India and in West Bengal in particular have more or less been rehearsing the same liberal politics since its genesis. In course of their long practice of liberalism, the leaders of these political parties cease to think of a basic fact that the issues of poverty, whatever its nature may be, have been the outcome of unemployment. They began to nurture a belief that the poverty is a real challenge of governance, and that the management of poverty would strengthen economic development and thus democracy. As a result of this practice, the postcolonial politics continues to focus on the management of poverty only to marginalize the issues of unemployment. Even if these political parties opt sometimes for tackling unemployment, they would try to do it from the perspective of poverty or its alleviation.

We have discussed the way in which the leaders of the political parties like, on the one hand, the Congress party, and on the other, the Left Front, interpret and tackle the issues of unemployment not only in the same fashion but in a stereotypic way. The Congress party, while in power both at the centre as well as at almost all the states in the initial period, never endeavoured to understand rural unemployment in its fullest sense. Whatever it intended to carry out on the employment front in rural areas was not a plan of action to directly attack unemployment. I explain that these interventions were at best an effort of employment generation for a short while with a definite aim of capitalist productivity in agriculture. The capitalist expansion in agriculture that began with the introduction of GRT though initially been helpful to augment in employment at least for some days seasonally, had been of no use in the long run as far as employment is concerned. While growth in agriculture slowed, the opportunities of employment also slumped. While this is the policy in essence of the Congress party in so far as livelihoods and employment are concerned, the Left Front trod mostly on the heels of the Congress on the issues of rural unemployment. After examining critically the performance of the Left Front in the field of rural livelihoods in general and land reforms in particular, my research finds that the Front partners could hardly surpass in its implementation the recommendations made by the Floud Commission. Although the ruling Left Front had utilized the GRT to accelerate the growth in agriculture, and subsequently to create some additional employments in agriculture, it couldn't keep that increase in production as well as in employment due to some anticipated reasons. The market-dependant agriculture which already manifested the signs of obliteration just after a short break became worse after the liberalization of Indian economy. The rural economy didn't seem turn around after this stagnation. No political party seems to have the courage to portray itself as the savior of this rural predicament particularly on the employment front, while the Left Front government came up with a more aggressive measure, i.e. land acquisition for industrialization.

Needless to say, after more than three decades, the rural masses finally put the last nail in the coffin of the Left Front rule in retaliation against the government's land acquisition move. Making use of the political potentials of the oppositional political parties as well as of the civil society endeavours, the peasantry at large in the state signaled a message that the big hi-tech industry whatever it would promise, it could hardly create employment at the very least for the land losers. However, the political party, the TMC, which got the custody of the state and its ailing economy in particular, did nothing different from the earlier ruling party as expected as far as rural unemployment is concerned. It could not perform differently because it too tried to construct its policies based on the same ideological framework as its predecessors did. The capital-based farming which had consistently been turned into a loss-making vocation during the last few decades became thus worse only to decrease the opportunities of employment in rural areas. Mechanization in agriculture has put the agricultural labourers out of work as well as forced migration, and vice versa. While all the political parties played the same role in (Kohli 2012, 2) 'opening of the Indian economy to global forces' since all 'agreed on the basic approach to the economy: a commitment to economic growth', and were not in a position to solve the problem of rural unemployment, no political party could afford to ignore the predicament of the rural unemployed masses. The political parties could not afford to ignore the case of rural unemployed simply for the reason that it might have some political implications. It is undeniable now that the rural unemployed mass who constitute the major part of the voters are actually the solid base of all kinds of political parties in rural areas. Therefore, the political parties are always in search of such policies that would manage the consequences of rural unemployment or, as they focus on, poverty. However, these initiatives, I have argued, that have been taken on the part of the political parties as well as of the government are palliative in nature.

The palliative measures are sought by the concerned stakeholders due mainly to three different kinds of reasons. While the purpose of governance is a major reason in the political sphere, the purpose of capital productivity is hardly a negligible reason in the economic sphere. Furthermore, the power relations that exist among different classes as well as among social groups also matter to an extent why these kinds of palliative measures have been undertaken on the part of the government. Taken the MGNREGA as an instance, I have explained the way the act has been constructed, interpreted and, above all, translated at different planes of the society based on the socio-cultural as well as political dynamics in the state. I explain that the people who constitute the power bloc and influence the fate of the policies both in the state institutions and in political institutions, on the one hand, and both at the level of central and at the state, on the other, belong mostly to the proprietor classes and the privileged social categories. The issues of rural unemployment do not concern as much them as the issues of poverty do. Why the issues of rural unemployment do not concern them is due mainly to the existing hierarchy related to class, caste and other social categories. Owing to their social position, neither do they realize the extent of predicament of rural unemployment, nor do they imagine a reasonable pathway to free the rural unemployed from abject unemployment. In fact, the people at the helm of power never consider the rural unemployed as equal to them; rather, it seems, they treat the rural 'poor' as the other who has to be managed through various policy interventions. Even the policies that are framed by the sections of people so as to manage the rural poverty clearly betray the fact that, apart from being palliative, these are having a supplicatory aspect. As a result of this sheer cognizance among all the stakeholders in general and among the policy makers in particular, the employment instead of being a right for all is still just a dream.

The civil society

Foucault's discussion of neoliberal governmentality (1984,1991) shows, as Rose and Miller (1992) and Lemke (2000, 11) also argues, that

> the so-called 'retreat of the state' is in fact prolongation of government…. What we observe today is not a diminishment or a reduction of state sovereignty and planning capacities but a displacement from formal to informal techniques of governments and the appearance of new actors on the scene of government (e.g. NGOs) that indicate fundamental transformations in statehood and a new relation between state and civil society actors.

Our context seems to show the same phenomenon, as theorized by Foucault, when it witnesses the prolongation of government in the field of welfare with the inclusion of new actors i.e. the NGOs 'on the scene of government'. The state, instead of being in retreat, has been on the go both in planning and in implementation of new kind of techniques, and thereby strengthening its structure at the grass roots. The contemporary techniques of the government include formal as well as informal procedures to govern the people in a new fashion. We have observed in the preceding chapters the way the government of India exhorted formally the NGOS and the so-called civil society in its efforts to transform India since the beginning of post-reform era.[8] Since then, as the policy trends reveal, the government and the market have been complementary with each other, and the government has shown enormous interests to work hand in hand with the NGOs with an aim of making a new India. This new India is having nothing but a (Kohli 2012) 'pro-business tilt' of its state aimed at, as the scholars perhaps rightly identify, accelerating the economic growth with a new direction. However, the 'pro-business tilt' of India's state matters a lot as far as unemployment is concerned at the bottom of the society.

Since the 1990s, India has set out on a journey with a new direction and has regularly been resolute to adopt newer measures aiming at welfare only to govern the mass who are prone to unemployment and subsequent poverty in the new situation. While the economic growth has fared well, and a new middle class has emerged at the apex as a result of ongoing economic reforms, the people in general and the rural people in particular have experienced a crisis in the field of employment and other basic securities during the same period thanks to economic reforms. To take the responsibility, and bear the consequences of its actions, albeit in a limited way, the post reform state of India has structured a number of policies and acts in collaboration and negotiation with the representatives of the so-called civil society in order to deal with the predicament in the sphere of unemployment and livelihoods. The launch of these new measures in policy domain has been interpreted and named in diverse ways, e.g. neoliberal governmentality, neo-welfarism, inclusive growth, etc. Whatever its name may be, the objective is, without a doubt, to manage the issues of unemployment and the loss of livelihoods only with an aim to maintain a status quo at least in terms of governance. Notwithstanding its failure to make any difference on the employment front, these measures must have some implications in political terms. The political implications are such that the means of welfare has begun to be thought as a goal of the policies by a section of concerned stakeholders. For instance, take the MGNREGA. While there is hardly any assurance of right in the said act, the protagonists are trying to demonstrate it as a right to employment. The policy interventions on the part of the government are such effective particularly in the popular discursive field that the causes of the rural distress are turned blurred, or become a non-issue. The people at large who are concerned about India's rural distress, while seeing immense potentials in the Employment Guarantee Act, are otherwise unbothered about the causes of unemployment.

I have discussed at length in a preceding chapter the way a section of representatives belonging to the civil society would express concerns out of their normative sincerity about the emerging rural distress throughout the country, and eventually playing a role in formulating various acts and policies related mainly to rural livelihoods. They are to engage in course of this policy process with the government, and members of the political parties in general and the ruling party in particular for negotiating the welfare issues of the distressed people in rural India (Chopra 2011a, 2011b; Ruparelia 2013). Their pressing concern often urges the government to initiate newer policy intervention into the rural predicament. The question that arises at this point is why the people of civil society who are in general so concerned about the lack of welfare initiatives on the part of the government don't bother at all to take into consideration the causes of unemployment in rural areas. In other words, why is the same section from the civil society least concerned about the causes of rural unemployment? Had they been concerned about the causes of predicament, we would have witnessed another development at the rural fringes. The majority of civil society does not bother as much about the causes of unemployment as it does about the alleviation of its manifestation. The concerned section of the civil society does really rarely bother, as I have argued, since it believes in, and so endorses, the path of economic growth that has been pursued by the government consistently as an all-purpose remedy of all socio-economic deficiencies. That the enhancement of economic growth can't ensure generation of employment is a truism to say, but most of the civil society still takes it as an axiom that the economic growth would make a positive difference on job front.

In fact, the people from civil society in general are swayed immensely in the theory that the benefits of economic reforms or, in other words, of the escalating economic growth would automatically trickle down to the poor strata of Indian society. However, this trickle-down theory, whatever the extent of trickling down may be, doesn't consider in any case the issues of employment opportunities of the poorer sections of Indian societies. Conceptually, the phrase trickle-down means dripping, and the trickle-down theory explains the dripping of wealth from the strata of riches to the strata of poor in a particular society. Neither does the theory consider the issues of employment for the poor, nor does the civil society realize the problem of unemployment of the rural poor. While the rural poor do continuously suffer from rising joblessness since the trickling-down effect fails to make any positive difference in their lives and livelihoods, the interpretations of the civil society broadly reflect a conservative mindset by way of approving the trickle-down theory. I have described throughout the pages of this book the way the concept of trickle-down effect gets ground among the people of civil society, and eventually shapes the activities of respective civil society as well as the civil society–led NGOs. The people from the civil society who belong mostly to the upper class-caste category in India, particularly in West Bengal, are not only engrossed in the popular rhetoric of trickle-down, but are also strongly in favour of philanthropic initiatives on the part of the government in order to alleviating poverty. Upon analysing the dynamic activities of three NGOs in West Bengal, I have argued that the guarantee of employment have become ever more elusive as a result of various interventions of the NGOs in the domain of employment.

The reason why I am proposing the idea that the interventions of the NGOs in rural sphere have aggravated the level of unemployment instead of resolving the same is that the NGOs neither attack the rural unemployment directly nor do they address the causes of rural unemployment in our country. Rather, the NGOs are more concerned with the palliative measures in order to make unemployment as an endurable phenomenon in rural areas. In other words, the intervening language of the NGOs is mostly apolitical and administrational, and thus meant for a managerial solution of the so-called poverty. These apolitical measures, while virtually ineffective as far as the guarantee of employment is concerned, are often seemingly the ploys in the hands of the ruling class or the government in their efforts to manage the rural poor. These measures are really very effective as far as the management of poverty, rather the poor, is concerned. The rural poor do not raise their voice as such against the lack of employment in most part of the year as they do regarding the non-availability of governmental benefits. Furthermore, the NGOs would aid in strengthening the state formation in course of implementation of various measures undertaken both by them and the government. In the name of inclusion of civil society in the process of so-called development, the government has been utilizing the potentials of the NGOs in its efforts to govern the rural people effectively. That the NGOs are the representatives of the civil society is a deliberate attempt of the international aid community, as Jenkins interprets (2001), in order to achieve a specific goal. The goal is nothing but to depoliticize the rural terrain with an aim of better management. When the NGOs are treated as the civil society, the people belonging to the civil society really have roles to play in ongoing 'development dramas'. What role they will play would depend not only on their class-caste position but also on their ideological standpoint.

Undoubtedly, most of the people belonging to civil society accept the line which promotes the enhancement of economic growth as a path of development by virtue of their class position. If any one section can benefit due to the enhancement of economic growth, it is the civil society obviously in employment term. The people of this section, while suffering time and again from the negative consequences of economic growth by way of uncertainty in the sphere of employment, are swayed by the rhetoric of economic growth. The discursive power of economic growth is such that the people from the civil society, though constantly being letting down in question of employment, are hopeful that the enhancement of economic growth would ultimately solve the problem of their unemployment. I argue that the people of civil society in general are in favour of the economic growth theory owing not only to their class position, but also to their validation of the narrative of economic growth. Notwithstanding the fact that the economic growth theory has achieved a kind of supremacy over other theories throughout the history of modern state, it is high time to critique economic growth and problematize the liberal theories. It is high time to say that the economic growth in itself can hardly deliver social justices, particularly, in employment term. The condition of rural economy would have been different if the civil society had questioned the legitimacy of the economic growth as a sole provider of employment. The future of rural economy would depend on the extent to far the people of the civil society critiquing the economic growth theory, thereby emphasizing only on issues of employment. As the people of the civil society dominate both the political institutions and the state institutions, particularly in West Bengal, a little shift in their standpoint could definitely make a difference in the domain of employment.

The class/caste

I have described the way the upper class (or the upper castes) has dominated the political as well as the state institutions in the state, and thereby determined the process of policy intervention in the lives and livelihoods of the rural poor. Unlike in other states where the lower strata (both in caste and class term) have a hold in the political institution at least to some extent, the lower strata in West Bengal can hardly influence the formation and implementation of governmental policies. The state policies, be it the economic or the welfare, are the product of the upper strata in West Bengal. The question that arises is the way in which the class-caste plays a role in generation of employment and unemployment. We are supposedly well aware of the fact that the nature of alignment of state and class has always been a factor in matters like what kind of policies are going to be grown out of that class politics. While it is undeniable that the big landholding class including the rich peasants aligned with the state forces, and that India has witnessed a (Kohli 2012, 3) 'basic realignment of state and class forces' in most of the states since the 1970s–1980s, West Bengal made an exception to this general pattern. Despite the successful implementation of the GRT in rural areas, the 'affluent' landholding class in West Bengal could exert its power neither in the Assembly nor in the Parliament, whatever its reasons may be. But the absence of alignment of landholding class with the state didn't make a difference to the employment opportunities in rural areas. Notwithstanding the increase of growth in agriculture, it could not put the rural poor in West Bengal out of their misery. Why did the increasing growth in agriculture fail to put the rural poor out of misery? Kohli attributes both the economic dynamism and the lingering misery to the alignment of the state and the business. Upon agreeing with Kohli's statement partially, I attribute the failure of solving the problem of rural unemployment, and the alignment of the state and business which, as Kohli rightly argues, is actually a cause of lingering misery to the prioritization of economic growth on the part of the government.

The prioritization of economic growth seems to have prompted the government not only to realign with the business class, but also to ignore the issues of employment opportunities for the sake of increase in growth. I have argued that the prioritization of economic growth has never been secondary in the policy domain of the country. However, the issues of economic growth have obtained immense priority during the period which is recognized by many as the neoliberal period. Contrary to Kohli's view, I argue that the process of economic liberalization is the reason why the realignment of state and business class has been possible. In the period of economic liberalization, the issues of economic growth have not only been prioritized by the government, but have also become well-liked among the people belonging to the affluent class as well as to a section of middle class. Therefore, what prompted the prioritization of economic growth has further prioritized the enhancement of economic growth. Where enhancement of economic growth is the focus, the question of employment must be ignored. The preceding pages of the book have just portrayed the way the opportunities of employment in rural areas, particularly for the land-poor, have become uncertain during the last two decades. While this is the situation all-over India, the configuration of the rural economy as well as of the rural classes did not remain the same. The concentration of assets among rural households in India has increased from 1991–1992 to 2002–2003 (see GOI 2011, 105).[9] When nothing remains the same, the condition of one class, i.e. the land-poor, seems to remain unchanged at least in employment term.

I have explained that the growth in agriculture had increased enormously for a short while after the implementation of the GRT during the two successive decades of 1970s and 1980s in West Bengal as was in other 'green' Indian provinces, and had subsequently begun to impact different economic class categories in different ways. Barring a small section of agro-entrepreneurs who otherwise belong to the large landholding class, most of the sections across the peasantry have experienced a negative backlash afterwards, at least, as far as their livelihoods are concerned. However, the class of land-poor who are thought to be the most ben-efitted from GRT has not profited at all from the implementation of the said tech-nology in the long run. Though this class of landless peasants got an opportunity to obtain some more days of wage-labour throughout a particular year subsequent to the relative success in implementation of the GRT in rural West Bengal, their good days did not presumably last long as farming itself ceased to flourish. The expansion of capital, which was considered as a key factor in achieving economic growth in rural areas and particularly in agriculture, and the ensuing increase in rural employment, whatever its proportion may be, has actually undone the achievements. While the GRT made the farmland relatively unproductive in due course, the market that related to agriculture turned the farming into a loss-making vocation particularly during the period after liberalization of Indian economy. As a result of this, the class of land-poor relapsed to suffer both in terms of wage-employment and of self-employment in cultivation whatever the nature of their ownership and occupation of land may be. Even the landowning community in the state would also witness the same economic predicament.

However, the nature and extent of growth in agriculture and of the ensuing expan-sion of capital would fluctuate in different rural settings based on the local specifici-ties and ethnographic components. This research finds stark variation in capitalist expansion as well as in application of the GRT in three broad zones, namely, the north zone, south zone and the western zone in rural West Bengal. While the trajec-tory of economic transformation in the southern zone of West Bengal manifests a rapid application of the GRT and the subsequent expansion of capital at the rural grass roots since the moment at which the then central government led by Indira Gandhi determined to apply the GRT in agriculture, the development in the western zone as well as in the northern zone of the state transpires the fact that the eco-nomic transformation both in terms of the GRT application and capitalist expansion had not been as significant for the same period. The factors which made a differ-ence in case of the latter from the transformation of the southern part of the state included the irrigation deficit, the structure of land ownership, the nature of the soil and, above all, the ethnographic elements. The difference in economic trans-formations did, however, necessitate a diverse kind of class configuration as well as employment opportunities at the rural fringes. Whatever the difference in class configuration may be, the employment condition of the land-poor varies a little. The land-poor in all three zones are still suffering a severe crisis in employment within their respective rural sphere throughout the year.

However, a considerable number of researchers (Kumar 2016, 70; Gupta 2005) have tried to attract our attention towards the phenomenon that the village econ-omy has changed increasingly from agriculture to rural non-farm services, and that the 'non-farm employment accounts for more than 50 per cent of all employ-ment'. While there is no doubt that non-farm employments are emerging nowadays as a major field of employment, it is also not undeniable that the nature of rural non-farm activities are essentially more casual and informal. My work reveals the same phenomenon as revealed from the research of Himanshu et al. (2016) that the disadvantaged villagers are more responsive to non-farm work, and thereby experience the social inequality that has resulted in the domain of employment. While among the relatively prosperous caste/class like among the Patidar community in western India, as revealed in Tilche's work (2016), many are trying to move out of the village and of agriculture, the land-poor community in West Bengal, and possibly everywhere in rural India, still does aspire to have a small piece of agricultural land in order to pursue a livelihood. Land remains a marker of status among the land-poor, as my research reveals, whereas securing 'a job away from land' has 'come to constitute new markers of status' among the agriculturally prosperous villagers (17). That the stable land ownership and the cultivation based on small-scale landholdings can ensure the relatively higher share of rural employment in agriculture has clearly been exemplified in Nagaland, where agriculture that is still based on self-land (Kuchle 2016, 56) 'remains more important for rural livelihoods … compared to India in general'. If such is the effect of economic policies undertaken by the government, and the processes driven by the market on the rural economy of West Bengal, the welfare policies meant for the disadvantaged section in rural areas are nothing different.

Ever since the inception of planning commission in India, the problem of rural unemployment has always been a concern of the policy makers. Although it was thought initially that the extent of unemployment would gradually lessen with the enhancement of production in agriculture, it was soon understood that a mere increase in production can't resolve the problem of unemployment in rural areas. Special efforts to generate rural employment at least for some days a year were felt, and subsequently undertaken by the government. These special efforts, as I argue, were aimed more at enhancing the labour or capital productivity than generating employment for the rural unemployed. The problem of rural unemployment, therefore, persists as an ever-present phenomenon throughout the country. The problem has taken a new incarnation in the post-GRT period only to be culminated in a devastating phenomenon during the post-reform era.

The future

Owing to the devastating crisis in agriculture and overall rural economy, and the subsequent out-migration of the male members of rural families in search of jobs, the women are conspicuous by their presence in agriculture. The more the male members flee the rural landscape, the more the women get hold the vocation of agriculture. This is to say, agriculture and in particular small-scale agriculture has become women's enterprise. Instead of indicating a positive trend, the feminization of agriculture signifies a grave insecurity that is emerging in the said sphere. The question that arises is the way these processes are going to shape the rural economy: what is the future of rural economy? In concrete terms, is there any prospect to transform the rural economy towards a better future in terms of equal opportunities in rural employment? What kinds of economic policies are required to curb rural distress? Do the welfare policies have any role to play in supplementing the rural livelihoods in India? The answers to these bunch of questions seem vital to find a fruitful future of the rural space of India. I would like to merge all these aforesaid questions into one single major question: how do we imagine essaying an alternative politics with an aim to compel the postcolonial state to adopt a strategy for effectively regulating the capitalist expansion with a skew to employment? Admittedly, there is not one definitive answer; however, one might instantly think of a possible politics which calls for withdrawing the neoliberal project which guarantees unfettered freedom of the market, and, instead, puts into place, as Harvey puts (2005, 10), 'embedded liberalism' which could ensure 'some sort of class compromise between capital and labour'. While the neoliberal state uses its power to preserve private property and the institution of the market (2005), the embedded liberalism endorses the idea that the state should be freely deployed in market processes to achieve goals such as full employment for citizens and the welfare of the citizens (2006). However, the real challenge is how effectively the state could manage the capitalist processes in a particular context, and thereby achieving 'full employment'. A 'progressive annual tax on capital' could control 'inegalitarian accumulation of capital', as Piketty (2014) postulates, but could hardly act as the one and only solution as far as employment is concerned.

As my research suggests, the liberal system, whatever it may be, can't automatically ensure full employment and welfare of the citizens unless a conscious effort is made on the part of the concerned citizens to prioritize employment over other issues. I have showed the way the issues of economic growth were prioritized even during the pre-neoliberal period in India. In the name of enhancement of economic growth, the capital has always dominated labour without a minimal compromise with labour. Some sorts of compromise between capital and labour are the prerequisite for the guarantee of employment for all. Instead of focusing on the issues of investment and economic growth, employment has to be a main focus of attention in all policies. Within the limit of liberal framework, this is the only option which the future policy makers could pursue in order to construct a better economic planning for ensuring 'equal' employment opportunities. However, there is hardly any sharp distinction between the two so-called economies, corporate economy and the non-corporate economy, as proposed by the scholars (Bhattacharya and Sanyal 2011; Chatterjee 2004). While the corporate economy as defined by them as a space of accumulation of capital, the non-corporate economy is imagined as a space of the subordinate classes for their mere survival (ibid.). However, I argue, the non-corporate space or the need economy is also a vibrant space for exorbitant accumulation of capital. This space is, rather, more prone to capitalist exploitation due to the lack of any effective state regulation. To sum up, the regulation of market processes by the state and a clear focus on full employment in every policy is necessary so as to make the country free from poverty.

Notes

1 I am here keeping aside the dichotomy between the rural India and urban India since the two are rarely dichotomous in terms of poverty, unemployment and governance. In other words, the masses of both India do experience the same precarious condition.

2 Rammohan Roy would also believe that the European settlement in India would aid to enlighten the Indians in light of western science and reasons. See for details Chatterjee (2011).
3 Chatterjee (2011) rightly argues that it was impossible to construct an idea of nationalism during Roy's time. He was the product of a specific historical time wherein the discourse of nationalism was yet to emerge.
4 Farming had become a loss-making vocation more and more on foot of the marketization of the production system. Moreover, the surplus from agriculture had hardly been used for developing the field of agriculture. Instead, the most part of the surplus from farming went to pay the exorbitant revenue to not only the intermediary zamindars but, in many cases, also to various kinds of other owners, occupants and leasers.
5 Flood Commission actually recommends that the John Kerr's bill should be restored, 'by which it was proposed to treat as tenants bargadars who supply the plough, cattle, and agricultural implements'. After anticipating that some difficulties may arise in the way of defining the bargadars who supply the aforementioned components, the commission recommends that all bargadars should be considered as tenants.
6 Their work reveals massive reductions in land owned per household as well as per capita with a sharp increase in landlessness from one third of village populations in the late 1960s to nearly a half by 2004. See for details Bardhan et al. (2011).
7 The foreword of the 8th Five-Year Plan (1992–1997) also mentions that 'planning is essential for macro-economic management, for taking care of the poor and the downtrodden, who are mostly outside the market system and have little assets endowment'. This is to say that one of the main objectives of the government as the policy directive indicates that the poor people are to be connected with the market.
8 See 8th Five-Year Plan, Planning Commission (Indian Government).
9 Top 5 per cent of rural households owned 35.7 per cent of total rural assets in 1991–1992, whereas the same portion of rural households owns 36.1 per cent of total rural assets in 2002–2003.

References

Bernier, Francois. 1891. *Travels in the Mogul India (AD 1656–1668)*. London: Archibald. Downloadable at Archive.org
Bhattacharya, Rajesh and Kalyan Sanyal. 2011. 'Bypassing the Squalor: New Towns, Immaterial Labour and Exclusion in Post-Colonial Urbanization.' *Economic and Political Weekly* 46 (31): 41–48.
Chatterjee, Partha. 2004. *The Politics of the Governed: Reflections on Popular Politics in Most of the World*. New Delhi: Permanent Black.
Chopra, Deepta. 2011a. 'Policy Making in India: A Dynamic Process of Statecraft.' *Pacific Affairs* 84 (1): 89–107.
Foucault, Michel. 1991. 'Governmentality.' In *The Foucault Effect: Studies in Governmentality*, edited by Graham Burchell, Colin Gordon and Peter Miller, 87–104. Chicago: University of Chicago Press.
Foucault, Michel. 1984. 'Space, Knowledge and Power.' In *The Foucault Reader*, edited by P. Rabinow, 239–254. New York: Pantheon Books.
Gupta, Dipankar. 2005. 'Whither the Indian Village: Culture and Agriculture in "Rural India"?' *Economic and Political Weekly* 40 (8): 751–758.
Harvey, David. 2005. *A Brief History of Neoliberalism*. Oxford: Oxford University Press.
Himanshu, Bhavna Joshi and Peter Lanjouw. 2016. 'Non-Farm Diversification, Inequality and Mobility in Palanpur.' *Economic and Political Weekly* 51 (26&27): 43–51.

Jenkins, Rob. 2001. 'Mistaking "Governance" for "Politics": Foreign Aid, Democracy, and the Construction of Civil Society.' In *Civil Society: History and Possibilities*, edited by Sudipta Kaviraj and Sunil Khilnani, 250–258. Cambridge: Cambridge University Press.

Kohli, Atul. 2012. *Poverty Amid Plenty in the New India*. Cambridge: Cambridge University Press.

Kuchle, Andreas. 2016. 'Inequality on Rural Nagaland: Changing Structures and Mechanisms.' *Economic and Political Weekly* 51 (26&27): 52–60.

Kumar, Satendra. 2016. 'Agrarian Transformation and the New Rurality in Western Uttar Pradesh.' *Economic and Political Weekly* 51 (26&27): 61–71.

Marx, Karl. 1853. 'The British Rule in India.' *New York Daily Tribune*, June 25. Downloadable at www.marxists.org/archive/marx/works/1853/06/25.htm

Mukerjee, Madhusree. 2010. *Churchill's Secret War: The British Empire and the Ravaging of India during World War II*. New Delhi: Tranquebar.

Piketty, Thomas. 2014. *Capital in the Twenty-First Century* (Translated by Arthur Goldhammer). Cambridge: The Belknap Press of Harvard University Press.

Rose, Nikolas and Peter Miller. 1992. 'Political Power beyond the State: Problematics of Government.' *The British Journal of Sociology* 43 (2): 173–205.

Roy, Dayabati. 2013. *Rural Politics in India: Political Stratification and Governance in West Bengal*. New Delhi: Cambridge University Press.

Ruparelia, Sanjay. 2013. 'India's New Rights Agenda: Genesis, Promises, Risks.' *Pacific Affairs* 86 (3): 569–466.

Sen, Asok. 1975. 'The Bengal Economy and Rammohan Roy.' In *Rammohan Roy and the Process of Modernization in India*, edited by V. C. Joshi. New Delhi: Vikash Publishing House Pvt. Ltd.

Sharma, Aradhana and Akhil Gupta. 2006. 'Introduction: Rethinking Theories of the State in the Age of Globalization.' In *The Anthropology of the State: A Reader*, edited by Aradhana Sharma and Akhil Gupta, 1–41. Malden, India: Blackwell Publishing. Downloadable at www.antropologias.org/files/.../2012/.../Gupta-Sharma-Anthropology-of-the-state.pdf

Tilche, Alice. 2016. 'Migration, Bachelorhood and Discontent among the Patidars.' *Economic and Political Weekly* 51 (26&27): 17–24.

Newspapers, magazines, reports and other media

Bardhan, Pranab, Michael Luca, Dilip Mukherjee and Francisco Pino. 2011. 'Evolution of Land Distribution in West Bengal 1967–2004: Role of Land Reform.' Working Paper No. 2011/31. Helsinki: UNU WIDER, World Institute for Development Economics Research, United Nations University.

Chatterjee, Partha. 2000. *Itihaser Uttaradhikar [The Legacy of History]* (In Bengali). Kolkata: Ananda.

Chatterjee, Partha. 2011. 'Abar Rammohan' [Again Rammohan] (In Bangla). *Baromas* 33: 47–54.

Chopra, Deepta. 2011b. 'Mediation in India's Policy Spaces.' Chapter 6. Downloadable at http://epress.utsc.utoronto.ca/cord/wp-content/uploads/sites/82/2014/05/Chapter-6 Chopra.pdf

Government of India. 2011. *Human Development Report 2011*. New Delhi: Planning Commission.

Gupta, Akhil. 2016. Farming as a Speculative Activity: The Ecological Basis of Farmers. Downloadable at www.academia.edu/Farming_as_a_Speculative_Activity_The_Ecological_ Basis_of.Farmers

Harvey, David. 2006. 'On Neoliberalism: An Interview with David Harvey', by Sasha Lilley. *Monthly Review*.

Lemke, Thomas. 2000. 'Foucault, Governmentality and Critique.' Paper presented at Rethinking Marxism Conference, University of Amherst, Amherst.

Planning Commission, Government of India. 8th 5 Years Plans. Downloadable at planning-commission.nic.in/plans/planrel/fiveyr/welcome.html

Report of the Land Revenue Commission, Bengal (Floud Commission Report). 1940. Downloadable at Archive.org

Glossary

Adhiar Adhiar is a kind of sharecropper during the British Period who would pay half of the produce as rent to the landlord.

Aman A kind of paddy cultivated during the monsoon season.

Babu The term babu in Bengali means the landed gentry or those who are at the helm of rural power.

Bagdi A caste under the SC category.

Bahir Bahir in Bengali means the outer world beyond the home.

Bandh Bridge on the river.

Bangla Congress Bangla Congress was a regional party in West Bengal. It was formed through a split in the Indian National Congress in the year 1966.

Barga land The land which has been recorded in the name of the sharecroppers who cultivate the land.

Bargadar A cultivator who is legally entitled as a sharecropper.

Benami land Above ceiling land illegally held by the landlords sometimes through recording those in fictitious names.

Bhagchashi Sharecropper.

Bhumij Kshatriya A tribal group recognized as Scheduled Tribe.

Bigha Bigha is a traditional unit of measurement of an area of land though the size of a bigha varies from place to place. In West Bengal, 1 bigha equals 0.3306 acre.

Boro A kind of high yielding paddy cultivated during the summer season.

Chasi Kaibartya Chasi Kaibartya is a caste group mainly based in West Bengal, Odisha and Assam, and traditionally engaged in occupation of fishing.

Cottah Cottah is a traditional unit of measurement of an area of land in Bengal, equal to 720 square feet.

Dan Dan is a Bengali word which means charity or donation.

Dewani A system of supervisory of a landlord's estate.

Gram Panchayat (GP) The lowest tier of the PRI, constituted with members elected from each election booth.

Gram Sabha Gram Sabha means a body consisting of all persons whose names are registered in electoral rolls for the panchayat at village level.

Gram sansad Village Council constituted with the voters of each rural election booth.

Jotedar Substantial farmers, principally employing labour to cultivate his/her lands.

Khas land Government land acquired or vested with the government.

Kishan Kishan is a Bengali word which means labourer.

Krishak Praja Party Krishak Praja Party was a political party which had a considerable influence on the peasants for a short period of time in the late 1930s–1940s.

Mahishya An agricultural middle ranking caste in West Bengal.

Operation Barga Administrative measures for registering the names of the sharecroppers, giving certain right over the land they cultivate as *bargadars*.

Panchayat Pradhan Chief of the Gram Panchayat.

Panchayat Samiti The second tier of PRI, functioning at the block level.

Panchayati Raj Institutions (PRI) Conceived in the Indian Constitution as the tools of rural 'local self-government'.

Patta Legal entitlement of land, distributed by the government to the landless people.

Raiyat Raiyat is a cultivator during the British period who would enjoy some occupancy right to land and could hold land for the purpose of cultivation.

Raiyatari area A kind of economic system prevalent in India during the British Period. It was based on the system of peasant proprietary system. The land revenue was imposed on the peasants who were the actual occupants.

Rashtriya Sam Vikas Yojana The Rashtriya Sam Vikas Yojana is an area-specific programme for addressing the problems of backward districts.

Sanja Sanja is a system that existed during the British period. In this system the peasants had to pay a fixed quantity of produce as rent to the landlords.

Saree A long piece of cloth worn by women principally in the Indian sub-continent.

Tili A caste under the SC category.

Ugrakshatriya An agricultural caste in West Bengal, and also termed as Aguri.

Underraiyat Underraiyat is a subordinate raiyat during the Mughal and British period. He would enjoy some occupancy rights to the lands he cultivates.

Zamindar Landlord.

Zamindari A kind of landlord system, prevalent during the colonial rule in India.

Index